BOY ON A BICYCLE
A Mandarin's Memoir

BOY ON A BICYCLE
A Mandarin's Memoir

Hayden Phillips

Foreword by Peter Mandelson

Marble Hill London

BOY ON A BICYCLE

First published by Marble Hill Publishers in 2023
Flat 58 Macready House
75 Crawford Street
London W1H 5LP
www.marblehillpublishers.co.uk

A CIP catalogue record for this book is available from
the British Library.

ISBN: 978-1-8383036-9-3

Printed and bound by Biddles Books
Text and jacket design by Paul Harpin

CONTENTS

Foreword by Peter Mandelson		1
Acknowledgements		3
Prologue:	July 1967	4
Chapter 1:	London - The Private Office	7
Chapter 2:	Brussels – The *Cabinet*	23
Chapter 3:	Terrorism and Riots – Promotion on the Field of Battle	31
Chapter 4:	Immigration – The End of Empire	46
Chapter 5:	Finishing School – the Cabinet Office and the Treasury	61
Chapter 6:	A Ministry of Culture	78
Chapter 7:	The Majesty of the Law	103
Chapter 8:	The Theatre, the City and the Prince	125
Chapter 9:	Party Funding – A Farewell to Westminster	134
Chapter 10:	A Professional After-Life - Advertising, Art and the Movies	139
Chapter 11:	Government Service in Retrospect	154
Chapter 12:	A Sense of Place	162
Chapter 13:	Boy on a Bicycle - A Cambridge Childhood	175
Chapter 14:	University Life – Cambridge and Yale	184
Footnotes		190
Index		210

LIST OF ILLUSTRATIONS   *Between pages* 60 *and* 61

1. A Press Conference with Roy Jenkins in Brussels
2. The SAS assault on the Iranian Embassy – 5 May 1980 *(Getty Images)*
3. Windsor Castle on fire – 20 November 1992 *(Getty Images)*
4. On stage with Charlie Falconer in a *Yes Minister* sketch
5. In Court dress in the Royal Gallery of the House of Lords
6. In death make-up as Spectre Agent No 4 in *No Time to Die*
7. The author's wife, Laura Phillips, at the premiere of *No Time to Die*

Between pages 126 *and* 127

8. The National Theatre's screen says "Farewell to Hayden" as Chairman
9. Behind the wheel of a Rolls Royce Silver Ghost
10. The River Ebble at the bottom of the author's garden
11. Kingfishers on the river at Homington Farm. Husband and wife
12. A longhorn cow emerging from the undergrowth
13. In masked conversation with The King (then the Prince of Wales) at Salisbury Cathedral's 800th Anniversary

For Laura

FOREWORD
by Peter Mandelson

A T FIRST SIGHT, the Hayden Phillips of this book sounds like someone from a bygone age. But therein lies its importance. He both represents governing standards that have sharply declined but which must return if Britain stands a chance of recovery.

Although I had known him socially for many years before, Hayden and I first worked together when I became Minister without Portfolio upon Labour's election in 1997. It was not a distinguished let alone high ranking office of state (although my actual office was roomy and grand enough in 70 Whitehall) and I felt frustrated by its limitations. But a source of endless amusement was the contact I had with Hayden who as Permanent Secretary at the Department of Culture, Media and Sport oversaw the building and fitting out of the Millennium Dome for which, as an early expression of friendship, I was given ministerial responsibility by Tony Blair.

Let's not go into the merits and demerits of this particular project. I would just point out (as Hayden and I often reminded each other) over 80% of the public who visited the Dome enjoyed the experience according to opinion polls and it is now the most popular live entertainment venue in Europe. It did not feel like it at the time.

Endless brickbats were hurled at me by the right wing press similar to those suffered by my grandfather, Herbert Morrison, when he oversaw the Festival of Britain in 1951. The experience it gave me, however, taught me the importance in ministerial life of maintaining a sense of humour at all times which was made ten times easier with officials like Hayden Phillips around you. You will discover why as you read this book, from the moment of his narrow miss of Burials, Cremations and Exhumations upon entry to the Home Office to his fast track promotion to Roy Jenkins' private office.

By the end of this book most readers will agree with me that, for all the battering it has taken during the last ten years, the British civil service is still extremely good at what it does and a model for much of the rest of the world. It has, however, been politicised and undermined, especially under Boris Johnson's premiership.

To devotees of *Yes Minister* there may seem nothing new about civil servants being political. Of course they are political – but that is not the same as politicised. The basis of a permanent Civil Service is that they do not change with elections, ministers are not free to hire and fire on the basis of party as opposed to national interest and that officials can speak truth unto power without fear of losing their jobs. Yet since the start of Johnson's tenure at No 10, at least five permanent secretaries have been sacked or forced out (from the Home Office, the Foreign, Commonwealth and Development Office, the Ministry of Justice, the Department for Education, the Treasury and finally the Cabinet Secretary himself). This is corrosive of basic Civil Service principles of independence but also of morals and morale. It puts in place an incentive for senior officials to get ever closer politically to ministers and to find ways round established rules.

Some close to Conservative ministers have pursued a narrative about 'Whitehall blocking' and argued that the Civil Service should be radically improved by opening it up to new talent. Yet 'blocking' becomes self-fulfilling if government becomes an unattractive place to work and especially if fast-stream entry is cancelled as it has been. Perhaps Labour might start thinking about this now. The Civil Service can be both more porous and more motivated. Forty year careers in a single department have to be a thing of the past. People should be expected and encouraged to go in and out between government, think-tanks and private sector to develop more skills and complement Whitehall's warriors and lifers.

Perhaps in this and other ways it will be possible to revive the attractiveness and liveliness of civil service life including the virtues of constructive disagreement and the visible promotion of people who disagree into senior roles. More not fewer like Hayden Phillips, I would say.

Peter Mandelson

ACKNOWLEDGEMENTS

This book began as a story for my children and grand-children about what it was like to grow up in Cambridge in the 1950s, with a ration book and on a bicycle. I then just kept on going on the basis that I had been lucky enough to have had a varied enough life, professionally and personally, to make a story.

I am grateful to Peter Mandelson for agreeing to do a Foreword. We share the view that relations between Ministers and their Civil Servants work well because of personal not political rapport.

I owe a great debt to the wisdom and experience of my publisher, Francis Bennett. We found out that we shared a happy coincidence in that his father, Ralph Bennett, a Medieval historian and Fellow of Magdalene College, Cambridge, supervised me in my Special Subject in my last year as an undergraduate. I should record it was on Pope Pius II, Aeneas Silvius Piccolomini: the first Renaissance Pope.

I must also thank my daughter Flo for pointing me towards Francis as a possible publisher and my sons Alexander and Thomas for their proof reading help and in Tom's case, especially, the work on all the footnotes. I had a problem to solve over permission to quote from Evelyn Waugh's Officers and Gentlemen and I thank Annette Day at Taylor & Francis for resolving that, and Hugh Taylor for having kept a copy of the Minute I sent round the Home Office in 1976 quoting the Waugh passage as a model to follow in writing speeches.

The book is a thank you to my wife, Laura, for her love and for organising everything in life.

Hayden Phillips
Homington Farm
December 2022

PROLOGUE:
July 1967

IT WAS A WARM and sunny morning as I crossed Westminster Bridge from Waterloo Station and made my way to the Home Office, walking across Whitehall at the Cenotaph. I climbed up the grand but gloomy staircase to the office of AR Bunker CB[1], the Principal Establishment Officer. There was another young man waiting. We were ushered in and greeted by a man in a black jacket and striped trousers, his bowler hat on a peg behind the door. He greeted us with a courteous smile and explained there were two vacancies; one was in Police Research, Firearms and Forensic Science, and the other was in Burials, Cremations and Exhumations. He asked us whether we had any strong preference and, as this was still the age of good manners, we both shook our heads in denial. "In which case," he said, "we had better toss a coin to see who can be first to choose." Suddenly my new companion and future colleague burst out that he actually had a strong preference. What I thought of him at that moment was unprintable. He then said he really wanted to go to Burials, Cremations and Exhumations. My feeling towards him changed to one of profound gratitude. (I may have raised my eyes to Heaven and said, "Thank you.") And so my professional career as a civil servant began, in late July 1967.

I could have started two years earlier but I had been offered and accepted a Mellon Fellowship[2] to Yale University. When interviewing me to discuss delaying my entry to the Civil Service the official concerned warned me that in starting two years behind my normal entry cohort I would be unlikely to catch them up during my career. Within seven years I had been promoted past my interlocutor. He may not have been on a "how to motivate people course" given what he said to me but unknowingly it may have served as a tiny spur to healthy ambition. I had listed my preferred Departments as the Treasury, then the Home Office and then the Ministry of Power (because the father of a girl I knew and liked worked there and he talked about it engagingly). I was offered the Home Office.

I had become an Assistant Principal in the Administrative Class, a system of entry which was like being an officer in military service rather than a non-commissioned rank: that, the non-commissioned class, in the Civil Service of the day, was known as the Executive Class. In the civilian world this now defunct distinction was still of its time. In cricket the annual match at Lord's between the Gentlemen (amateurs) and the Players (professionals), in which the two teams entered the pitch through separate gates, had only recently been abolished. Looking back at the way this class system felt then compared to the time I left the Civil Service thirty seven years later, it was another world, long gone by.

CHAPTER 1:
London — The Private Office

Early days • economics • stationary road traffic • summoned to Roy Jenkins • IRA terrorism • bombs everywhere • visits to Paris and Bonn • the 1975 Referendum • Washington • a problematic speech in Anglesey •Wilson resigns and Roy withdraws from the race to succeed • how to write a speech with help from Evelyn Waugh • planning for Brussels • learning French in the south of France.

MY FIRST FEW YEARS in the Home Office were entirely un-conventional. I had only done three months in police research/ firearms (where I met a delightful woman in charge of forensic science called Phyllis White who I discovered was the crime writer PD James[1]), when I was summoned to see the Home Secretary, then Jim Callaghan, who told me he wanted me to set up a charity for the dependants of policemen killed on duty (called the Police Dependents' Trust). He said I would be working with Lord Stonham, a Minister of State. So I joined the latter's Private Office and became, in effect, an amateur events organ-iser and fundraiser. The project lasted a few months and people seemed to be satisfied with my contribution so I expected to be returned to a normal posting for an Assistant Principal in a Home Office division, but that did not happen. The Private Secretary to the other Minister of State, David Ennals[2], had become very ill and I was asked to stand in for him. I was actually there for almost a year. I much enjoyed the Private Office life but knew this was not the way a conventional career was meant to begin. I

7

never knew how all this came about but as it was all full of fun and variety I did not ask.

However, rather than being given a conventional job, I was asked if I would go to work with the Home Office's new Senior Economic Adviser, Gordon Wasserman; as it turned out I was the only person of the latest intake of the right age who had done any economics (when I was at Yale). The main task was to set up a new Programme Budgeting system for the police service if the planned research and pilot schemes worked. This method of accounting – on the basis of outputs rather than inputs – had become very fashionable in the USA, and the Treasury wanted to try it out in Whitehall. In this role I was promoted to be an Economic Adviser, stayed for almost three years, then, seeing that I was moving (or not moving) into a possible dead end, switched myself back into the Administrative Class, went on the then new six month, post-Fulton[3] course at the Civil Service College, and was promoted into my first conventional Civil Service job. It had taken five enjoyable nomadic years before I had the sort of posting which was normally expected of a trainee mandarin.

In May 1974 I was sitting at my desk in the Home Office Police Department in Horseferry House, rather bored, perhaps unsurprisingly, as I was in charge of the policy towards stationary road traffic offences.

The only excitement that had come my way was when Ted Heath, then Prime Minister, had been late getting from Downing Street to the House of Commons. He complained to the Metropolitan Police Commissioner, Sir Robert Mark[4], who said the traffic congestion he had suffered was created by parked cars. There was a problem in enforcing the parking laws because the only person who could be prosecuted was the driver, and getting a driver to admit to being 'the driver' was very difficult and if someone denied they were driving at the time it was almost impossible to demonstrate they were lying. This enforcement problem (and the congestion) would be solved, he argued, if the owner of the vehicle was made liable. The Prime Minister agreed and I had my first, and, as it turned out, only piece of legislation to shepherd through Parliament. It was a rewarding intellectual exercise in which I much enjoyed working with the brilliance of some Parliamentary Counsel. But that brief flutter of stationary traffic excitement had passed, and I was bored.

Then the phone rang and my secretary said that the Principal Establishment Officer wanted a word. (This is the second of two appearances in this book by AR Bunker). He asked me to go over to the main building in Whitehall to see the new Home Secretary, Roy Jenkins, who was looking for a new Deputy Private Secretary. I duly went and, although I recall being both nervous and slightly overawed, he and I had a very enjoyable conversation, mostly about the USA, as he was interested in the fact that I had been at Yale after Cambridge. It is possible that as I left his enormous and very gloomy office – where in the past Home Secretaries had written on capital punishment case files "Let the law take its course" – Roy had said something like "Thank you - that was most agreeable". As I emerged, the Principal Private Secretary, Syd Norris[5], asked if I had been offered the job. I said that we had not discussed it at all. He shot past me back into the Home Secretary's room only to emerge saying that Roy wanted me to come and to start the next day. Thus began almost five years working for him in London and then in Brussels. I was no longer bored.

Both at the time and in retrospect the year 1974 was dominated by IRA terrorism on mainland Britain. But in the early summer that depressingly lowering period began not with bombs but with how to handle the hunger strike of the Price sisters, Marian and Dolours, who were in Brixton prison. What they wanted was to serve their sentences in Northern Ireland and Roy was under great pressure to enable this to happen. In some ways the easiest course would have been to decide that if they gave up their hunger strike then they could be transferred at some future date. But Anthony Lester[6] (one of Roy's two Special Advisers) argued firmly and persuasively that this would be seen to be giving in to pressure. As a result, Roy then produced two draft statements setting out the alternative decisions he faced and the different reasons for each. He decided that the one that said they would no longer be forcibly fed but gave no commitment about their future location was much the more compelling. He delivered it most convincingly in a television broadcast (it was that big an issue at the time), concluding, "After deep thought, I am clear that I must not be forced into a decision about their future location or an unwarranted promise as a result of any intimidation, however harrowing may be the consequences."

The following week I was dispatched to Brixton prison, with Shirley Summerskill[7], to visit them and report back. They were very young (twenty three and twenty), very pale and they left me with the impression that they were under pressures not of their own making. Using further go-betweens they were gradually persuaded to take liquid food again. After six months they were moved to Durham Prison and the following March to Northern Ireland. Everyone was then satisfied. It was the only occasion on which I observed a senior politician use the "alternative drafts" technique to help to decide on the most convincing course of action. No doubt it has often occurred and, of course, the most recent alleged example is of Boris Johnson deciding how he would choose whether to be a Remainer or a Brexiteer in relation to our membership of the European Union. To my mind, it will not surprise the reader, he made the wrong decision but it could not have been because of his lack of journalistic drafting skill! He just got the substance wrong.

In August 1974 Roy took me to lunch at Brooks's (even though I had only worked for him for four months I had become something of a default lunch companion if his other planned arrangements had fallen through or if he had none). In the course of the lunch he said that if the Government was returned with a bigger majority in the expected Autumn election, and he was to come back to the Home Office, he wanted me to take over as his Principal Private Secretary. (The incumbent, Syd Norris, was a highly intelligent and very nice man but it was obvious that Roy had little feeling of a personal bond with him.) That came to pass and I found myself promoted to be an Assistant Secretary at the age of 31. My Permanent Secretary, Sir Arthur Peterson[8], observed drily that he had been even younger when he became the Principal Private Secretary to Chuter Ede[9]. I did not respond by telling him that he was then at a lower grade than the one I had now, with his help, managed to achieve. However the system reacted to my relatively youthful advance by providing me with a Deputy who was at least ten years older than me and who had come in from the RAF. Squadron Leader Bill Innes turned out to be a tower of strength.

Autumn 1974 was marked by a series of IRA bombings and it seemed to me that I was accompanying the Home Secretary to the House of Commons to make a statement on the latest atrocity on an almost weekly basis. And there were the sites of the explosions to visit and the Home Secretary to be photographed doing his duty, and visits to hospitals to sympathise with the injured. One bomb which exploded at the White Tower at the Tower of London badly injured a group of schoolchildren who were on a visit there. We went to see them in hospital via Hamleys in Regent St where Roy bought a number of presents for the children. Even at this late stage I can assure the reader that he paid for the presents himself.

The worst incident occurred in Birmingham on 21 November when twenty-one people were killed and nearly 200 injured in explosions at pubs in the city centre. This awful event had added poignancy for Roy as his constituency, Stechford, was in Birmingham. The following morning he first announced the introduction of emergency legislation; then we left for Birmingham. It was a deeply dispiriting occasion. As we drove into the centre of the city, in the rain, there were groups of people, mostly women, on street corners, scowling and shaking their fists at us as we drove past. Of this visit Roy himself wrote later of being oppressed by the "pervading atmosphere of stricken, hostile resentment such as I had never previously encountered anywhere in the world". The following Thursday night the emergency legislation which the Home Office had already prepared, the Prevention of Terrorism (Temporary Provisions) Act, went through all its stages in the Commons and the Lords. Roy intervened in the debate many times inviting protagonists and supporters to his room for a glass of champagne as the night wore on. Winston Churchill would have approved. When the exhausting all-night sitting was over we went to Brooks's for a restorative breakfast.

Brooks's Club itself was later bombed. No one was seriously injured but the dining room ceiling was badly damaged and that caused the only light-hearted moment in an otherwise miserable season of terrorist attacks. As we arrived at the scene the police officer on the door offered Roy a hard hat with the observation, "You should wear this Sir. Plaster is still falling from the ceiling." The Home Secretary was not persuaded to do so and with a dismissive wave of the hand he strode into the Dining Room where the Press were gathered. Ceiling plaster immediately descended on him making him look like the 'Abominable Snowman'. The cameras clicked away and he turned to me and said, "Hayden, tell them they can't print that picture." So I toured the room persuading each photographer not to publish as it would do terrible damage to our reputation for taking terrorism seriously. Not a single newspaper used the photo. (That was 1974. What would happen now I wonder?)

Reflecting on that terrible time I have thought about the qualities required of a Home Secretary in the midst of trouble and I know it requires a degree of steadfast authority that goes well beyond any political point scoring. In my generation Roy had it, so did Willie Whitelaw and Douglas Hurd and Ken Clarke. It is a job for calm statesmanship in Government in a way that other offices do not demand.

In the midst of all these bombings we had a short distraction as we had accepted an invitation to go on an official visit to Paris to see Monsieur Poniatowski, the French Interior Minister. Our party was Roy and his wife Jennifer, the Special Branch protection officer and me. On arriving at Charles de Gaulle, Roy's luggage appeared, as did our police officer's and then mine. Of Jennifer's there was no sign. An Embassy official was told to wait for it and bring it on but without success. That evening there was to be a reception and dinner (black tie and long dresses), and then visits and a lunch the following day. Jennifer had no clothes for any of this. So I telephoned the Chairman of British Airways, Sir John King (later Lord King of Wartnaby) and asked him to agree to British Airways paying the bills for whatever it was that the Home Secretary's wife required. He agreed without demur and got his PA to read over the bank account details we needed. This done, Jennifer and Gilly Tomkins, the wife of our Ambassador in Paris, went into the Faubourg St-Honoré and spent a good deal of someone else's money. The highlight purchase was an elegant long dress of green and yellow. Jennifer became very fond of it. (Indeed she wore it years later for her 80th birthday dinner which my wife and I gave for her.) She was reunited with her luggage when we returned to Heathrow. It had been to Faro in Portugal. Looking back, and reflecting on this incident and my handling of it, I wondered whether it meant that I was almost unsackable. While as a Private Secretary your Secretary of State is your primary focus, if you were also there successfully for his or her wife or husband and retrieved them from a great personal disaster you became nearly indispensable. This theory was never tested. Although I do remember once saying to him, "Home Secretary, I fear that was my 14th cock-up". He replied: "My dear boy, when we get to number 114 we can discuss what is an unacceptable total." In my view personal relationships matter more in terms of effectiveness in Government than official ones (a theme I develop further in Chapter 11).

In the summers of both 1974 and 1975 I had to telephone him on business while he was on holiday in a house in Southern Italy. Unfortunately the house had no telephone then and to receive calls he had to go to a refrigerator shop in the small coastal town of Policastro. I had to call at a pre-arranged time. I did not know then that the house – Casa Bussento and the nearby town – would become very familiar to me as it was and still is partly owned by the person who would become, in 1980, my future mother-in-law, Leslie Bonham Carter. I have had no reason to visit the refrigerator shop.

We travelled quite often in Europe on official Home Office business, for example to Bonn and to Hamburg and to West Berlin, all in West Germany as it then was. Our Ambassador in East Germany invited us to go there so we crossed into the East at Checkpoint Charlie and did a small tour of the back streets of old East Berlin, past large numbers of tenement blocks of pre-War housing, their walls still pitted with bullet holes from the time of the Soviet Army's advance into the city.

1975 was a brighter year as we did not experience the buffeting of bombs to the same degree and, for Roy, there was the cheering prospect of leading the pro–EC umbrella group, Britain in Europe, into the first Referendum on our membership. There was a charming Euro prelude to that in the Königswinter Conference held in Bonn in March. I went with Roy and Jennifer and stayed with them at the Residence as guests of our Ambassador, Nico Henderson[10] and his wife Mary. In his diaries Nico records our arrival and the issue of room allocation. "Roy was also insistent that we should give his Private Secretary, Hayden Phillips, a good room and treat him with the respect due to his rank. He said that people in the Diplomatic Service had the reputation of treating home Civil Servants as though they were inferior beings." That visit to Bonn introduced me for the first time to quail at dinner (very tricky to carve given how tiny they are) and to a long term dancing partner in Sylvia Rodgers, Bill Rodgers's[11] wife. I did not feel I was treated as an inferior being either then or later when in the presence of my Foreign Office colleagues, some of whom became lifelong friends.

From my point of view the Referendum campaign was immensely rewarding. It was also a restorative for Roy. He was released from much of the day-to-day grind of Home Office business (the Permanent Secretary had agreed to make arrangements to consume as much of it as possible without his involvement) and he was doing something to which he was wholeheartedly committed. My good fortune was that I was able to travel with him around the country during the campaign to be the immediate channel for such Home Office business as there was for him to do which meant that I was also able to attend a range of public meetings in major cities which were very well attended and produced some good old-fashioned heckling with which Roy, and the others in the team, Ted Heath, Willie Whitelaw, Jeremy Thorpe and Shirley Williams dealt with skilful professionalism. A feature of the 1975 Referendum was the courtesy with which the opposing sides treated each other, especially on television and radio, and also the quality of the arguments on both sides. In that respect the 2016 Referendum was very much a second or third class affair, full of cheap but effective slogans, misleading messages (which some called lies) and very low quality debate.

The Referendum Count took place at Wembley Stadium. Sir Philip Allen[12], former Home Office Permanent Secretary, had been appointed Chief Counting Officer. The result was that 17.3 million people voted for staying in to 8.4 million for leaving. In the office the next day Roy asked me to draft a Minute to the Prime Minister recommending Philip Allen for a peerage, not just on the grounds of the superbly run Referendum but also on the grounds that the Home Office was one of the three great Departments of State but had never been allowed a fair (indeed any) share of appointments to the House of Lords, unlike the Foreign Office and the Treasury. Harold Wilson agreed and Philip became Lord Allen of Abbeydale and a much loved and greatly respected member of the House. However, his appointment did not set the precedent for Home Office Permanent Secretaries and peerages that Roy had hoped for.

During 1975 there were some other lighter moments. A small group of officials and special advisers had gone with Roy to the USA to look at how the American Freedom of Information Act worked. (Following the visit we put proposals to the Cabinet both on Freedom of Information and on Human Rights. Roy had not lost the impulse for liberal reform which had characterised his first term as Home Secretary but a rather tired and battered Labour Government did not have the appetite for such radicalism. It was not until the Blair Government that these pieces of legislation were enacted more or less as we had envisaged in 1975.)

Roy and I ended this visit at our Ambassador's Residence in Washington and we were having breakfast before getting the return flight when the butler entered and said, "I'm afraid there has been a leak, Sir." Roy asked me to go and find out how bad it was. The butler led me not to the telephone but to the bathroom where he pointed to a red box and liquid all over the floor. He said, "I am sorry, Sir, but I dropped it." Unfortunately he had dropped the official box in which I had packed our duty free alcohol together with a number of presents which we had bought for family and lady friends. When we handed the presents over on our return it took some explaining as to why all the presents, although their wrapping had dried out, smelt so strongly of whisky.

Back in London Ian Gilmour[13] was appointed Shadow Home Secretary. Knowing that he was a close friend of Roy's I bounced in, rather Tigger-like, to give him the 'good' news. "This is the worst news I could possibly have had," he said. "We shall have to pretend to disagree with each other when our views on most issues are virtually the same." The same political problem applied a year later when Willie Whitelaw[14] succeeded Ian. In some ways it was worse for me than for Roy as Willie had a habit of ringing me when Roy was making a statement in the House and asking me if it was okay i.e. had the Government got it right and was it safe for him to support what the Home Secretary was saying. It was very trusting of him to believe that I would be able to spot areas in which he might have problems, although he was always careful not to ask me questions on what were for him sensitive issues. On only one occasion did I judge the Conservative backbench reaction wrongly, and after I had told him it was safe for him to support the Home Secretary he was fiercely shouted down by those behind him. I rang to apologise for my misleading advice but he was, as ever, courteous and friendly. I believe these exchanges helped our personal relations when I returned from Brussels in 1979 and he became my Secretary of State.

In January 1976 Roy, disenchanted with the drift of Government economic policy, made a speech in Anglesey which was a provocative attack on the Government's position of allowing public expenditure as a proportion of GNP to reach 60%. He said: "I do not think that you can push public expenditure significantly above 60% and maintain the values of a plural society with adequate freedom of choice. We are here close to one of the frontiers of social democracy." Now it was then, and is now, a long-standing convention that if you make a speech touching on another colleague's responsibilities you clear it with him/her. Roy knew he was making a direct assault on the Chancellor's policies and that Denis Healey would try to stop him making the speech as it stood. So I was instructed to observe the form but not the substance of consultation. I was with Roy in North Wales and arranged for the Treasury to have a copy of the speech on the morning of the day in question. Telephone calls pursued me through the day which, steadfastly and under instructions, I did not take. I answered the last call from the Chancellor's office to say that it was too late to make changes as the Home Secretary was already on his feet.

Roy's own version of the day following this event went as follows: "Hayden Phillips, who was with me in North Wales, received various messages of protest during the day, but under instructions ignored them. He was more disturbed by the journey back when he claimed that as the car switch-backed over the hills of Wales I smoked three large cigars during the morning while working steadily through two Home Office boxes. He enjoyed lunch near Hay-on-Wye less than I did." The last comment is a massive understatement. Not only was Roy smoking cigars but in the front the driver and the protection officer were smoking cigarettes. Opening the window was out of the question as mid-Wales was freezing and covered in snow. Before lunch at Hay I was violently sick into a ditch unobserved, I think, by the Home Secretary. After that a cheerful lunch of good quality food and wine was a major challenge.

The next important event was not an official Home Office one and should not have concerned me at all as the Private Secretary. But it did – both at the time and for the future course of my professional career. The event was the election of the Leader of the Labour Party to succeed Harold Wilson. Roy had of course been the Deputy Leader and natural successor until he led his followers into the Lobby in support of Ted Heath's Government in the Europe vote of 1972. In consequence Roy resigned the Deputy Leadership and by January 1976 he was in a much less powerful position to challenge for the Leadership. On the first ballot he polled a respectable 62 votes behind Foot's 90 and Callaghan's 85. His supporters, or most of them, then joined him in his room in the House of Commons to discuss tactics. I was in the Outer Office. After a while he came out and told me that the overwhelming view was that he should withdraw which was what he was going to do. But he said that Shirley Williams[15] had not turned up (she was notorious for her unpunctuality) and could I track her down? I did and when she eventually appeared she said that Roy had made a mistake and he should have fought on. He was clearly very disappointed that she had not been at the meeting and her view jolted him a little on the decision he had put in hand. My view was less sympathetic. Too late, I thought; the lesson is if you want your advice to be taken, then turn up at the meeting on time! It is conceivable that had he pressed on he might have garnered a few more votes but not enough to have won.

Roy had already explained to me that in the event of his losing he had no wish to stay on at the Home Office. After the result he told me that if Callaghan, who had won, offered him the Foreign Office he said he would readily consider that and that I would have to go there with him. The alternative was to take up the firm promise he had in his pocket of the Presidency of the European Commission (from the German Chancellor, Helmut Schmidt[16] and, the French President Giscard D'Estaing[17], and endorsed by Harold Wilson) and would I please go with him there? I said I would be happy to do either. An offer of the Foreign Office was not made (perhaps it would have been if Shirley's too late advice had been available in a timely way), which was understandably churlish of Callaghan, so he and I knew we were headed for Brussels at the beginning of 1977. He left the Government in July 1976 and then began about six months of transition as we prepared ourselves for a very different life.

Reflecting now on almost three years as Roy's Principal Private Secretary in London and with the hindsight of having worked closely with a large number of senior political figures in subsequent years, that period was of singular significance for my future judgement of the quality of my political masters. Although out of sympathy with the drift of the direction of the Labour Party he brought to his work the most concentrated strategic intellectual focus of any Minister with whom I have worked (I would put Nigel Lawson[18] a quite good second). He was incisive and decisive. He was highly efficient but not a workaholic, and carefully guarded his private social and literary life. The Permanent Secretary, Arthur Peterson, with whom Roy did not always have a good relationship, recognised his quality as a Minister and said to me that I was right to go to Brussels on the grounds that if I stayed I would be immensely frustrated by having to work for Ministers of much lesser quality.

My Private Office years in London, produced two unusual documents of record. The first was a letter I sent to Robert Armstrong[19], then the Principal Private Secretary to the Prime Minister, following the Prime Minister's concerns about a leaked story which he felt could only have come from a Cabinet Minister. Robert had to send round a letter asking each member of the Cabinet to complete a questionnaire about the leak e.g. did they know the journalist; when did they last speak to him; etc. Roy instructed me to reply to explain that he had always made it a rule of his private and public life never to complete questionnaires "from however eminent a source they originated". I was also instructed to write, however, that the Prime Minister had the Home Secretary's personal assurance that he was not responsible for the leak. Robert replied to say that the Prime minister was quite content. (I reminded Robert of this unusual exchange on his 93rd birthday on 31 March 2020. Sadly he died three days later. Robert was a very great man, a loyal friend and one of the finest 20th century servants of the Crown.)

The second concerns a Minute I circulated round the Home Office on how to write speeches. Most Civil servants, however clever, are not natural speech-writers, because they have rarely given speeches themselves, and some of the official speech drafts that came in for Roy to deliver were execrable. I spent far too much of my time, sitting up into the night, re-writing these depressing efforts and I suggested that we might give some guidance to the Department on how to do better (and therefore let me go home earlier). This resulted in an unusual document, of which I remain inordinately proud, which explained to all my colleagues that they should study and take careful account of the first paragraph of Chapter VI of Evelyn Waugh's *Officers and Gentlemen* where the juxtaposed rhythm of short and long sentences offered an excellent discipline for handling the spoken word.

The Minute, headed SPEECHES WRITTEN FOR USE BY THE HOME SECRETARY went as follows:

"The Home Secretary has asked me to acknowledge the amount of work which goes into draft speeches written for his use. From time to time, however, he has commented that the style in which they tend to be written – long sentences containing long words as well as complicated subordinate clauses – tend to make them difficult to deliver and sometimes difficult to understand. This is apart from the soporific effect some of them may have on the audience. The Home Secretary has asked that I remind all those concerned with drafting his speeches of the stylistic and auditory value of the juxtaposition of the short sentence, containing perhaps longer words implying the more complicated concepts; and of the long sentence which reads and sounds better if shorter words are used. He has drawn my attention to the first paragraph of Chapter VI of Evelyn Waugh's novel *Officers and Gentlemen*; a copy of which I attach. In drawing this to my attention the Home Secretary commends no more than Mr Waugh's style, which he believes provides an excellent example of the approach to speech writing he would like to see taken."

The accompanying extract from Chapter VI reads:

"The Isle of Mugg has no fame in song or story. Perhaps because whenever they sought a rhyme for the place, they struck absurdity, it was neglected by those romantic early-Victorian English ladies who so prodigally enriched the balladry, folk-lore and costume of the Scottish Highlands. It has a laird, a fishing fleet, an hotel (erected just before the First World War in the unfulfilled hope of attracting tourists) and nothing more. It lies among other monosyllabic protuberances. There is seldom clear weather in those waters, but on certain rare occasions Mugg has been descried from the island of Rum in the form of two cones. The crofters of Muck know it as a single misty hump on their horizon. It has never been seen from Eigg."

There was sadly no noticeable improvement in the draft speeches which came in to us but there was a general belief in the Department that, despite appearances to the contrary, the Home Secretary and I had a lively sense of humour. Actually we meant every word of what I had sent round. Could such a literate observation for everyone in a Department to see be found in modern Government? I strongly doubt it.

The Private Office in Whitehall is a unique governmental arrangement and as I was about to go on to work in a different context, the

French *Cabinet* system, it may be worth a few transitional observations. The best authority ever on the Private Office is still Nico Henderson in his book, *The Private Office* (first published in 1984). Whilst his descriptions have some elements peculiar to the Foreign Office they are mostly generic to the rest of Whitehall. The opening sentences of the first chapter are graphically compelling. "The Private Secretaries to Ministers are the impresarios of Whitehall; and in their Private Offices the drama and friction between politics and the machine are theatrically audible." That was certainly my experience in the two and a half years I did the job in Whitehall.

Some very senior civil servants had to be coached in how best to approach the Home Secretary if they wanted their advice to be taken; some junior Ministers had to be reminded from time to time that they were not in charge. Rows had to be defused and feathers had to be unruffled. This was the nature of the daily task of oiling the wheels of the relationship between the Department and its Secretary of State.

Nico Henderson's book goes on to explain that whereas in the French *Cabinet* system the members of the *Cabinet* owe their jobs to the Minister who appoints them and when he/she goes so do they; in the British system the Private Secretaries are emanations of the Department and do not necessarily come and go when a Minister changes. During the summer of 1976, as we planned the membership of Roy's *Cabinet* as President of the European Commission, we were putting together a group of people whose loyalty would be to him personally. Some of them were British civil servants on secondment or on short-term contracts, others were Commission staff whom we chose for their sectoral experience and expertise, and national representative diversity, and others were neither of those, so the team was pretty eclectic.

The key appointment was that of the *Chef de Cabinet* – the person in charge. Roy began with the idea that I should have the job, about which I was extremely nervous. Fortunately I was helped out by Michael Palliser[20], the then Permanent Secretary at the Foreign office whom I went to consult. I was happy to agree with his view that I had neither the diplomatic experience nor the command of languages which the most senior job in the President's *Cabinet* required. However, while he was willing to take the strain of explaining to Roy that appointing me would not be wise, he went out of his way to make it clear that it was essential that I went to Brussels, as the number two, as Roy had formed a strong dependence on me as an individual. Roy then decided that I should be the head-hunter to help select my future boss and I was sent to see and sometimes to entertain for lunch various Foreign Office grandees. In the end Roy settled on the late Crispin Tickell[21] as his *Chef de Cabinet*. Crispin arrived at the Home Office on a bicycle, delightfully clad in a cream linen suit carrying a plastic bag containing two copies of his monograph on climate change which he had just completed while on a sabbatical at Harvard. His work in that regard was prescient and as it turned out he also handled my presence as the Number Two and my special relationship with Roy with great skill; which could have been a great irritant for a lesser person.

A generous Foreign Office helped plug a major gap in my formation by sending me on a month's intensive immersion course in French: the working language of the Commission. The difficulty was that the course was on the Riviera at Villefranche sur Mer in a September of glorious sunshine. But there was another difficulty which proved even more of a challenge than being indoors when the sun was high and warm and the sky and sea a luminescent blue. To judge the existing competence in French of a new entrant class, the School set a written test. Although I had only O Level French to rely on I had been well taught and had a good memory; so I did far too well in the test and as a result was placed in the top class. As all the work for the rest of the month was entirely in oral French I really suffered and longed to be in the bottom set. However, some of it stuck and when I got to Brussels I just about survived. I had a limited vocabulary and it concentrated on the language used on work subjects which meant that I was a boring dinner companion if the language being spoken was French. Most of the nationalities with whom I dealt in the Commission moved straight into English when talking to me except the Italians, whose French appeared to be as bad as mine. In conversation with them I had very limited vocabulary exchanges in highly operatic French, but we understood each other. Our language was 'Verdi-esque.'

'En passant', I found that when speaking French I was always thinking about what I wanted to say in English in my head first, and then turning it into French before I opened my mouth. I know this approach means you have not really grasped the language. This process produced some strange results as well as some long silences for careful thought. The worst but amusing example of the consequence of my lack of French occurred some years later when my wife and I returned to Brussels for a lunch which Christopher Tugendhat gave in Roy's honour on his departure as President of the Commission. I was placed next to the Comtesse Davignon a highly intelligent and elegant woman, wife of the Belgian Commissioner, who did not like speaking English. Our conversation was halting. She asked me whether I was still in the Diplomatic Service. How I wondered did I explain that I had always been in the Home Civil Service? So I said: "Non. Je suis toujours en service domestique." She roared with laughter as did the rest of the table.

CHAPTER 2:
Brussels —The *Cabinet*

The British and Europe • settling the role of the President • planning for monetary union • my role as Deputy Chef de Cabinet • appointments and expenses • Jimmy Carter comes to visit • Sudan and Egypt • Harold Wilson on Roy Jenkins • a farewell lunch • a present from Emile Noel • divorce and remarriage.

THE FIRST DAY IN Brussels in 1977 started badly. The President had been allocated two cars, a Rover and a Mercedes. Understandably Roy chose the British car to arrive in but unfortunately it broke down on the way and it had to be pushed into position in front of the Berlaymont, the Commission headquarters, so he could be photographed getting out of it.

In the first Commission meeting Roy's task was to achieve agreement on the allocation of portfolios which involved a series of bilateral consultations with individual Commissioners and, in the trickier cases, between them and their home Governments. In the end agreement was reached just before 5.30 am! Needless to say this was not the normal pattern of most Commission meetings. Roy had had a go at moving this process forward when he gave a dinner for all the Commissioners and their wives at Ditchley Park in Oxfordshire earlier in the previous December. As we moved into dinner he glanced at the place-à-table and moved a few cards around better to accommodate his preferences for those whom he would prefer to sit next to or nearby. Potential disaster loomed. But

Laura Grenfell (my future wife) was at hand, quickly noted the changes he had made, went into the Dining Room at speed and rearranged the place cards. Nobody knew except me and her. Genius.

The major issue in the first year in Brussels was to persuade the Heads of Government that the President of the Commission should be equivalent to them at Council meetings and at Summit meetings e.g. the G7. This turned out to be a lengthy and tricky diplomatic struggle to persuade – mostly the British and the French – that this was right and sensible. In the end it happened and it meant that Roy, as the first serious senior political figure to become President, was at one with his peers and not placed 'below the salt'. This was a good early example of 'grown-up' behaviour by the German leadership: a good helping of common sense without any self-regarding national petulance. I fear that cannot be said of the French performance or I have to say of the British. Indeed I observed quite early on a sceptical ambivalence in the British attitude towards the Community which I had not been closely aware of when working in London. As time went on I realised that the 1975 Referendum triumph had masked a deepening fault-line in domestic politics over Europe.

The British often seemed hesitantly half-opposed to Commission initiatives, which was a pretty useless negotiating position. I also noticed on my visits to the UK that when I undertook speaking engagements of a debating sort about Europe, while the pro-EEC votes were usually in a majority it was not always so. As a result one of the main points of British membership, namely for us to give a lead in Europe, was often under-mined at the start. Ambivalence and doubt are not leadership qualities.

In the summer of 1977 the *Cabinet* had an away-day at Roy's house in East Hendred in Oxfordshire to take stock of our first six months, of where we were and where we should try to take the Commission, and Europe, in the future. At that stage it appeared that none of the Big 3 – France, Germany or Britain – was ready to support a major Commission policy initiative (which was what in constitutional terms the Commission was there for; it proposed, the member states disposed) so if we wanted to strike out with a proposal to develop the role of the EEC we should have to go it alone and then try to drag others along. Roy decided that the issue of monetary union was the one to pursue, and it became one of the main preoccupations of the following year. In neither of the two great early battles did I play a leading role. Crispin Tickell supported Roy on the first, namely the role and standing of the President; Michael Emerson did the economic analysis to underpin the second. However, I did have the good fortune to travel with Roy to Florence where, on 27 October 1977, he used a lecture in honour of Jean Monnet to launch his arguments for a plan for monetary union. This was the intellectual and political origin of European Monetary Union, and later of the Euro.

The 13th floor of the Berlaymont (the headquarters of the Commission) was a series of pleasant glass boxes, some larger than others, with dramatic views over the city of Brussels. The most senior members of the *Cabinet*, and others whose work meant they were in daily contact with the President, had offices near to his; others were placed on the floor below. Crispin looked after the world outside; I dealt with the President's responsibility for running the Commission. Roy was more interested in the former, after all it was what he had joined for, so I had a free hand at trying to manage the latter and often presenting him with decisions to ratify, which I had made, rather than giving him advice on what decision to take.

The President was directly responsible for the Legal Services Directorate, the Information Directorate and the *Porte Parole* – the Commission's news handling and communications department. I was also heavily involved on his behalf in Personnel issues, especially in relation to filling senior vacancies and therefore promotions. And I had to approve Commissioner's expenses and those of the senior staff of the *Services* for which I was responsible on the President's behalf. The Legal services Directorate provided me with one monthly meeting to chair, which was often frustrating but mostly enjoyable. The meeting was titled *Infractions* and it decided on which breaches of EC law by member states should be taken by the Commission to the European Court of Justice. Each Commissioner's Cabinet was represented. The Italians were the most cheerful serial offenders; but the British Government implemented EC Directives with gold-plated precision and it was very difficult to find my own country ever in breach. There was quite a bit of horse-trading between the *Cabinets* as a country in the firing line sought allies to help plead its cause. On one occasion I recall having to deal with the export of German horse semen and the French Post Office *Tabac* monopoly in the same meeting. Evasion was quite widespread and imaginative. The British were boringly compliant.

The principal Personnel Appointments Committee was chaired by the Secretary General, Emile Noel[1]. He was an immensely experienced and very subtle operator. I liked him a lot. It was important to him and to the integrity of the system that the President's representative carried weight in the Committee and he was grateful that I attended and did not send a more junior member of staff. My only difficulty was that the meetings were entirely in French without any translation (as there was for every other collective *Cabinet* meeting). Although Emile's use of the subjunctive was legendary and to me often incomprehensible, I was usually well briefed and understood just enough to vote for the 'right' candidate. The wheeling and dealing in relation to such issues at first took my rather straight-laced English upbringing in a fair and responsible promotions system by surprise but I soon adapted to a less objective and more continental style. Later, after I had returned to London, my successor, Nick Stuart[2], telephoned me for advice as he said that three Italians in the Commission had each said that I had promised them promotion to the same vacancy. I said I probably had, as it led to much less grief in advance of the decision and once one of them had been promoted the resentment of the others would be directed towards him/her rather than to me. These were the skills of the Borgias or of Tudor England which I honed in Brussels before I returned to the auditable procedural correctness of Whitehall, as the dark arts I had learned faded gradually away; but not totally!

Approving Commissioners' expenses for foreign travel was an utter pain, but it had to be done and done diligently and it was my job to do it. On one occasion I was asked to approve the size and membership of a delegation to China led by Vice-President Haferkamp, the senior German Commissioner, who was in charge of foreign affairs. I noticed that it included Madame Van Hoof, the head of the Interpretation Service in the Commission, whom I knew did not speak Chinese. On enquiry I was told it was necessary for her to go in order to interpret between the members of the delegation. I did not find this a very compelling argument and refused permission, knowing it would be escalated eventually to the President. Roy buckled under pressure and she went to China. She was

Haferkamp's mistress. In 1986 she became Madame Haferkamp.

The Information Directorate included the Commission's offices in Member States and, on one occasion, I noticed when going through some expenses claims, that a small group of officials all of whom were British or Irish were making 'liaison' visits to certain capital cities on Friday afternoons. As it was winter I thought I would check when and where the rugby internationals were being played and it turned out that visits to Cardiff, Paris, Edinburgh, Dublin and London were on the Friday before a big match on the following day. I explained that I did not see these were allowable expenses claims even if a visit was made to the relevant Commission office as well as to the match. These Friday claims ceased. My friends could have their sporting pleasure but at their own expense.

Although the majority of my time was primarily focussed on the running of the Commission there were occasions when I was able to step away from minding the shop. Every month we spent two days either in Strasbourg or in Luxembourg for the meetings of the European Parliament, and we also made occasional visits to the European Court. Early in our first year President Carter paid an official visit at a time when Crispin was in hospital for a minor operation so I took over. It was a good and cheerful visit and Jimmy Carter was a pleasant and courteous man. In the private meeting in Roy's office Carter immediately went and sat in Roy's seat and with a certain over-eagerness I told him he was in the wrong place and he moved places with pleasing alacrity. On the way from that meeting in the corridor outside, full of staff members eager to see him, he spotted my 8 year old son Alexander, at the front of a small crowd, and immediately went over to him saying, "Do you work here?" which went down extremely well with my son. Jimmy Carter had won a new and lasting fan. On our return visit to Washington about a year later I also joined the team, although Crispin was back in charge. As Roy was presenting his entourage he first introduced Crispin as his *Chef de Cabinet*. I think the President caught the word *chef* and the look on his face silently asked why Roy had brought his own cook over. However, recognising me, next in the line, he cheered up a lot and asked me how my son was doing.

I did various other foreign visits but the most interesting and enjoyable was to Sudan and Egypt in early 1978. We flew from Munich to Khartoum. The in-flight food was awful. I had reindeer – never again. We were to attend an International Trade Fair and Roy was making a speech in opening the European Pavilion which went well despite the struggle to get there through an overexcited and poorly policed crowd. We visited President Nimeiri in his Palace; stood on the steps of the Palace on the exact spot where General Gordon[3] had been killed; and received a present of two carved ivory elephant tusks. (It was a world in which modern sensitivity towards and protection of wildlife had not quite caught on). We then took a small plane to Egypt. To my surprise the Sudanese Foreign Minister held my hand all the way from the terminal to the aircraft. It was explained to me that this was not a personal expression of desire but a customary practice of courtesy. We flew over the Nubian Desert to Luxor where I was detained for about an hour because I had an Israeli stamp in my passport. We had decided on a two day break so there were visits to the Valley of the Kings, Son et Lumiere in Luxor, and Chateau Omar Khayyam with omelettes for lunch and highly competitive table tennis. In the soft evening light there were trips on dhows on the Nile. When we got to Cairo I found that the elegant boxes containing the elephant tusks had not appeared at our hotel. Having summoned our Foreign Ministry liaison officer and having explained to him firmly that the President would like them back, they duly turned up two hours later. The regularly allowed pilfering percentage taken at the airport was not meant to include official gifts from a foreign Head of State.

There was one moment in my time in Brussels when I was starkly reminded of quite recent British politics and, indeed, why we were in Brussels at all. Harold Wilson came to visit and Roy asked me if I would look after him until he came back from a meeting with the Belgian Prime Minister. Harold was very chatty and after three glasses of sherry asked me if I would show him to the Gents. We were standing there as one does when he suddenly said, "You know it's a great tragedy." "What," I replied, "is a great tragedy?" He paused then said, "Well it's because Roy was meant to succeed me, that was the plan, everyone knew." I observed that he was presumably referring to the Europe vote and Roy's subsequent resignation as Deputy Leader of the Labour Party. He grunted assent and added "and to think that I was succeeded by an older man." When the 2016 Referendum result was announced I reflected on this conversation and felt glad that Roy was not around to witness the pulling down of so much of what he had fought for and for which he had sacrificed his chance to be Prime Minister. He wrote at the end of his autobiography: "I may have avoided doing too much stooping, but I also missed conquering." This was too modest an epitaph. In his great reforms of the 1960s as Home Secretary for the first time, as Chancellor of the Exchequer subsequently, and in his leadership on and in Europe in the 1970s, he conquered more in terms of his legacy than many of those who had climbed their way to the very top of the greasy political pole.

At the beginning of our second year I had to nerve myself to tell him that I had decided I should not stay for his full four year term but should leave after two. Roy recorded our discussion in his *European Diary*: "Lunch with Hayden, going on a long time while he argued with compelling logic that he thought he ought definitely not stay much beyond the end of the second year, that if he was ever going to leave me it would be time to go, that five years was about long enough to work for anyone, otherwise one became too much their creature. It was all done in the nicest possible way. I regretfully think it a sensible decision. God knows what it will be like without him, however."

I returned to London and to the Home Office just over a year later. When I left Brussels Emile Noel gave me a present of a large and beautiful volume of Picasso drawings and paintings entitled *Les Dejeuners*. With it was a charming card which explained in exquisite French how I had demonstrated a deep understanding of how both the Community and the Commission worked and then playfully recorded how decision-making in Europe was intimately bound up with breakfast, lunch and dinner. I had proof of this as when I went to Brussels I weighed ten stone and when I left I weighed eleven and a quarter.

I enjoyed my time in Brussels. Being in a *Cabinet* as opposed to a Private Office offered a role which was part Private Secretary, part senior policy adviser and part junior Minister, taking decisions on the President's behalf and representing him not only in private but in public too. This greater exposure to press and Parliament influenced me quite a lot in the way I handled my next two jobs when I returned to the Home Office. And some years later it led me to support changes which David Cameron wanted to make to the way in which Ministers were served (see Chapter 11).

My time in Brussels also changed my personal life, and most profoundly. I arrived a married man with two small children but I left having fallen deeply in love with someone else. All those who have gone through the painful process of divorce, especially when young children are involved, will know the agony of the challenge you face in reneging on the commitments you had made while deciding on those you know you have to make. Laura Grenfell had been introduced into my life by Roy who wanted her to help him in Brussels but whom he insisted I interview to see if she was good enough to join the *Cabinet*. I interviewed her. She was more than good enough. In July 1980 we were married in the beautiful Seaman's Church by the Thames at Battersea.

CHAPTER 3:
Terrorism and Riots – Promotion on the Field of Battle

An American prelude • Mrs Thatcher visits the Home Office • six days at the Iranian Embassy siege • drilling holes • the wrong Imam • ham sandwiches • my grandmother-in-law's sofa • an aircraft hijacking and all night with the PM • The Brixton riots, then Toxteth and Moss Side • Willie Whitelaw threatens to resign but gets his way • the singularity of Lord Hailsham • a water cannon debate • a man called Fagan and The Queen • sending policemen to Southern Rhodesia for the first independence election • promoted to be the Metropolitan Police Authority.

O N MY RETURN TO London and the Home Office in late January 1979 I was sent to run a Division in the Police Department in charge of terrorism, public order, royalty protection and other security issues. In retrospect I know I owed this appointment to Robert Armstrong who by this time was Permanent Secretary of the Home Office and with whom I had stayed in touch throughout my time in Brussels. I had no idea when I began that this job would turn out to be almost the most engaging of my whole career, with some dramatic terrorism to tackle, lots of riots and a certain Mr Fagan sitting on The Queen's bed in her presence. After all that I was promoted on the field of battle.

It was a slightly on/off start to this new job because I had been offered and had accepted a State Department Fellowship which enabled me to travel for a month in the USA. (The award was based on the recommendation by an American Ambassador for someone who had been helpful to the interests of the USA, in this case in the European Community.) I had therefore made arrangements to go to America in April 1979 and the Home Office had not objected. However, there was a lot of fluttering in senior dovecotes in the Home Office when they discovered my programme included a meeting with Senator Edward Kennedy in Washington (which I had arranged through Roy Jenkins). There was evident neurosis that it would come out that the head of anti-terrorism in the UK was meeting a leading US politician whose pro-Irish sympathies were well known. However, in the end, common sense prevailed and the objections were withdrawn. The trip was not meant to be just a holiday but had to include working visits which related either to my past or to my present jobs. I therefore looked at policing in New York and Chicago, solar energy in New Mexico, agriculture in Iowa and politics and constitutional issues in Washington. There Laura and I had an hour's meeting with Teddy Kennedy and spent an afternoon in the Supreme Court sitting beside Chief Justice Warren Burger. We had a holiday break in Texas, riding by the Rio Grande.

When we went to Chicago we stayed with Laura's great uncle, Volnay Foster, in Lake Forest. I took the train into town with him on the first morning. We climbed into the car and I asked him where I should sit. He pointed to a seat and told me to sit there. "That was George's seat but he died last week". He introduced me to the rest of the men in the car. I travelled back in the evening with Volnay. He and all his regular commuter companions played cards. The next morning when we arrived at the station I was greeted warmly by the others and by name, "Hi Hayden". By their reckoning I had taken George's seat and would be travelling with them for the rest of my working life.

Volnay was Laura's grandmother's brother, which was why we were there. She married Condé Nast[1] the founder of *Vogue,* and their daughter Leslie was my wife's mother. Condé is an immensely important figure in terms of style and culture in the life of 20th century New York and when my daughter Flo was a graduate student at Columbia she decided to do her thesis on Condé's impact on the cultural scene in New York in the 1920s. She went to the Conde Nast HQ and asked if she could see the archive. She was refused. After some consultation with my wife she returned and explained that she was the great man's great-grand-daughter. That worked; the gates were opened, the archivist became a friend and her thesis was then able to include original personal material which had not been published before.

This trip to the USA was an immensely enjoyable bridge back to what I assumed would be a return to a slightly mundane Whitehall routine. Indeed that was what it was for most of my first year with the exception of the day when the Prime Minister, Mrs Thatcher, made an official visit to the Home Office. When she had done the handshaking round she and the Home Secretary repaired to a large room with a selection of officials who were to be invited to talk about various policy issues. I was one of them. The Home Office was in charge of broadcasting in those days and the Under-Secretary responsible for that department was invited to open the proceedings. She began by telling the Prime Minister that the Home Office was responsible for Government policy towards the broadcasters, not for broadcasting itself. I could see from the expression on Mrs Thatcher's face that she was not best pleased with such accurate pedantry. My colleague pressed on but the Prime Minister became increasingly frustrated and burst out: "Why can't I have the range of choice of channels that I can have when I go to the USA?" The reply, that what she got in the UK was about quality rather than quantity, did not appear to improve her humour. Her Private Secretary suddenly appeared beside me and whispered: "This is awful, the Home Secretary will call you next." I then spoke about anti-terrorism policies and she smiled; I think with relief rather than because of anything I was saying.

The most absorbing part of my new routine was, at first, on the terrorism front, where we engaged in a lot of detailed practical training exercises of coordination between the various organisations that had to work together effectively in the event of a major incident – civil servants, on behalf of Ministers, the police, the security services and the SAS and the SBS, if we needed military aid to the civil power. We trained hard on different scenarios – hijacking of aircraft, taking of hostages, attacks on North Sea oil rigs and other vital installations. This induction into my new world included visits to Hereford to see the SAS in training; various trips to police forces; and practice at the regular convening of the Cabinet Office Briefing Room, the heart of central coordination, then known simply by its initials COBR, but now, and for the last 30 years, by the acronym Cobra.

In the course of these training sessions the various personalities in the different agencies got to know each other and became used to working with each other. This stood us in good stead when a group of young Iranian terrorists seized control of the Iranian embassy in Princes' Gate in Knightsbridge on 30 April 1980 taking quite a number of hostages. My allotted role was to be the Government's representative at the scene, liaising with the police, the military and with COBR. A police car swiftly took me from an anti-terrorism seminar I was attending to the scene (before any of the Press had arrived). The police had first set up our Headquarters in a building close to the embassy. Unfortunately, it was a Montessori Primary School and the chairs and tables, not to mention the male urinals, were not designed for adults. So we took over the next door building, the Royal School of Needlework. There, on the top floor I shared an office for the next six days with John Dellow[2], the police commander, and Michael Rose[3], the Lt Colonel in charge of the SAS. We could hear everything being said by the police negotiators and the terrorists to whom they were talking. I had a separate direct line to COBR. It was very tense. Despite all the training we had put ourselves through this felt like the first really serious terrorist attack in the capital (the sieges of the mid 1970s, when I had been Roy Jenkins Private Secretary, at Spaghetti House, down the road in Knightsbridge, and at Balcombe Street, looked, with hindsight, pretty minor affairs). It was also the first terrorist incident related to tensions in the Middle East.

Our policy was very simple: to be prepared to give the terrorists patience but nothing else. This placed a responsibility on the police negotiators which was very demanding in its need for subtlety and for using up time while retaining the confidence of the terrorists and continuing conversation with them. They did an immensely successful job in keeping the negotiations going until the end of the morning of Monday 5 May. Among other things this gave time for the SAS thoroughly to prepare detailed plans for an assault if it was needed. The overall story is well known, in books and on film, but I will mention two events in which I was closely involved, one of which was a success and the other a disaster.

It was important that the security services were able to drill into and through the walls of the Embassy so that listening devices and cameras could inform us of what was going on inside. On the second day this work began. The trouble was that the drills, although sophisticated for their time, were not silent so we had to create enough unrelated ambient noise to drown out the sound; and it would be best if it was obviously external to the scene so as not to alert or alarm the terrorists. So I telephoned the Civil Aviation Authority and asked them if they could reroute the aircraft going in to Heathrow over Hyde Park at a low enough altitude to give us plenty of covering noise. They agreed. There was suddenly a lot of ambient noise. The police negotiators explained to the terrorists that it was aircraft noise, which was true, and that weather conditions had dictated a change of flightpath into Heathrow, which was a lie. We were not however in a position to explain all this to the denizens of Knightsbridge who must have had a rather uncomfortable and bewildering afternoon.

On the morning of Bank Holiday Monday it was clear that the terrorists were becoming very volatile. Their demands for a flight out of the UK, assured, at their request, by the presence of some Middle Eastern ambassadors, had not been met and their patience, but not ours, was clearly running out. It was suggested that a Muslim religious leader should be asked to speak to them to see if he could calm them down and perhaps even persuade them to give up. I was therefore asked to ring the Regent's Park Mosque (the only one we really knew much about at the time). I spoke to an Imam there. He was charming and cooperative and said he would come. When he arrived he talked to the spokesman for the terrorists and it was progressively clear from the translation we were listening to that this intervention was having the precisely opposite effect to that we intended. What I had done was to invite an Imam from the wrong sect not knowing the crucial difference between a Sunni and a Shia.

An hour later shots were heard and the dead body of one of the hostages was placed outside the Embassy door. Michael Rose turned to me with a slight smile and said: "Well you've c....d that up completely, but don't worry, I will go in and rescue you by 3 o'clock this afternoon." (Michael denies he said anything as crude as that.) He was as good as his word except for the precise timing of the SAS assault. The Home Secretary approved an assault, which actually took place later that evening at 3 minutes to 7 pm. John Dellow had been authorised by the Home Secretary to judge when the timing was right. We thought the terrorists were moving the hostages around which would have delayed the assault further. When it was clear this had not happened, and that the SAS could rely on the location information they already had, John Dellow signed the piece of paper relinquishing command to the military. There followed the dramatic and successful denouement with tear gas from the assault drifting into our room and making us cry.

There were some, but not many, amusing moments during those six tense days. One concerned sandwiches. Catering was done in the basement and there was no lift so the police cadets who brought us lunch and other things had to climb five flights of stairs. One day we were brought ham sandwiches. I asked the cadet if they had mustard in them (as Winston Churchill would certainly have done) and he said no, so without a moment's thought as to what I was asking I told him to bring some mustard. He disappeared for what seemed a very long time. Indeed one of my colleagues wondered whether, in order to get me the right quality of mustard, he had run to Claridge's. When he eventually returned it looked as though he had. He was in a muck-sweat and it was only then I noticed that he was seriously overweight. It took John and Michael 41 years to make me feel a bit guilty about my behaviour and include this anecdote in my story!

The conclusion of the siege was an actual and symbolic success for British anti-terrorist policy both in the skill and discipline of the police negotiators, in the skill and courage of the SAS, and the effectiveness of our command, control and liaison arrangements. We had demonstrated the right balance between operational and political spheres of decision-making, and there were lots of invitations for us to travel the world and tell the story. I was able to go with John Dellow to Australia and Japan: Michael could not come and had to send a more junior officer. In Australia we flew from engagements in Perth to Adelaide where, after a welcoming dinner, the police host said, "Hayden, our colleagues in Western Australia tell us you like a drop of red so here is a small present of the best you can get." He then placed a case of red wine on the table. The next day we went to a game reserve where I made friends with a koala bear and I discovered that if you pick a koala up and give him a hug he is very responsive but his claws are very sharp and he digs them deeply into your back when returning the hug. I wish I had a photo of that moment of happy agony. In Tokyo we attended a martial arts demonstration and, as the leader of the delegation I was invited to take part in the combat, as an honour. Terrified, I said that I had brought my 'champion' with me and he would fight. The SAS major I sent into battle acquitted himself well; he knew how to fall without causing himself too much pain.

In my house in the country there is a physical legacy of my involvement in the Iranian Embassy Siege. For five nights of the six days I did not go home to sleep but went to nearby Victoria Road, no 49 to be exact, where I slept on my wife's grandmother's sofa. This meant I could leap up early and get back late without asking the police to drive me home. My wife's grandmother, Lady Benson, who despite all her years in England had never lost her American accent, bequeathed the sofa to me in her will on condition it had a plaque that explained its use in early May 1980. I think the sofa is too large for any of my children to find it a home when I am gone so there is some negotiation to be had about the future of this piece of our national heritage; perhaps the National Army Museum would like a sofa?

I also went to the USA to talk to our anti-terrorist colleagues there. Our reputation of being able to win a "small war" was enhanced by the fact that days earlier, on the 24th and 25th of April, American forces, directed by President Carter to try to end the hostage crisis in Tehran had failed disastrously, before the troops could even get near to the American Embassy where the hostages were held. One helicopter and one transport aircraft were destroyed and five helicopters were abandoned or captured. But there was no crowing on our part. A long range rescue operation was quite a different thing from our achievement at Princes' Gate but it did lead to a serious re-assessment of US military preparedness for such operations at long range. Years later the assassination of Osama bin Laden told the world a different story about American capability.

I visited the SAS Headquarters in Hereford on a number of occasions. The first time was to observe their training at close hand; and it was very close. I was placed in a chair in a mocked-up room as a captured hostage surrounded by cardboard cut-out terrorists. The soldiers coming into the room had to shoot the terrorists but not me. The ammunition was real. On another occasion Michael Rose and his wife invited us to the Mess for dinner and to stay the night. We had retired to bed when we heard a lot of gunfire around the house. When I went into the corridor to see what was afoot there was the commander of the SAS in pyjamas and dressing gown descending the stairs, revolver in hand. The drama was simply the local RAF Regiment on exercise and no one had told the Colonel it was happening.

I was actively involved in only one other major terrorist incident, at the beginning of March 1982, when an Air Tanzania aircraft which had been hijacked landed at Stansted .This was an entirely different experience as on this occasion I was in the COBR and not at the scene. It began on a Saturday. The Home Secretary (Willie Whitelaw) had to be brought down from Cumbria to chair the COBR meeting but the Prime Minister was in London, with no engagements, and she decided to attend throughout the first day. At about 7 pm on Saturday evening, when police negotiations with the hijackers were rather stalled and with threats in the air of them blowing up the plane, some brave or foolish soul in the COBR asked whether and when there would be some supper. One of the support staff had to confess that they hadn't had time to ask the Metropolitan Police Catering Department to make provision so there would be no supper. At which point Mrs Thatcher stood up, said "Leave it to me" and strode out followed by her entourage. About 40 minutes later she returned followed by her staff bearing many plates of sandwiches, a large iced cake and two bottles of whisky. "There you are," she said. "No more complaints, boys."

Discussion about what to do carried on late into the evening and although there had been no breakthrough it looked as though the young terrorists might be settling down for a while. We broke up just before midnight. I was to be on duty through the night so I turned to the Prime Minister and asked her when I might ring her in the morning. She asked me to ring her in an hour's time. I rang at 1 am and reported that all was quiet. She asked again to be rung in an hour's time. That pattern continued throughout the night during which the police had done well to track down a former Tanzanian Foreign Minister who was in England and who was likely to have some persuasive clout with the hijackers. After a while a pregnant hostage and her 5 year old son were released. So things were looking up when we all resumed at 8 am. I was tired and unshaven when the Prime Minister appeared looking as fresh as the flowers in May. Before she handed over to the Home Secretary as COBR Chairman, she said: "Perhaps before we begin I can say thank you to Hayden Phillips who has been up all night on our behalf while the rest of us were sleeping. And it now looks as though we may be able to close this incident without too much trouble. I suggest we all thank him and let him go home to his wife and family." This was very generous; a real political touch of class. During the Sunday all the hostages were gradually released.

The year in between, 1981, was very dramatic, marked by serious riots breaking out in many cities. They began in Brixton over the weekend of 10 – 12 April. There were fierce battles between young rioters, mostly black, and the police; many people were injured; shops were looted; petrol bombs were thrown. I was asked to come up to London on Sunday morning to meet the Home Secretary and to go with him and the Commissioner of the Metropolitan Police to visit the scenes of devastation. We were filmed for the news programmes. If anyone looks at that old footage I can easily be found as the only civilian wearing a tweed jacket rather than a suit as I had not had time to go to my house in London and change. We went back to the Home Office for a discussion about what steps we should take, one of which was the Home Secretary deciding to ask Leslie Scarman to conduct an inquiry into the reasons why the riot had occurred. (This turned out to be a wise and farsighted choice.) Lord Scarman agreed to do it. His appointment was announced on the Monday, and he asked me to accompany him to Brixton on Tuesday morning. I said I thought I ought to let the police know we were coming but he said no; we were going incognito. As we walked round some miserable scenes of damage, with groups of police on patrol and groups of depressed looking civilians on street corners, he described every street to me and told me what it was like when he was growing up in the area as a boy. It seemed to me then that if anyone could give back confidence to a broken community then it was this highly intelligent, humane and sensitive Law Lord who knew Brixton like the back of his hand. And so it proved. He went straight to work, consulting widely and skilfully, and produced his report in November. This was not an Inquiry which vanished into long grass, and it provided a platform of recommendations to improve police community and race relations which were acted on and made real. It was a masterpiece of its time.

Unfortunately, although swiftly accomplished, his report was not available to help us in responding to even worse rioting that broke out on 6 July in Toxteth, Liverpool and then spread to Manchester, Moss Side, and beyond – to Birmingham, Preston, Leeds, Wolverhampton and Hull. Toxteth was the first occasion in which CS gas had to be used on mainland Britain. The Chief Constable, Ken Oxford, rang me very late at night as he had to get the Home Secretary's authorisation to fire CS gas. I rang the Private Secretary who spoke to Willie Whitelaw who agreed. Back down the chain I recorded that approval. (I did this, I recall, whilst holding my 6 month old baby daughter in my arms.) This process was a crazy way to take an urgent operational decision and I would not be surprised if the CS gas had been fired before my final message of authorisation arrived. (In his later Statement to the House of Commons on the riots the Home Secretary sensibly announced that while he would approve guidance for the use of CS gas, rubber bullets, etc, their actual deployment was an operational decision not a political one.) The following day I flew up to the scene with the Home Secretary. While driving through Liverpool into Toxteth everything seemed normal enough, but when we got to the scene of the rioting there were damaged buses, and fires still smouldering and hostile looking groups of people. I was strongly reminded of my visit to Birmingham with Roy Jenkins in 1974 after the pub bombings; visiting a community in pain and grief with the question in their minds: "What are they going to do about it"?

We had a meeting with the Leader of the Council, the Mayor, the Chief Constable, and the Anglican and Roman Catholic Bishops[4]. During the discussion another man, also wearing a clerical collar and present at the meeting, launched a furious attack on the Home Secretary. Bishop Worlock said something like, "I am sure you are wrong, as Mr Whitelaw is a good Christian gentleman." This was said with such authority that the man with the clerical collar subsided. As the meeting ended he approached me and offered me a pile of paper asking me to persuade the Home Secretary to intervene in his case. He was a de-frocked priest facing various criminal charges. How he got in to the meeting was never satisfactorily explained.

On Friday 10 July we went to Manchester following two nights of rioting in Moss Side and afterwards I drove back with the Home Secretary to London, while the radio reported on further minor disturbances, and journalists speculated about what might happen and where, over the forthcoming hot summer weekend. And there were indeed further sporadic out-breaks of violence, even as late as Monday evening, again in Brixton. It felt as though England was on fire.

There was to be a Debate on the riots in the House of Commons on 16th July and it fell to me to draft the statement with which the Home Secretary would open it. I worked at it hard and it was sent over to No 10 with very few ministerial changes. On the morning of the debate I had a call from the Home Secretary's office saying could I go to see him. He told me he was summoned to discuss the speech with the Prime Minister and I was going with him. We met in the Cabinet Room – Mrs Thatcher, Clive Whitmore[5] (her Principal Private Secretary), the Home Secretary and me. She began by saying the speech was excellent, at which the Home Secretary beamed outwardly and I beamed inwardly. But then she told us that there was one sentence that she would like taken out as it implied that unemployment might be one of the causes of the riots when in fact the rioters were simply criminals with no excuse whatsoever. (I can hear her saying that even now.) The passage that offended her read: "Many of the people committing criminal violence on the streets in recent weeks live in inner city areas, which have suffered relatively from a range of disadvantages, including unemployment, over a number of years." Willie Whitelaw's response to her request for the removal of the sentence was instant and decisive. "If you want me to remove that sentence then you will have to find a new Home Secretary to open the debate." This was my only experience of being present when a Cabinet Minister threatened to resign. It worked. She smiled and patted him on the arm saying she didn't really mean it. She did of course, but she needed him much more than she wanted the removal of a sentence that offended her.

The Statement was to be repeated in the House of Lords, by the Lord Chancellor, Quintin Hailsham, later that afternoon, and I was asked to go over and brief him at 2 pm. I was ushered into his enormous Pugin room overlooking the Thames (which was to become a very familiar part of my life in my final job in Government service). He was seated at the far end of the room like an Indian Mogul, feet on the desk, two walking sticks in his in or out-tray and the statement in his hand. During my long walk across the room he said the statement was very good – "I presume you wrote it" – but he also said that he wanted to add a short paragraph about the importance of nursery education in encouraging learning, good behaviour and discipline at an early age. Apart from the slightly far-fetched, or should I say original, nature of the suggestion, I was very conscious of the fact that a statement repeated in the Lords had to be exactly the same as that which had been delivered in the Commons. I explained this correct but boring procedural point to him, adding very quickly (to head off any explosion of irritation) that it seemed to me the best way to get his important point on the record was to arrange for one of his backbenchers to ask him a question when he sat down. He seemed to think this an admirable solution so, after drafting the Question and his Answer, I left him a happy Lord Chancellor. He was an extraordinary man. On one occasion visiting the Home Office to try to settle a dispute between the two departments, he straightway told the Home Secretary that he disagreed with his own officials and agreed with the Home Office view. They looked as surprised as we were. The meeting lasted three minutes.

During this extended period of public disorder we had a number of discussions about equipment for the police and the Home Secretary made it clear he was rather keen on the police having water cannon, on the simple grounds that people didn't like a fierce burst that would make them both very wet and very cold. The police were reluctant to endorse the use water cannon and I wrote a paper which came down against their use largely on the grounds that rioters chose where to riot and they tended not to select broad avenues like the Mall or Whitehall but locations with narrower streets where the mobility of water cannon would be severely limited. We had a perfectly friendly discussion in which Paddy Mayhew observed, "I know we are going to agree with what Hayden says but these people really don't like a blast of cold water up 'em." The Home Secretary's decision, reluctantly to his mind, went against the use of water cannon but I was asked to go away and produce a list of other actions he could take which would be helpful. As I left the room the Home

Secretary said to me, out of earshot of others: "Hayden, I really need the *Evening Standard* to carry the headline 'Whitelaw Acts.'" I came back with a paper containing a range of smaller measures which when added together I felt looked pretty good and would have some real impact on press and public. Willie was very pleased. However, as we left the room my Permanent Secretary observed that I had produced a number of excellent Christmas decorations but he couldn't discern a tree of policy on which to hang them. I could not challenge this impeccable logic; but the Home Secretary got the *Evening Standard* headline he wanted.

Towards the end of my time in a job in which things went unexpectedly 'bump in the night' a man called Fagan entered Buckingham Palace and got as far as The Queen's bedroom. She showed remarkable sangfroid at this unknown and unexpected arrival and kept him talking until help arrived. That was on Friday 9 July 1982. The Home Secretary took this serious security lapse very personally and offered to resign. This was not accepted. On the morning after I was asked by the Commissioner of the Metropolitan Police to go to see him. He told me that Brian Cubbon had been to see him very early that morning and had told him he ought to offer to resign, and he asked what my opinion was. This put me in a rather uncomfortable position given the advice my boss had given so it seemed best to avoid a straight answer. I muttered about the decision being one for him but that I was absolutely sure that if he did offer to resign his resignation would not be accepted. He decided not to accept Brian's advice so perhaps he did not have much faith in my advice either. Willie's subsequent statement to the House on Palace security was preceded by two IRA bombings, one of the Household Cavalry in Hyde Park and one of the bandstand in Regent's Park. I felt very sorry that someone who was a substantial and respected Home Secretary and a noble man, could be hit by such a series of blows. But I had been able on one occasion to offer him some compensation.

It is very rare for any Home Secretary to say that in their professional life they enjoyed a moment of unalloyed pleasure. But I think I can say that I was instrumental in providing one for Willie Whitelaw. It came about as follows.

In February 1980 there were independence elections in Southern Rhodesia. The last Governor General, Christopher Soames[6], had known me through Roy Jenkins as Christopher was leaving Brussels as a European Commissioner and we were arriving. About 10 days before the elections I received a call from him at home on a Sunday. He told me that he was being advised to have armed soldiers on duty at each polling station for security reasons but he was against that; it was the wrong departing image of British rule. Could I therefore arrange to send him 600 British policemen in helmets and tropical kit armed only with truncheons and whistles? I consulted the Home Secretary who agreed with alacrity and on the Monday I sent a fax (very modern in those days) to every police force in the United Kingdom asking for volunteers. The replies pounded in and by Wednesday I had 14,000 volunteers. This joyful embarrassment of riches meant we had to find a way of a defensible rationing of places, and it was worked out (not by me but by a more numerate member of my staff) that if Christopher Soames was willing to feed and water 800 police officers every police force in England, Scotland, Wales and Northern Ireland could have at least one representative on the expedition. This was agreed. The Metropolitan Police took over all the logistics and arranged for the volunteers to gather on Friday morning in Central Hall Westminster. I gave them a boring address about all the rules they had to observe and the pills they should take to avoid getting a variety of diseases and then the Home Secretary spoke. I can't remember exactly what he said but it was a very rousing end of Empire address about passing on the values of freedom and democracy, and the reputational symbol that those going out to serve in the Election would represent. It led to a standing ovation that went on and on. As we left the platform there were tears in his eyes as he turned to me and said, "Hayden, thank you. I wish you were my agent."

The Election was free of abuse and fair and Robert Mugabe won. A few weeks later a large box appeared in my office with a letter addressed to me from President Canaan Banana of Zimbabwe thanking all the policemen who had served during the Election. He added: "I enclose 800 Zimbabwe Independence Medals for you to distribute to the volunteers, and one for you." I have never had occasion to wear it.

Towards the end of my time in this job the Home Secretary had to appoint someone to review the effectiveness of the Prevention of Terrorism Act. This was very much a part of my personal history following the all-night session in which the Act was passed in 1974. He asked me if I had anyone to suggest and I replied, "George Jellicoe." He was absolutely delighted and George was asked and accepted. Thus Lord Jellicoe was brought out of public service exile, after his resignation from the Heath Government because his surname had been confused with the apartment block – 'Jellicoe House' – in which he had used call-girls. His resignation was, in my view, a good example of that signally British conflation of prudishness with an obsession with sex, which can drive otherwise extremely able public servants out of office for a private matter which affects neither their ability nor their value. We ought to have stopped doing that long ago. I tried to help stop it 10 years later but that is for a later chapter.

In mid-1982 I was promoted to be an Under-Secretary in the Police Department and took on the mantle of being the de facto Police Authority for the Metropolitan Police. This was a serious job and Brian Cubbon asked me to review the way the Home Office had carried out its role and recommend any changes I felt necessary. It lacked the operational excitement and occasional glamour of what I had been doing but it was a job of real substance. I was relatively young in Home Office terms to be promoted to that rank; a friend, passing me at lunch in the canteen that day, paused to congratulate me adding my promotion was a "triumph for wit and energy". My friend, a clever man and five years my senior had not been so promoted, so I took his words in the spirit in which I think they were intended.

CHAPTER 4:
Immigration – the End of Empire

*Lunar House in Croydon • the Home Secretary gives me advice •
marriage and the primary purpose test • a hillside in Azad Kashmir
• "running the empire that has come home" • an awkward dinner
in Delhi • passion for India • Mr Kottawallah • tummy trouble in
Bangladesh • the future of Hong Kong • deporting the Libyan Peoples'
Bureau • the General Synod and the Archbishop • inner city ethnic
minority meetings • how to write letters to applicants • Ted Heath's
musical cases • Zola Budd • judicial review begins • I talk at the
Treasury and the Chief Secretary falls asleep.*

IN THE EARLY SPRING of 1983 Brian Cubbon[1] called me in to
say it was time I moved on and, "by acclamation," it had been decided
I should become Head of the Immigration and Nationality Department
(IND). He preceded this mildly depressing statement – its headquarters
were in Croydon and I lived at the Fulham end of the King's Road –
with the observation that I had danced attendance on Ministers for long
enough and the time had come for me actually to run something.

And there was something to run: 3,000 staff both in Croydon and
at the ports and airports and expenditure of about £45 million a year. My
reaction was not however full of joy. I asked how long the sentence was
and was told three years. I had never been to Croydon and it felt as if I
was being sent into the fields to labour as in Mao's Cultural Revolution.
My step-father-in-law, Mark Bonham Carter[2], had been the founding

Chairman of the Race Relations Board, and in my very liberal extended family, Lunar House, the IND HQ, was known as "Looney House" and as a centre of post-imperial oppression. Architecturally it was a 1960s tower block about as unprepossessing on the eye as you could imagine; and a grim place of necessary pilgrimage for would-be immigrants, those wishing to continue their stay and applicants for citizenship. Whatever the surroundings, and despite the fact that we had to buy a second car so I could drive to work, there and back against the traffic, Brian Cubbon had been right about the value of such an appointment. I did learn to manage a relatively large organisation and to give some leadership to large numbers of people of greatly varying abilities.

It was a charming irony that as I left the Permanent Secretary and plodded rather gloomily along the corridor the Home Secretary emerged from his room and, seeing me, came over and said how enormously grateful he was that I was willing to go and run the Immigration Department. He asked me whether I minded if he gave me some advice. You do not say no in those circumstances to your Secretary of State. He said something like: "I don't mind how you do it but please try to keep immigration out of the newspapers." I said I understood, and indeed I did, and he knew I did. At Conservative Party Conferences, as a liberal one-nation Tory, he had suffered fierce personal attacks on two emotive subjects: capital punishment and immigration. He had just emerged from a bruising parliamentary experience in 1982 over proposals for revised rules over the admission to the UK of partners or proposed partners. In his Memoirs he wrote: "the Government was criticised by two absolutely opposing factions – on the one hand, by the opposition parties who were prepared to see an increased entry of husbands and male fiancés and, on the other, by our critics on the back-benches who feared that the new rules would allow in too many husbands and male fiancés.... These diametrically opposed factions made common ground ... and succeeded in defeating the Government..."

That issue, the admission of proposed marriage partners, mainly from the Indian sub-continent, was the principal policy preoccupation of my time in charge of IND, and given our imperial history this was not surprising. Decisions about entry were made either by entry clearance officers (ECOs) in the subcontinent or by IND staff at Lunar House and those decisions turned on how to interpret, in any individual case, what was known the 'primary purpose' rule.

This legal test for admission to the UK on the basis of marriage had become and was to remain highly contentious. Before 1982/3 an applicant for settlement on the basis of marriage had to demonstrate that the parties had an intention to live together as man and wife and that the primary purpose of the marriage was not to obtain admission to the United Kingdom. A husband could be admitted only if the female sponsor was a British citizen, who either had been born in the United Kingdom, or had a parent who was born in the UK. However, following a challenge at the European Court of Human Rights the law was changed in relation to the primary purpose part of the rules. The burden of proof was now placed on the applicant; entry clearance was to be refused unless the applicant could satisfy the ECO that the primary purpose of his marriage to a British citizen was not to obtain admission to the United Kingdom.

It didn't take me long to see the problems this rule caused both for my staff and for the applicants. The issue was a matter of central personal importance for the two applicant parties but the outcome was dependent on a judgement that an IND or ECO official was persuaded that their arguments were wholly believable. Parliament was asking my staff, abroad or at home, to look into the hearts of men and women and make a judgement as to whether they were telling the truth or not. This was an everyday confrontation with a delicate moral and ethical issue. Some of the most difficult individual cases came occasionally to me. If a very senior MP wrote to the Home Secretary protesting about a decision, I knew he would want it to be considered at the most senior official level. However, the majority of MPs' correspondence was dealt with by the Minister of State, David Waddington, and there was a lot of it. I was under no illusion that the arranged marriage system could be abused to get young men into the country, but making a judgement about that was an uncomfortable dilemma. Were the couple really in love and wished to marry or was his request a cynical rationale for simply getting into Britain. Maybe Lunar House in Croydon was the last Government outpost that believed that real romance could exist? It was certainly the only one to my knowledge that had to police it.

A graphic illustration of the moral issues that confronted my staff also confronted me when David Waddington and I were on an official visit to the sub-continent to see how the system worked on the ground. We were in Pakistan at a mountain village in Azad Kashmir and a table and chairs had been set up so people could bring their petitions to us. We were approached by a middle-aged man in smart traditional Pakistani national dress accompanied by a very beautiful young woman and a rather dishevelled youth. The older man told us in English with a very strong Yorkshire accent that he and his daughter had flown over from Bradford so she could meet the young man with the intention of their marrying and him joining her in the UK. Could we approve that then and there? I asked her some questions. She was bright and quick; in the 6th form at a grammar school and hoping to go to university. The young man spoke hardly any English and was clearly ill-educated in comparison. I whispered to my Minister that we did not have enough of the facts to make a decision and it should be remitted to us in London. When we returned home I gave the details of the case to my staff and asked for the application to be sent to me. After looking at all the evidence I refused the request on the grounds that I could not be satisfied that his primary purpose was not admission to the UK. Even with hindsight I do not know whether that was right or fair; all I do know is that I felt it was in the best interest of a young intelligent English woman. I would have liked to know what happened to her. I do hope she prospered personally and professionally, and that I did not misjudge his motivation.

Continuing with this post-Imperial theme, in June 1984, Peter Hennessy[3] wrote an article in *The Times* about my new Department. The headline was "*Running the empire that has come home.*" The first paragraph said: "There was a time when the best we bred were sent abroad to become the sons of Empire. Nowadays, apart from the odd colonial governor, most of the work is done from an office block in Croydon by Mr Hayden Phillips, an energetic under-secretary aged 41." There was a real strand of truth in this; although he said I did not altogether relish the image of being Whitehall's super district commissioner wrestling with the problems that had accumulated since the Empire came home with the large scale immigration of the 1950s.

Returning to the sub-continent itself, and to the official visit which I made with David Waddington[4] and his wife in 1985, after visiting Lahore and Islamabad in Pakistan, we went to Delhi. There we stayed with the High Commissioner, Robert Wade-Gery[5], whom I knew well having worked with him in London in the COBR context and having stayed with him and his wife on the first private visit to India which my wife and I had made in 1982. At dinner on the first night Robert turned to David Waddington and asked him what he was doing coming to India – an unusual welcome to a Minister of the Crown from your host at dinner. The High Commissioner explained that the question of immigration to the UK was not a controversial issue in India but the Minister's presence might make it so. (No speeches at this dinner other than bromide, I thought to myself). A large silence fell so I filled the embarrassing gap by saying that we were simply there to visit our staff and understand their problems; we had no plans to meet Indian Ministers; and then I asked Robert some topical questions about Indian politics to try to move the conversation on. He cheerfully engaged with the change of subject as did Mark Tully[6] who was also a guest. However, for the rest of dinner our High Commissioner addressed all his remarks across the table to me and others and none to my Minister or his wife, on his right and left respectively. Robert Wade-Gery was a singular and very able man but he did not, that evening, present the Foreign Office at its courteous best. At a drinks party in Delhi on another occasion I asked a distinguished Indian journalist for his view of our High Commissioner. His reply was "I like him but it is a problem that he speaks to one as if from top of elephant."

The following morning we were to have the day off for sightseeing. David did not appear for breakfast and his wife, Gillie, said he had gone down with Delhi Belly. I was not surprised; so it was I who escorted her to Agra, the Taj Mahal and Fatehpur Sikri. I was a happily relaxed guide/companion as I had been to these sites many times before; and it was always a treat to go there.

Indeed through the 1980s and 1990s my wife and I developed a passion for India. Over twenty years we visited almost every state including some where special permits were required for entry – e.g. Shillong, Tripura and Megalayah; and some which were "dry," which was fine once you had registered as an alcoholic and collected your special permit to buy alcohol. I think the most 'Indian' place we visited was the Jain Temples at Palitana in the Gujarat. The sight was magical as you saw the temples rise up out of the early morning mist. We were greeted by a senior retired official of Indian railways, who was also an academic. We descended the mountain as the midday heat came upon us. My wife and I were accompanied on our journey down the mountain by elderly but very fit 'doolie-men' carrying on their shoulders hammocks on poles to offer us a more comfortable descent. Smiling they kept asking whether we needed help. With about a mile to go, my wife had had enough and climbed into a hammock as her very elderly carriers speedily disappeared over the hill. I was delighted to see her alive when I eventually pottered down in a muck-sweat.

The most 'Last of the Raj' place we stayed at was not an Imperial monument of which there are many – State buildings, stunning railway stations, and churches and Cathedrals not to speak of Lutyens in Delhi - but a large bungalow in the jungle above Ootacamund in southern India owned by a Mr Kottawallah. He had been the Master of the Ooty Hunt and seemed to live his life entirely from news from the BBC World Service. He had many dogs (labradors), horses and he shot. Once we were stuck in another place to stay nearby as we had been told his house was full – the other place was called Jugle Hut because the 'n' had fallen off the sign, and in the Reception room when we arrived there was on the wall a knitted picture of the Last Supper. Faced with the grim prospect of actually having to stay there, my wife and my intrepid mother-in-law set off to try to persuade Mr Kottawallah to take us in. They arrived and Laura introduced her mother, Lady Bonham Carter. "Ah, there's a name to conjure with," he said. By the time my wife had engaged with him in dog and horse conversation we were in and, indeed, we watched a troop of other guests leaving – perhaps being sent to the accommodation we had just rejected. The current topic of the day for him from the BBC World Service was Edwina Currie and 'eggs' (the salmonella saga). Staying with him was an absolute delight but pretty exhausting as he found he had a trapped senior English official whom he could question voraciously about current events in England. His affection for Mrs Thatcher was voracious.

Returning to the narrative of our official visit to the sub-continent after Delhi, David Waddington and I then took three days off from work and from each other before flying to Bangladesh for the third and last leg of our journey. I went via Varanasi on the Ganges only to find when I was due to leave that the flights to Calcutta had been cancelled because of bad weather. Three other English-speaking travellers were stuck at the airport and, after some debate, we decided to be driven by taxi to the nearest place we could find a train to Calcutta. The monsoon rain was incessant and each time we came across a flood in the road we persuaded the taxi driver to go through it by passing large amounts of rupees over his shoulder. Eventually we arrived at the railway station and found the train for Calcutta had already arrived. We rushed onto the platform towards the first class air-conditioned carriages, without tickets. We were found seats! More rupees were handed over. I got to Calcutta and stayed with the Deputy High Commissioner.

I joined David Waddington again in Dhaka, Bangladesh, a sprawling over-populated city, where we settled down to meetings with the Government and visits to our entry clearance officers. Of the three countries we were visiting it was Bangladesh that presented us with the biggest immigration problems in terms of numbers. The next day we flew off into the countryside to Sylhet, the region which was the major source of immigration to the UK from Bangladesh. It was a mixture of jungle and paddy fields which seemed to me to be remarkably full of people going backwards and forwards in different directions. We were driven a short way from the airfield to a charming-looking bungalow with a veranda and a flagpole. Here we were offered breakfast, which consisted of fried fish (warm) and fried eggs (cold), and were then asked to take the salute at a parade of the local militia. This was slightly chaotic in terms of drill and one young man succeeded in putting his bayonet up through his uniform jacket when told to salute. Fortunately the blade only nicked him as it sliced into and then out through his uniform. But he was bleeding and was carried from the field.

We then set off for a tour of various villages in the jungle and I began to feel progressively more unwell as breakfast, and no doubt other unrelated local bacteria, took hold, until I was violently sick. One of our local guides shinned up a palm tree and brought down two large coconuts which he sliced open and made me drink the milk. This palliative kept me going until we caught the plane back to Dhaka but I was too weak to go out to dinner and, indeed, for any work on the following day. However, I managed to go to supper on the following evening which was on a boat as we cruised up and down the river. On one side I had a Bangladesh

Foreign Office Minister who said to me: "You must understand that my country is a patchwork of dried-up river beds that too frequently are over-filled with water." I understood. On a previous visit to India I had stood on the edge of the escarpment at Cherrapunji (a place which, in the state of Meghalayah, has the highest rainfall in the world) looking down on Bangladesh. From high in the sky it looked exactly as the Minister had described.

There was one other ex-Imperial theme in my work beyond a necessary preoccupation with the Indian sub-continent, and that was the future immigration status of the residents of Hong Kong when our 99 year lease came to an end in 1997 and Hong Kong reverted to China. During my first year and a half in IND I was much concerned, under the leadership of Sir Percy Cradock[7] and with the Foreign Office, in working out issues around the future status of the people who lived there. The result was the British National (Overseas) Passport which, after the Hong Kong Act 1985, was first issued in 1987. After the transfer of sovereignty to China it became the most popular travel document among the people of Hong Kong although the status it conveyed – visits to the UK did not require entry clearance or a visa – could not be inherited. One of the trickiest issues we then faced was how best to protect those Chinese in Hong Kong who had given exemplary service to their British rulers (both openly and covertly) and who might be targeted by the Chinese when they took over. We made arrangements for them to be able to come to Britain without creating a sense of panic and, interestingly and admirably, most chose to stay on after independence. At the end of 2020 and the beginning of 2021 what would happen to "our passport" holders, after the crackdown by Beijing, had again become a very live issue. The denial of Hong Kong's pledged freedoms under China remains a tragic failure of a country to honour its treaty obligations.

As an aside, there was a brief moment in 1984 when I was drawn back into anti-terrorism action. After PC Yvonne Fletcher was killed by someone shooting from the Libyan Embassy, called the Libyan People's Bureau, I was summoned to the Foreign Office to see the Foreign Secretary, Peter Carrington[8], who asked me to arrange for the deportation, inter alia, of the Head of the Bureau, Moussa Koussa, as he put it in his dry humour "to name but only two of them." Moussa Koussa subsequently became the Head of the Libyan Intelligence Services and had a very successful career. Lord Carrington retained his laconic and wry sense of humour for the rest of his life. He ticked me off once, many years later, when he overheard me telling another guest at a lunch, that Willie Whitelaw was the only Cabinet Minister under Mrs Thatcher not to have had a Special Adviser. "That was not so," he intervened to say, "I took the same view." Working with him from time to time was an immense pleasure.

Not long into my time in charge of IND I became increasingly concerned about its public reputation. This came to a head, at least in my mind, when the General Synod of the Church of England voted by an overwhelming majority that the Immigration Department of the Home Office was a racist organisation. I was much incensed, and told the Home Secretary that something had to be done. He was at his avuncular best: "Hayden, never take on the Bishops in public. Let's have a private meeting with the Archbishop of Canterbury and you can explain your concerns."

The meeting was duly arranged. Robert Runcie was then Archbishop. I was allowed to explain why I was worried: I said the vast majority of staff were fair-minded, and many were practising Christians; my objective was to get them to open up and be less defensive about their work but the Synod vote had set this policy back; and it was one thing for the Synod to vote against immigration policy, a political matter for the Government of the day, but quite another to criticise the staff who had to implement it for being racist. The Archbishop replied very simply that the Synod had no proper conception of how Government worked and had, as I had implied, muddled its view about immigration policy (which it didn't like) with the work of my Department, through a process of guilt by association. He said he was really sorry and suggested that I met and discussed the issues with the then Bishop of Birmingham, Hugh Montefiore, who was the Chairman of the Board for Social Responsibility. When the Archbishop left, having quite disarmed me, I congratulated Willie Whitelaw for his handling of the meeting. He said something like: "I knew it would be all right; Robert served under me in the Scots Guards in the war."

As it turned out Hugh Montefiore was a personal friend, at one time being the Vicar of Great St Mary's in Cambridge where my parents and I had worshipped for many years. He had also conducted the service when I first married in 1967. He asked me if we could meet at Heathrow. I collected him and as we stepped off the escalator in Terminal 3 we were greeted by the Senior Immigration Officer on duty: "Morning, Padre, Sir," he said while saluting with a slight click of his heels. This was not the (militaristic) impression I had intended to convey. What I wanted to get over in the press and in the public mind was a distinction between policy on immigration (a matter for Ministers and Parliament) and how it was administered (a matter for my staff in the UK and for entry clearance officers abroad). It was not an easy task. The Peter Hennessy article was a part of this explanatory campaign as was a very good "fly-on-the-wall" documentary for TV on the work of the department by Michael Cockerell.

In addition, and with the Home Secretary's approval, I embarked on a series of visits to inner-city immigrant areas across the country, holding open public meetings organised by community and/or race relations bodies locally. I recall we went to Leeds, Bradford, Birmingham, Manchester and Brent. I always took the Chief Immigration Officer with me and two or three other members of staff, so they could experience what these occasions were like. The format was simple. I would introduce who we were and then encourage people to ask questions or put their concerns to us. The meetings were invariably well attended, about 100 people, and there was no shortage of contributions, and some questions. The meetings usually lasted about two hours usually beginning with a not very well disguised hostility but gradually becoming more positive as the audience realised we were genuinely trying to explain what we did and were actually trying to respond properly to their grievances. I knew I was getting through when on our visit to Brent (where the meeting lasted about three hours) I was fiercely attacked by one man as a figure akin to Adolf Hitler when a large chunk of the audience sprang to my defence and told him to leave the meeting. He departed to their ironic applause. Each outing ended with our giving supper to the organisers in a local Indian, Pakistani or Bangladeshi restaurant.

Over a period of about 18 months in the areas we visited I believe we built up a greater understanding in the communities we visited about what we did, helped by some very positive local press coverage. So good was it that the Home Secretary had to tell me that his Junior Ministers in the Home Office were rather put out at the favourable coverage I was receiving.

I always put one of my staff who had been at the meeting in charge of regular liaison with the particular community we had visited. This sort of openness works for a while but needs to be sustained over a long period. I much enjoyed getting out and about but not everyone has the temperament or inclination to expose themselves personally in that way. When I moved on from IND these visits ceased. It had been different a few years before when, in the Police Department, I had similarly been round the country holding public meetings on the problem of racial attacks. That led to a report being published which began a series of pieces of work to try to tackle the problem. But in IND I was trying to do something trickier and counter-cultural. I regret that I failed to find a way of entrenching a practice of greater public openness.

For a while I was successful also in encouraging direct recruitment into the department from local ethnic minority communities within easy travelling distance of Croydon. However, coming back to see what had happened some five years later I was disappointed to find that only a few of 'my' recruits had broken through to more senior positions. Again, I had learned a self-evident truth that to make such sensible positive discrimination take root requires persistent and consistent energy and application and, above all, personal commitment at a senior level.

Another, and more obviously bureaucratic way, of trying to be more user-friendly to our customers, was by looking at the way our letters were written to people. This was the principal form of communication of decisions in those days and therefore the main means by which the Department's performance was judged by those who dealt with us. I was very conscious that whether the decision letter on a case came from a Minister to an MP or directly from an official to the recipient it could be a life changing moment for the person who received it. Personally, I dealt only with difficult deportation or asylum cases. So in my second year I thought I should look at a sample of more routine immigration and citizenship cases. This revealed a pretty standard approach; rather long letters which rehearsed the history of the whole case right from the beginning with the decision being conveyed only set out right at the very end. Immaculately

Cartesian I thought, but why should someone have to plough through the whole history of their case before they knew their fate? So I asked all our case-workers to draft the decision letters the other way round, setting out the decision at the start then saying: "the rest of this letter explains our reasons for this decision". People struggled at first to adapt their ways but we gradually got there and it was, in my view, a substantial improvement in the way we handled our customers - and the Department won a Plain English award a year later.

An exception to my lack of ordinary casework came about rather strangely. The former Prime Minister, Ted Heath, whom I had met during the 1975 Referendum campaign, discovered that I had become the Head of IND. He wrote to me saying he did not need the Home Secretary to write to him about his constituency immigration cases and he would be grateful if I would deal with them and him directly, as that way they would get more detailed attention at a senior level than if Ministers replied. His experience of how Government worked was self-evident. However, even more graciously, he added that he would accept my decisions and would not appeal to the Home Secretary if he didn't like one. As this was to my knowledge a highly unusual request to break the normal correspondence convention, I knew I had to ensure that the Home Secretary was content. He said he was and so began two and a half years of correspondence that was not at all dull or indeed conventional.

As his passion for music and commitment to help young musicians was well known, both here and abroad, foreign musicians who wanted to study or work in the UK came to him. They were usually highly gifted players who had either been scouted out by a British orchestra, or soloists, who were making their mark, but often under a rather repressive East European regime, for example, and desperately wanted to get to the UK. I did my best to help where there was some discretion I could use to solve a problem on the grounds that their arrival here would enrich our cultural life and that was, by definition, a good thing. Whether or not between us we managed to import a whole orchestra I don't know. I hope we did. It certainly felt like it.

However, there was one case I handled personally which I do not look back on with any pride. It concerned a request for the grant of British citizenship to Zola Budd, a barefoot South African distance runner of great promise, so she could represent the UK at the Olympic Games in 1984. A campaign was led by the *Daily Mail* to get her citizenship application on a fast-track on the grounds that her grandfather was British and this would enable her to circumvent the international sporting boycott of South Africa. While we would not do that sort of thing for an ordinary applicant, most of whom had to wait a very long time, I had to balance the inevitable criticism of unmeritorious favouritism, which of course occurred, against an outburst of criticism of an unthinking bureaucracy getting in the way both of common-sense and sporting success. I confess I was a bit affected by the argument that we were "going for Gold", as she was expected to do very well, but I was conscious that if she did not win our reputation would be tarnished.

The result of my risk-taking was an all-round disaster. In the 3,000 metres Budd began as second favourite to the US world champion Mary Decker. The unfolding of the race is well known. There was a lot of bumping and shoving in the pack; Decker spiked the barefoot Budd, then collided with her and fell heavily. Decker was out of the race and for a short while Budd led but to my dismay she gradually fell behind finishing 7th. I always regretted the decision to give her a preferential advantage in getting citizenship; one of the worst decisions I made or gave advice on in 37 years of public service. Had she won that would have been consoling but, on reflection, no more than that.

The main casework policy development during my time at IND was the growth of Judicial Review. Immigration was a natural target for the judicial review of administrative decisions. My case-working staff were understandably worried about what this would mean for them so I suggested to the top of the Home Office that I should go and talk to the senior judiciary in charge of the administrative list. My senior Civil Service colleagues were against this, largely, as far as I could see, on the grounds that this sort of contact was unprecedented and the Lord Chancellor's Department (LCD) wouldn't like it. So, behaving badly or well, depending on your point of view, I wrote directly to Leon Brittan, then Home Secretary (and a distinguished lawyer) explaining that there was a division of opinion in the Office and I would like him to decide what I should be allowed to do. He approved of me talking to the Judiciary. With the consent and support of the LCD I went to see Lord Justice Tasker Watkins[9]. I took with me the heads of the case-working Divisions in IND and the Chief Inspector. Tasker was flanked by some High Court Judges. He talked us through what the Judges would be looking for: a fair process; a balanced assessment of the evidence and the arguments; and a reasoned and defensible decision. If a judicial review found these elements were present we had nothing to fear. It was after this that the first guidance to Civil Servants on Judicial Review, *The Judge over Your Shoulder,* was published. (Incidentally it was not until 2015 that a decision of mine was taken to judicial review – but that was in another context and I was in another role.)

On a quite separate judicial matter, it seemed wrong to me that I was in charge of appointments to the Immigration Appeal Tribunals who were there to sit, allegedly independently, in judgement over whether my staff had made the right (i.e. legally defensible decisions). I went to see Tom Legg at the Lord Chancellor's Department to try to persuade him that he should take on this responsibility. There was a clear reluctance on his part but in the end I got my way and 25 years later, when Permanent Secretary of the Lord Chancellor's Department, found myself in charge again of the same tribunals; but by then without any conflict of interest.

A lot of my time, as had been intended by my Permanent Secretary, was taken up with management issues. I was offered no special advice or training and learned by doing the job, but it was made easier when IND became one of the first experiments in Whitehall under the new Financial Management Initiative (FMI) devised between Derek Rayner, Mrs Thatcher's management guru from M&S, and the Treasury. My department became a "responsibility centre" taking to itself all the decisions about resources, human and financial, which had formerly been scattered across 14 bits of the Home Office. This meant I could change and redirect resources provided I lived within my means and could, after the event, justify the decisions I had made. I know this now sounds quite anodyne and normal but at the time, within the Civil Service, it was revolutionary. After about two years working at this I was summoned to the Treasury to talk to a seminar about my experience. One other 'guinea pig' was invited to present alongside me, Richard Wilson[10], who had been given the same responsibilities in what was then part of the Department of Trade and Industry. The whole of the top tier of the Treasury seemed to be in the room in Great George St – Permanent Secretaries, Second Secretaries, Third Secretaries, Under Secretaries and the Chief Secretary himself; who fell asleep or appeared to do so, during our presentations.

Being the Head of the Immigration Department of the Home Office turned out to be more interesting and rewarding than I had expected. It was the sort of job that given the managerial ethos of the Thatcher years those who might want to advance their careers would be expected to do. I relished the degree of independence I was allowed and gained in confidence in taking decisions. If there was any group-think lurking in the Home Office it was certainly not where I was. I was the last single Under Secretary Head of IND. When I left I was replaced by two people so I must have enlarged the scope of the job in ways I was not really conscious of at the time.

My time in charge of Immigration came back to greet me years later when my wife and I returned from a trip abroad. When we got to the desk to show our passports the Immigration Officer said, "How very nice to see you, Sir." He then explained that he remembered me very well because he was the representative of the Trade Union side when I arrived in Lunar House in 1983 and they had to give their approval for my request to have a fridge in my office. He reminded me that my argument – that I wanted to be able to offer a glass of wine to those working late – went down very well with the Trade Union side. On reflection, how extraordinary it was that even in those days such a process was thought necessary.

At the beginning of 1986 I went to see Brian Cubbon and gently reminded him that my three years in charge of the Immigration Department had been done and I wondered what might come next. He said he had some plans for me but he needed more time before they could come to fruition. He called me back to see him at the beginning of June and told me I was to go to the Cabinet Office on promotion to Deputy Secretary, in charge of Education, Training and Development for the Civil Service and, in particular, to run the recently created flagship Top Management Programme for high fliers from both the private and public sectors. Thus at the age of 43 I became the Headmaster of a coeducational boarding school for the middle aged.

A Press Conference with Roy Jenkins in Brussels.

The SAS assault on the Iranian Embassy – 5 May 1980 *(Getty Images)*.

Windsor Castle on fire – 20 November 1992. *(Getty Images)*

On stage with Charlie Falconer in a *Yes Minister* sketch.

In Court dress in the Royal Gallery of the House of Lords before a State Opening.

In death make-up as Spectre Agent No 4 in *No Time to Die.*

The author's wife , Laura Phillips, at the premiere of *No Time to Die.*

CHAPTER 5:
Finishing School — The Cabinet Office and the Treasury

Running a boarding school for the middle aged • selling the TMP to the private sector to collect its magic dust • country houses and tennis • Roy's election as Chancellor of Oxford • the great storm of 1987 • the Sunningdale phase of the course • the Summer Node in Winter • moving to the Treasury • NHS reform • an outing to Addenbrooke's • the NHS today • some mysteries of working in the Treasury • the agony of understanding local government finance • Nigel Lawson and my pink hair • Mrs Thatcher and the Thyssen Collection • John Major and slopping out • cigars and Ken Clarke • pay policy and civil service management • battles over the creations of agencies.

THE MANAGEMENT and personnel side of the Cabinet Office lived at the St James's Park end of the Treasury building. The setting was a pleasant change from Lunar House in Croydon. My room looked out over the Park and down onto the fine statue of Clive of India (in modern times no longer just the early heroic imperial figure he once was but a part of our 'contested heritage'). My remit covered a Training Division, which was the main policy engine, the Civil Service College, at Sunningdale and in London in Belgrave Road, and the role of being the Director of two residential development programmes for senior people, one of long-standing called the Summer Node - the Node being the place where it met in Bedfordshire – and the other a recent 1985 creation, the Top Management Programme (TMP), of which I was its second Director. Both the Node and the TMP reached out beyond the Civil Service into the wider public sector (e.g. local government, the universities, the armed forces) and into the private sector, for their participants. The Node occurred once a year and lasted only a week and its principal mode was the members of the programme talking about their own professional lives plus a daily visiting speaker. The TMP was longer and more didactic. It lasted four weeks for all the participants and they were only allowed home for the middle weekend. It consisted of a demanding series of daily lectures by high-powered academics, other visiting speakers and participant-led sessions and projects. There was also a lot of reading. The civil servants on the programme were then required to do two further weeks at Sunningdale without their newly-made private sector friends. The TMP was no holiday camp as the work rhythm was incessant and the content often demanding but it did take place in rather attractive country house conference centres and the ageing boarders were well supplied with too much food and wine.

Although I had a variety of roles to perform in my new job it had been made very clear to me that the priority was to embed the TMP as a successful change programme for the future top ranks of the Civil Service and for future leaders in the private sector and the wider public sector. This meant spending a good deal of time overseeing the selection of speakers, both academic and non-academic; marketing the programme to the private sector and reporting on its progress regularly to Permanent Secretaries as a collective; persuading senior politicians from the three main parties to come and speak; and chairing all the formal sessions. I was greatly assisted in putting the programme together by two Assistant Directors (who helped run alternate programmes) and they were in turn supported by two Administrators. It was a small niche-market educational business operation at the heart of Government. It was a complete change, for me, from the normal Civil Service working environment. Ministers were not involved at all.

The formal academic subject matter was wide ranging – a fair amount of economics (macro and micro), social policy, international policy matters (especially Europe), the environment (glimpses of global warming), education, and public and private sector management issues. There was a lot of recommended reading. Most days consisted of three morning sessions, each of an hour and a quarter; a lunch break from 1 to 2.30; four afternoon/evening sessions, again each of one and a quarter hours; after dinner (from 7 pm to 8.45) there was a final session until 10 pm. In addition courses tackled a "problem" set by someone externally which the participants had to try to resolve and then give a presentation of their chosen resolution. One course I recall had four "problems" to solve – prisons, inner cities, airports and dockyards. It seems to me that all of these, except possibly the last, are by definition chronic problems and will probably continue so for each succeeding generation.

During my time I ran six such courses and so for a period was, boringly perhaps for dinner table companions, surprisingly and eclectically well-informed of the latest fashionable thinking on a wide variety of issues. The most demanding part of the job was the chairing of sessions. If the speaker was really good and the course members really engaged I basically had nothing to do. But this was often not the case so I would have to intervene to try to prompt discussion and I was conscious of the risk that I might not have fully grasped the detail of the subject under discussion and thereby make a fool of myself. The worst sessions to chair were those after dinner when we usually had a guest speaker. If we had had a tiring day and a little too much wine, overseeing a useful, intelligent and courteous discussion was challenging if the visitor did not grip the audience. We did not persist in inviting speakers who failed to grasp the dynamics of the process on which we were engaged. Course members bonded with each other, it was "their" course, and they could present a formidable critical audience to an 'outsider' if they chose to do so.

I much enjoyed marketing the programme to the Chairmen and/ or Chief Executives of private sector companies. Many of them were very generous in coming to the programme and speaking. For example, James Hanson used to arrive and depart by helicopter which much impressed course members. I remember calling on Derek Rayner at Marks & Spencer and as I walked in he said, pointing at the great pile of spreadsheets on his desk, "I am glad you are here as this is all your fault." He showed me the print-outs and explained that he received the sales results of every store in the land on a daily basis (this was his hands-on period of the day) and when he rang to ask why the results at a particular store weren't good enough he was often told that the person in charge was away on a training course. "I hope it wasn't yours," he said. Then he smiled and we had our planned discussion.

The TMP had been launched to secure at least two enduring prizes: to encourage the public and the private sectors to learn to work together; and to train people to take a more strategic view of how their organisations might develop and play a part in the way the whole of the UK economy and society could work better. It was infected, and I don't mean that critically, by Mrs Thatcher's view of what was needed by way of change. I imagine the Prime Minister felt that the public servants on the course might have some of the magic dust of the private sector rubbed off on them and that we might all (public or private) be encouraged to lift our eyes beyond the silos in which we often lived our professional lives to embrace a wider vision of the contribution we could make to a successful United Kingdom in the longer term. On the courses I ran I think this sense of purpose worked for most participants and the learning was mutually beneficial and was not just one way. And as usual friendships were made and sustained and useful links were formed and developed.

My life as the Director of the TMP, was peripatetic. For example, we did a month at Elvetham Hall near Fleet in Hampshire (three times), a month at Nuneham Courtenay by the Thames in Oxfordshire (twice), and a month at Uplands, a more modern Conference Centre near High Wycombe (once). Tessa Blackstone[1], then at or about to go to run Birkbeck College, was on the latter course and was my extremely good tennis partner. A lot of tennis was played on these courses. While the intellectual demands of the programme exercised the brain, the quality and quantity of food and wine were a challenge to the body mass index and strenuous tennis was a good and necessary response.

During one of the Nuneham Courtenay courses in 1988 there was the Election for the Chancellorship of Oxford University. Saturday 14th March was the day for voting personally in Oxford. I and my wife had a special interest in the election as our former boss and friend Roy Jenkins was standing against Ted Heath (a fellow Balliol man) and Lord Blake (Provost of Queens and historian of the Conservative Party); the contest was between a liberal democrat radical who should have been a Labour Prime Minister against a Conservative who had been Prime Minister, both passionate Europeans, and Blake a conservative masquerading as non-political. So we motored the five miles to Oxford for the day. As a Cambridge graduate this sort of fun had been denied me. Queues of graduates of all ages in gowns (you could not vote if you were gown-less) thronged the streets and lined up to vote. We wandered along the various queues meeting and greeting many friends. Had we been in Italy we would have called it a 'fiesta'; it was certainly a "passeggiata." We stayed for the result. When it came, in the evening, it was: Roy Jenkins – 3,249 votes; Lord Blake – 2,674 votes: Edward Heath – 2,348 votes. We were obviously delighted, although sorry for Ted as perhaps Blake had split the Conservative vote. We assumed Roy would be carried off in triumph to an uproarious 18th century style bibulous and bucolic dinner given by his most well-heeled supporters, but he turned to Laura and to me and invited us to his house at East Hendred for a celebratory modest supper for four, with a lot of delicious wine.

A fierce extraneous event hit TMP 11 in October 1987. The great storm which ripped up trees across southern England came to us overnight at Elvetham Hall in Hampshire. I woke up early to find, that having left the bedroom windows open as I normally did, I and the bed and the floor were fully carpeted with leaves and the trees outside that were still standing, had no leaves. I rang my wife to describe my bosky experience only to find she had done even better and that the temporary roof on our house in London had ended up in a friend's garden five houses away. Some of the participants on the course, particularly those who lived in Kent and Sussex had to be allowed home to assess and deal with the damage. I do not know whether this event had a particular bonding impact on the group but of all the courses I ran it is the only one that continues with an annual reunion lunch and a planned discussion of serious topical issues of the day.

When at the end of four weeks the civil servant members of the programme turned up at the Civil Service College for the final fortnight there was a palpable sense of anti-climax and bereavement; apart from a serious decline in the quality of food and wine. With the benefit of hindsight I cannot say that I am sure this more introspective period of study and debate was really necessary. The important impact had already been made. Perhaps all that was needed was, at most, a week discussing the value to the civil servants of the previous part of the programme, plus a few seminars on current governmental issues, interspersed with some entertainment from visiting speakers, like, I recall, the occasional Field Marshal. A week rather than two would have been enough for that. However, this was our time to reflect on the timeless values of the Civil Service – of objectivity, impartiality and a committed loyalty to implement the policies of the Government of the day- of which we were the guardians on behalf of the Crown, so that the course members as they moved onwards and upwards could re-embed them in their hearts and minds and live them out as examples for their staff.

There was some reading set for this part of the programme but I doubt if it matched up to the prescription in the Macaulay Report on the selection and training of entrants into the "Civil Service of the East India Company" published in 1854, the same year as the Northcote – Trevelyan report, which led to Civil Service appointment on merit rather than by patronage.

The Macaulay Report said:

"The new recruit should study Indian history, not merely in the works of Orme, of Wilkes, and of Mill, but also in the travels of Bernier, in the Odes of Sir William Jones ... He should understand the mode of keeping and checking accounts, the principles of banking and the laws that regulate the exchanges."

On the TMP there was plenty of accounting and banking and the regulation of the City but not much history and no officially prescribed poetry. There were, however, lectures on Time Management from business school and management consultancy gurus. Not as good as poetry (the Poet Laureate of the day should surely have been a regular visitor but why didn't I think of that?) but at the time I was, in my naivety, impressed by the Time Management sessions. It seemed terribly grown-up and creative to plan your diary with periods in which you deliberately settled down for reflection and strategic thought. I later discovered when attempting to practise this discipline that it only worked if you were totally in charge of your own time. It turned out it was difficult to tell the office of the Chancellor of the Exchequer or the Secretary of State or the Cabinet Secretary that you couldn't go round for a chat, however urgent they thought it was, because it was your time of the day or week for a pause for private undisturbed strategic thought.

The Node, as I have mentioned, was a different and more relaxed animal. It had distinguished Joint Chairmen in the Cabinet Secretary, Sir Robert Armstrong and the head of BP, Sir Peter Walters. I had to attend a meeting with them to get my marching orders which were not at all demanding. The Node had been going for years and was one of those public/private sector institutions, created in the post-war years to rekindle something of that powerful mixture of people from the public and private sectors working side by side during the war and afterwards. (Another such institution was the Whitehall Dining Club made up of Permanent Secretaries and Captains of Industry and Commerce, which was a 'one night' version of the Node, with one of its members giving a topical after-dinner talk. I was its Chairman in the 1990s.) My first, and indeed only, chance to lead The Node should have been in the summer of 1987 but Mrs Thatcher called a General Election and it seemed sensible to postpone the course. Therefore in late November - early December 1987 the only ever known "Summer Node in Winter" took place. Its title sounds like a ballet, either by the Ballet Russes[2] or by Fred Ashton[3].

The format of the week, mostly participants talking about their own professional lives, was very popular with the participants – there is nothing easier or more enjoyable than talking about yourself - and there were also good visiting speakers. However, it is memorable in my recollection for an event that had nothing to do with the course at all. My wife was then expecting our third child and on the 3rd of December she told me she was going in to hospital the following day to have the baby. I asked my then Permanent Secretary, Anne Mueller, if she would cover for me and she kindly did so. Our son, Tom – at the time of writing now an actor – was born on the 4th of December and I returned to the course which was coming to an end on the following day. I was greeted with presents – boxes of nappies, other useful baby equipment and various soft toys. As it turned out it would have been a nice way to bow out of a rather extraordinary job but I had one more TMP to run, TMP 12, at Nuneham Courtenay in Oxfordshire. However, after I had moved on, on 9 June 1988 I attended the Node's Silver Jubilee Dinner; it had been created in 1963 when I was an undergraduate, in what was still a period of post-war consensus and one of growing optimism. An optimism which, twenty five years later, I then still shared. I do not do so now.

Training and development programmes are subject to great fluctuations of fashion but the TMP managed to last for 20 years having become part of another ephemeral creation, the Centre for Management and Policy Studies (CMPS) in 1999. The Civil Service College, which had existed since 1967, the year of the Fulton Report, was however abolished when the CMPS was created. Things have moved on since.

While I was running TMP 12 in early 1988 the new Cabinet Secretary, Robin Butler[4], asked me to see him. He said that everyone ('omnium consensi') thought I had done a good job but it was time I moved on and I was to go to the Treasury to take over from a Deputy Secretary, Peter Kemp, on the public expenditure side of the Department. Peter, whom I had met, was a man of considerable but quirky intellect and great emotional volatility. When Robin Butler left for the Cabinet office Peter had been greatly put out that he had not succeeded Robin as Second Permanent Secretary in charge of public expenditure. He protested hotly, talked about resignation and was moved, on promotion as a sort of consolation I presume, to the management side of the Cabinet Office in charge of the Next Steps reform programme.

I walked across the road to the Treasury to meet Peter Middleton[5] my new boss. He told me that my principal initial task was to lead the Treasury input into the review to reform the NHS, which had recently been agreed. The Prime Minister had announced in a TV interview that she would put many more millions of pounds into the NHS but without having cleared what she had said with the Chancellor, Nigel Lawson. He was, understandably, pretty cross and said that not a penny would be released unless there was a thorough review of the NHS, the way it worked, its organisation and its ability to know how to provide evidence it was giving value for money. On my second day in the new job I went to meet the Chancellor at No 11 Downing Street. After some brief pleasantries he said to me: "They tell me you are good at strategic thinking and you'll need to be as this review is to set the long-term direction for the NHS. Do you know much about the NHS and health policy?" "No," I replied. "Nor do I," he said, "so at least we approach the task with an open mind."

The whole process of the review of the NHS was conducted very simply. The Prime Minister chaired a trio of Ministers — herself, Nigel Lawson and the Health Secretary (at first John Moore[6] and then Ken Clarke[7]). She was helped by Brian Griffiths[8] at No 10 and Richard Wilson in the Cabinet office and I supported the Chancellor. The three senior civil servants met with Brian to prepare for the meetings of the Ministerial trio. It was a highly efficient process. To help fill in the vast gaps in my lack of knowledge about the NHS I did a very non-Treasury thing – I went out and met doctors and nurses and health service managers in the places where they worked. The most memorable of these visits was to Addenbrooke's in Cambridge to talk to the renowned liver transplant surgeon, Sir Roy Calne. When I arrived I was told to go to the ward where his patients were and there I met him in his uniform white coat accompanied by his registrars and house-men and women, all similarly dressed. Thus I set off on my first and only ever ward-round. When we reached the first bed there was a woman who seemed to be attached to very many tubes and machines. Roy Calne leant over her and, in a quiet voice, said: "This is Mr Phillips from the Treasury who is going to help us." She looked at me rather nervously and then I saw her eyes run towards one of the main tubes to which she was attached. I think she was not entirely convinced that "The Man from the Treasury" was really there to help and was concerned that I might decide to unplug her life-support machine on grounds of affordability and value for money.

There followed an intensive year's work until we produced a White Paper on 31 January 1989 entitled *Working for Patients*. It presaged the first radical reform of the NHS since its creation in 1948, and broke up the centralised monolith the NHS had become. Delegation of decision making from Whitehall was the order of the day. Hospitals would be given self-governing status as NHS Trusts earning revenue directly as an incentive to attract patients. Trusts could set their own rates of pay and they could borrow. And money would follow the patient across the system to offer him/her services both public and private. In the foreword to the White Paper the Prime Minister said: "We aim to extend patient choice, to delegate responsibility to where the services are provided and to secure the best value for money." The Leader of the Opposition, Neil Kinnock, said the White Paper should have been called *Working for Accountants*.

Perhaps the Treasury influence on the outcome had, after all, been what Nigel Lawson wanted.

Most of this book was written during the Covid-19 pandemic which prompted me to reflect on the state of the management of the NHS now compared to thirty odd years ago. In the last few years I have seen the NHS at work closely, as happens as you get older, in terms of clinical, including nursing, care; and loud applause should rightly ring out for the service that countless doctors and nurses provide. But I find it difficult to connect that with our 1989 reforms and I therefore worry that there is too much preoccupation with structures and systems and that successive Health Secretaries, wanting to produce their own legacy, seek to change the current arrangement for the sake of it. I know that no organisation, however successful, can stand still, but I do believe the NHS, in terms of structure, has too frequently been mucked about with. I will end that little rant at this point. But my best 'in hospital' moment was when I was recovering from some necessary procedure and I was visited by a Bishop, a Dean and a Canon all together. When they left one of my fellow patients said: "What a relief – when we saw that lot we thought you were a goner."

The Treasury was a wonderful working environment but to a newcomer a rather strange one. As a very senior official I lived in an office on the rotunda looking down into the central courtyard of the building, while Ministers lived at the corners of its square surround. There were regular ritual meetings; the weekly meeting of Second Secretaries chaired by the Permanent Secretary and, on the public expenditure side, weekly meetings called PEX and COGPEC chaired by the Second Permanent Secretary in charge of Public Expenditure. I cannot recall the precise purpose of these acronymic creatures only that on one occasion the Chairman asked: "Any views from the sofa?" on which three officials were seated. One of the main things that struck me about the culture in the Treasury was the speed with which it was necessary to comment on drafts that people circulated before they went to the Chancellor or to the Chief Secretary. If you missed the boat you were not heard. The other thing was that at the top of the office it felt very collegiate compared to the relative solitariness I had in previous jobs elsewhere, including my time in the Home Office. While it was intellectually competitive it was personally cooperative which produced a powerful and compelling working ethos which I much liked.

In August 1988, after I had been in the Treasury for five months, Peter Middleton called me in and told me that as all the other top brass were on leave for the next two weeks I was in charge so he hoped nothing serious would happen! I said I agreed. He told me I had one task to complete and nothing else mattered. I was to ensure that a young man named Jeremy Heywood became the Private Secretary to the Financial Secretary. Jeremy was interviewed and got the job. He was undoubtedly one of the best officials with whom I worked. At No 10 in later years as the Prime Minister's Principal Private Secretary he always made time for me however busy he was. His early death when he was an elegant, wise and efficient Cabinet Secretary was a tragedy.

In the Treasury I was responsible for the oversight of the expenditure of a number of non-economic departments: the Home Office and the Lord Chancellor's Department, Health and Social Security, Education, Scotland, Wales and Northern Ireland, the Office of Arts and Libraries; and Local Government expenditure. In addition, I was also responsible for the thematic subjects of Value for Money, for the Next Steps agency creation programme and for the Civil List. The only one of these which I found really challenging intellectually was local government finance. It was one of those areas which required, so it seemed to me, a high degree of profoundly arcane knowledge. (I remember Willie Whitelaw saying that to me years before when he had to chair Cabinet Committees on the subject.)

Most people who join the Treasury enter it at relatively lower levels but to go in as I did as a Deputy Secretary (a Director General in today's Whitehall currency) was like becoming a direct-entry Bishop in a religion of which you did not have complete embedded theological command. So it was with local government finance in my case; but I had an Under-Secretary who knew it inside out, Andrew Edwards. There was only one occasion when I had to appear without his comforting presence which was a Nigel Lawson economic policy meeting in which conversation turned to how public expenditure numbers affected the interpretation of the overall economic position. He looked to me to explain the local government figures and how they influenced the position. Nothing except blind panic came into my head when I heard the voice of Rachel Lomax[9], then a senior economist in the Treasury, saying, "Perhaps I should respond to that as it is really quite technical". A true friend and ministering angel. She reappears later in the context of the National Theatre.

Nigel Lawson's meetings were always interesting although in my limited experience there was often little need to contribute. He seemed to have complete mastery of most of the issues under discussion and whether we were meeting in the Treasury or at No 11 he tended to open the discussion for a while and then invite comments on what he had said. But I recall one meeting at which the format took a different shape and that turned out to be largely my fault as he appeared to be staring at me, first with incredulity then with increasing curiosity, because a lot of my hair was dyed pink. I had just returned from two weeks holiday in India and the festival of Holi had occurred. We were in a small town, Samode, in Rajasthan. I, a much younger sister-in-law and a male cousin-in-law, went out into the town in the evening to see what went on. We came across several groups of revellers who threw pink paint and dye over us and sprayed us with water, all done with the utmost friendly cheerfulness. We had taken the precaution of wearing old and disposable clothes. Back at the hotel I tried to wash out the pink dye in my hair – to no avail. And although some of the colour had faded by the time I returned to England it was still very obvious at that first meeting in the Treasury. As the meeting ended and people began to leave I walked over to the Chancellor and told him what had occurred. He said he was greatly relieved.

Public expenditure concerns threw up some interesting moments. Very early in my time the Chief Secretary, John Major, called me in and told me that in the last public expenditure round the settlement that the Secretary of State for Social Security, John Moore, had accepted was inadequate in relation to housing benefit, and it would be better to ask him to accept more money now than to allow a demand driven programme to become a controversial failure. So I had to cross Whitehall to Richmond House and tell John Moore he had to accept an extra £180 million, or else! He did as he was told. For me it was an early lesson that Ministers must be careful to curb their affection for austerity in the economic interest of the nation because the politics of agreeing with the

Treasury's proposals could mean their impact on the voters might point in a quite different direction than one of approbation.

The most curious public expenditure issue I had to deal with very early in my time in the Treasury was the Prime Minister's request for £50 million to buy the Thyssen Collection[10] for the nation. I rang Neil MacGregor[11] at the National Gallery for advice. I asked what should be the priority purchase for the nation if I had £50 million to spend on a collection of works of art in private hands. Without hesitation he said that in terms of the UK it was the Duke of Sutherland's collection; if I was looking only to England then the answer was the Radnor Collection at Longford Castle[12]. I accordingly advised No 10 that her idea was bad value for money and there were better prospective purchases closer to home. I know my advice had no impact whatsoever but her plan came to naught anyway. I was later told that the Prime Minister had enlisted the Prince of Wales in her quest. I subsequently understood that the Countess Thyssen's dog died on the morning the Prince of Wales flew out to see her and she was too distraught to meet him in a timely way. I am told while having to hang about waiting he became rather disenchanted with the project. Whether true or not the story has a certain predictive charm as the Collection went to Madrid; which is probably what she wanted anyway. Value for money, for the UK, was in the end achieved.

Even in such a case, public expenditure choices often raise ethical and moral issues in some ways more powerful than those I had faced in the Home Office when dealing with riots and their causes, with racial attacks and with difficult immigration or asylum decisions. One small but evocative example occurred when I was going through with John Major the Home Office's bids for more money and our brief to him about how we should respond to their arguments. He said that he saw that I had advised against giving them the funds to end slopping out in prisons and asked whether I believed that slopping-out was acceptable. I replied that, of course, it wasn't, that it was a reprehensible practice and should go. So, he asked, why reject the bid to end it? So I said the normal boring thing that we couldn't afford to do it except by taking the money from elsewhere. So he said that that was what we would do. This was a 'good' decision but we were still left with finding the money from elsewhere; and, of course, we did, despite it involving another moral judgement not to favour another good cause.

My two years of engagement with public spending policies were a remarkable period in which instead of working within the context of a PSBR (public sector borrowing requirement) we had the context of a PSDR (public sector debt repayment). The amount of public money we were, therefore, able to give out in response to good arguments for worthy causes and to the public good was very satisfying; but in every case, however much money there was available, most decisions always involved an ethical decision or choice. I still wonder whether the public fully understands the difficulty of the decisions which Ministers and their advisers face in this area, when they have to balance the arguments about a whole range of desirable objectives and outcomes.

There was a ritual to the public expenditure round of bilateral meetings between the Treasury and the whole series of Departments. In later years the Government moved on to three year expenditure settlements. But when I was in the Treasury it was done a year at a time. The meetings to discuss a settlement with any particular Department were long; they often took a whole day, and sometimes more. The Chief Secretary was in the chair flanked by his relevant officials; across the table sat a Secretary of State flanked by his or her officials. One item of an expenditure bid was taken at a time. The best, i.e. most amusing, exchange on an agenda item at which I was present was on Health expenditure. Norman Lamont[13] was Chief Secretary and we were having the bilateral with Ken Clarke as Health Secretary. He asked, after about half an hour, whether Norman minded him lighting a cigar. Of course not, Norman replied, and said he would have one too. I smoked small cheroots in those days and joined in. The next request, said Ken, was for £25 million for a "Look after your Heart" campaign. We all paused and looked at each other and the Secretary of State, smiling, said, "In the circumstances I think I should drop that bid." He went on to secure everything else he wanted. Brilliant.

Early in 1990 Peter Middleton asked to see me to explain that Anne Mueller, who had come into the Treasury when Peter Kemp went to lead the Next Steps team in the Cabinet Office, was about to retire and he wanted me to take charge of her portfolio of Civil Service Management and Pay and also take my Next Steps and Civil List work with me.

Peter quickly added that while I would not be promoted (Anne had been a Second Permanent Secretary) I would be placed at the highest point of the Deputy Secretary pay scale.

While the role was not as central to the impact on the outside world that my public expenditure job had had it was a very independent command, important to the internal life of the effective working of Whitehall and it made me an Accounting Officer[14] for the first time (for the gripping subject of Civil Service Pensions) and the Chairman of the regular cross-departmental meetings of the heads of personnel in all departments (known as the Establishment Officers Meeting – EOM). Pay policy, and meetings with the Trade Unions, were a regular preoccupation but I found the most intractable issues I had to face were the pay of Ministers and, above all, Members of Parliament. I was very conscious that compared to legislatures in most other democratic countries our MPs were quite seriously underpaid. I discussed this with John Major, who by now had become Chancellor, and we agreed that whatever the merits of the arguments, we had to accept that the time for a serious increase in pay for Members of Parliament was "never ripe".

This chronic problem can only be tackled without MPs being involved at all. The pay review Bodies make recommendations to Government and then Government decides. It might be better if the relevant Pay Review Body was allowed to decide; but I know that would be difficult to achieve.

A lot of time was spent attending the meetings of the various Pay Review Bodies but one of my principal day-to-day preoccupations was what the Treasury's response should be to the creation of a whole series of Next Steps Agencies. Their purpose was to get a greater focus on the better delivery of services and the chosen mechanism was to separate large "delivery" chunks of the Civil Service from the smaller cores of policy advisers with whom Ministers had the greatest day-to-day contact. I had played so far a small part as a reformer in the Thatcher programme to improve management in the Civil Service by running the TMP, the flagship training programme for change, but in the Treasury my role was different as there had been a troubled history about the Next Steps programme. The Next Steps plan was to move about 75% of civil servants into autonomous agencies. As the Institute for Government's summary history of the programme put it: "Thatcher was reportedly wary, primarily because of the enormity of the proposed change and the prospect of Treasury hostility .... The Treasury, as expected, was highly resistant, fearing a loss of control over public finances and upward pressure on agency expenditure." Through a large part of 1987 there had been a continuing battle with the Treasury but Nigel Lawson was eventually won round when he became convinced that Next Steps fitted with the political commitment of using market models for public service delivery. During 1988 therefore I found myself in charge of the Treasury role in two great change programmes – of the NHS and of the Civil Service.

But whereas in the former I could be the protagonist for change towards a market model for NHS services, in the latter my role was that of the diplomatic guardian of cautious advance to ensure control of expenditure was not thrown to the winds. Every single draft Agency Agreement in all its detail therefore had to be cleared with the Treasury. And this meant in practice a whole series of detailed negotiating meetings between Peter Kemp, who was not a natural delegator, and me. These occasions were rarely easy as his personal style was highly argumentative and sometimes deliberately confrontational with added intermittent walk-outs. As a former senior Treasury official he had become a complete and often fanatical convert to the new religion, looking on his old Treasury home as a primitive place full of creatures from a past unenlightened age. Many of the agency proposals were utterly straightforward to agree to and, bit by bit, a great deal of useful progress was made. But some of them it seemed to me were pointless and some others were not at all easy or wise. In the first category I never saw the purpose of re-creating the Inland Revenue and HM Customs and Excise as agencies as they would go on working exactly as they had been before. I suppose it helped hit a number of "agencies created" target and one of "the numbers of Civil Servants in Agencies"; and it may have offered them some new financial freedoms, but it seemed to me no more than a process of cosmetic re-labelling.

In the second category, and knowing life in the Home Office as I did, I was able to offer particularly dire warnings about turning the Prisons Service into an agency which would be at arms-length from the policy interests and political preoccupations of Ministers. I had too often seen how some operational prison crises escalated inevitably to the Home Secretary and I made it clear that the apparent rigidity of a framework agreement between Ministers and the parent department, and an agency Chief Executive, lacked the necessary flexibility to enable the system to adapt well when under pressure. I would have liked to block the proposal but knew I could not do so without an enormous row, with the then Home Secretary turning to the Prime Minister against the Chancellor, if the latter had agreed with me. In retrospect this was feeble of me to choose not to fight that battle. So, I was not at all surprised when some years later Michael Howard[15], then Home Secretary, sacked the Prison Service Agency Chief Executive, partly because of a confusion over their respective roles and accountabilities. (Around this time I had an ironic moment of 'prison' panic when Peter Middleton told me that the Home Secretary, then David Waddington, had asked for me to return to the Home Office to become Director-General of the Prison Service. Before I could gather my protest together he went straight on to say that "we have said no as we have other things in mind for you". And so it turned out.)

CHAPTER 6:
A Ministry of Culture

Where new Departments begin their lives • what the new Department did • hanging on to David Mellor • John Major at the Banqueting House • Olympic Golds in Barcelona • David has to resign • DNH gets press regulation and, eventually, a new home of its own • Peter Brooke arrives • Windsor Castle on fire • The Queen pays tax • the Duke of Edinburgh's Committee • Canada geese in St James's Park • Peter Palumbo locks himself in a cupboard • creating the National Lottery • the Churchill Papers • the Dome (Jocelyn Stevens, Michael Heseltine and Peter Mandelson) • the awful Millennium night • the PAC applauds a sacking • flirting with statutory press regulation – giving Horseguards Parade back to the people • the week after the death of Princess Diana • exploding flowers into compost • my wife gives me a racehorse • not becoming Cabinet Secretary • almost going to the Home Office.

O**N THE MORNING** after the remarkable, against the predicted odds, General Election Conservative Party victory in April 1992, the Cabinet Secretary, Robin Butler, asked me to come to see him. He said John Major wanted to offer me the job of Permanent Secretary in charge of his new creation, the Department of National Heritage. While he had had a different future in mind for me he would understand if I wanted to accept. I said I would like to do it and I left him to go to try to find somewhere for us to live. By 'us' I meant David Mellor[1], the first Secretary of State, and myself and our immediate staff. I was able to take my old Cabinet Office room at the back of the Treasury building overlooking the statue of Clive of India, while David had grander and more cavernous rooms along the corridor looking out on to St James's Park. My Treasury PA, Alison Yearley, agreed to come with me and she subsequently stayed, becoming central to the life of the new Department until she retired in 2018. The following day a young woman called Heather Wilkinson[2] asked to see me. She said she was the Home Secretary's Deputy Private Secretary but wanted a change, loved the idea of what the new Department was there to do, had not heard anything bad about me yet, and could she be my Private Secretary? Thus seduced, I said yes. It was a charmingly chaotic beginning.

The Horseguards Road end of the Treasury building, or the parts of the Cabinet Office which were not in the Cabinet Office in Whitehall, was the place where new departments began. I was delighted to find some excellent black and white newsreel footage from 1964 showing George Brown entering the new Department of Economic Affairs though the same door. However, I hoped the fate of that new creation's brief life would turn out not also to be ours. (Thirty years later the rechristened Department of Digital, Culture, Media and Sport, appears to thrive.)

I had a real sense of excitement at this new beginning. I had to create a new Department out of a number of parts of existing departments – museums, galleries and libraries from the Office of Arts and Libraries (a semi-detached part of the Cabinet Office); broadcasting (the Home Office); the built heritage (Environment), tourism (DTI) and sport (Education). I had to create a National Lottery to provide new funds for these and other sectors which would (in John Major's view) never be a priority for public expenditure, although they needed and deserved public support. And I needed to attract new and good senior staff. Fortunately, the process of change had shaken out a number of those on the verge of retirement so I was able to bring in some seriously good people. And I had to find us a permanent home. But despite all these potential problems to be resolved, I thought to myself, most happily, that I was being paid to take charge of the Government's responsibilities towards all those parts of our cultural and sporting life which were my personal passions and those of millions of my fellow citizens – theatre, opera, ballet and music; works of art; test matches and the Cup Final and Wimbledon; film premieres; and our heritage of great buildings and landscapes. I could not have said no to such a job offer, although the hint from the Cabinet Secretary had pointed to a quite different future.

But being able to enjoy the fruits of my new inheritance was yet to come as the growing preoccupation in my first few weeks was the fragile personal political position of David Mellor as my Secretary of State. He rang me on a Thursday evening in June 1992 to tell me that on the following Sunday, *The People* would publish a story about his affair with a young actress, Antonia de Sancha, The next day he asked me to be present at a meeting with Tim Bell[3] to discuss the media handling of his personal crisis. I was careful to ensure I took no active part in the plans and decisions they discussed. I was telephoned in the evening at home by the Prime Minister. He said he wanted my advice on what he should do: should David go or be allowed to stay? I said that my view was very clear; that if in all other respects a Minister was professional and effective in his public duties his private life should not be allowed to undermine his official position, unless what he had done affected the Government's position or policies directly. John Major said he was grateful for that advice and that he agreed with it. He said he understood that I was holding the first gathering of the whole department to celebrate its creation on the following Monday in the Banqueting House in Whitehall. He said he would come but no-one was to be told.

His Private Office arranged the logistics of his arrival and, at the precise time agreed, I was at the door to greet him and take him upstairs. As we went in to one of the most beautiful of grand rooms in the whole of London (albeit the one from which Charles I walked through a window to his execution) I asked for silence and the Prime Minister spoke: he spoke in praise of the Department's birth and its purpose and of his support for David as its political leader. It was magisterial and moving. The applause was a real thank you. He then worked the room and shook every hand. He had turned a potentially depressing moment into a celebratory triumph.

It had been a difficult time for David, and this was to continue while adverse media comment was regularly present. From time to time

he asked me to take on speaking engagements he could not face but gradually office life and our proper respective roles returned to normal. We
went to the Olympic Games in Barcelona ('we' is David, me and my wife,
Laura, whose costs, I hasten to add, I paid for myself – not a wholly fa-
cetious observation in view of what was to happen to David later). As we
landed in Spain a departmental press aide bounded on to the plane and
told David that 'hordes' of pressmen were waiting for him. He went very
pale and I asked the man why were they so keen to question the Secretary
of State. The man said there were allegations of drug abuse by our weight-
lifting squad. This was wonderful news compared to what he expected
and David approached the Press Conference with a big smile.

We were to do two full days at the Games. David took one look at
the programme for the first day which was, understandably perhaps, full
of 'politically correct' things for the Secretary of State to be seen to do,
and said that was all to be cancelled and, instead, we were going north
to the lake for the rowing. How right he was; that was the place for gold
medals for Britain and for a Secretary of State to be in the photos. Our
haul, with no effort from us other than from our driver getting us there
on time, was five golds. The next day we were in the stadium for some of
the athletic finals. We had three seats in the row below the Royal Box right
above the finishing line. We were there for Linford Christie's[4] Gold Medal and then for Sally Gunnell's[5]. Being the Minister or the Permanent
Secretary for Sport was a pretty 'fun' berth when things were going well.

But the clouds were gathering for him. In August David told me
he was going to have to give evidence in a libel case involving a woman
called Mona Bauwens, the wealthy daughter of the Treasurer of the PLO.
He told me that it would come out that he had taken free flights from
her and free holidays too. I told him that when this emerged the Government and the Party would be less forgiving than it had been over his
affair. Extra-marital sex was risky, interesting but not fatal; taking other
people's money to support your preferred lifestyle, if you were a Government Minister, was quite another matter. David was forced to resign on
24 September 1992. He had been in office only since 11th April.

Before turning to the arrival of my second Secretary of State I
should say that in the real world of real work some progress was being
made despite all the personal political turmoil. On the policy front David

had a particular preoccupation with the regulation of the Press, having commissioned the review of the performance of the press by David Calcutt[6] when he was in the Home Office. This had led him, David Mellor, to describe the press as "drinking in the last chance saloon". He was cross to find that while the new department was in charge of the regulation of broadcasting it was not in charge of press regulation, which remained with the Home Office. He asked me to see if I could persuade them to hand it over to us. It was with no expectation of success that I telephoned Clive Whitmore, then the Home Office Permanent Secretary. Unless transfers of responsibilities between departments form part of an agreed, or imposed, change in the machinery of Government, they are hard to secure as people's natural position is to want to keep all they have. I said to Clive that David wanted the responsibility very much indeed and produced arguments of logical fit with broadcasting. I felt this was pretty unpersuasive. Clive said he would go and have a word with the Home Secretary. I assumed this meant I would have to wait quite a while before the inevitable 'no' came. Fifteen minutes later Clive rang back and said we could have the responsibility for press regulation. I then knew that he had happily passed me what was, in his view, a poisoned chalice which Ministers would do best to keep well away from. A couple of years later in 1994 I discovered why. (And many years later, after the Leveson Report in 2014, I found that press regulation had continued to pursue me and I agreed to be in charge of appointing the next new regulator, the Independent Press Standards Organisation –IPSO).

During the first year of the new Department's existence I found a building for the Department to live in and got agreement for us to be there. It was not easy to achieve this. David had made up his mind that the new DNH had to make a statement through where it was located, and he had lighted on a modern building, owned by the Qataris, the address of which was No 1 Knightsbridge. It was almost exactly opposite No 1 London, i.e. Apsley House, the London residence of the Dukes of Wellington. David and I had a meeting with the Qataris in the Lanesborough Hotel to settle the rental cost. I put their proposal to the Treasury who turned it down fast, as the rent being asked for was, in their view (and in mine), exorbitant. I was not very surprised, having so recently, when in the Treasury, been in charge of saying no to most of such importunate demands, but I had not expected the profound visceral parsimony of my former colleagues when 'helping' to set up a new Department. Their counter-offer was that we could go to Elizabeth House, rent free. This building, occupied at some point by the Department for Education, was essentially a part of Waterloo Station. I did not see how I could sell this location, with however redolent a connection to the Iron Duke, either to David Mellor or to anyone else of any intelligence as a fitting home for the nation's first ever "Ministry of Culture." I could hear the French amusement at our 'typical' barbarism, and Lady Bracknell deeply intoning "your headquarters is a railway station?"

Fortunately, I had a compromise which my excellent search team had found. This was an elegant modern building in Cockspur Street on the edge of Trafalgar Square and close to the National Gallery. This felt like a good cultural location, albeit it was putting Nelson ahead of Wellington in my property preferences. The Treasury predictably said 'No' even though the rent was a precise compromise between their preference (no cost at all) and the Qataris' demands. How to escape from this dilemma was a serious preoccupation so I decided I had only one shot left, called 'force majeure'; in other words, the Prime Minister. My Private Secretary, Heather, was despatched on her scooter to take photos of Elizabeth House which were popped in an envelope and delivered to No 10 so the Prime Minister could fully appreciate the barbarism of the Treasury's preference. I then rang No 10 and told my sad story about how the bloodless Treasury mandarins, who knew the "price of everything but the value of nothing" but who should have been our closest friends, were trying to destroy his newly born child. It was then rapidly agreed we could go to Cockspur Street and this remained the Department's headquarters for many years. Amusingly, the private company that occupied the upper floors of the building took legal action to prevent us moving in on the grounds that the presence of civil servants in the building would lower the tone and put off their clients. Despite their well-paid lawyers search for arguments – did civil servants dress badly? Did we wash frequently enough? – the Judge threw out their case as wholly unfounded. At last we had a home to go to, but it took another year, until autumn 1993, before we could move in.

On the day after David had resigned, No 10 called to ask me whether I had any suggestions for the Prime Minister as to who my new

Secretary of State should be. They and I knew that what we really needed was someone of wisdom and experience who would steady a rather battered young ship. I suggested that the Prime Minister should welcome Peter Brooke back into Government. The next call from No 10 told me to be in the Prime Minister's Office in the House of Commons at 2 pm. When I arrived he was in a very good practical joking mood and decided he would give me various clues so I could guess who my new Secretary of State was to be. It was quite funny because as I tried to guess the answer to each clue he would say, "Well, what do you think of that?" and I would say, "You couldn't do that to me," or "You must be joking." The game ended, a door was opened and there was Peter Brooke. This could not have been better in personal terms. I had worked with him in the Treasury; my wife and I had bought his parents' house in Wiltshire in 1984; and I knew he was wise, intelligent and was seriously interested and committed to the work of the department. He would steady the battered ship. And he did so until July 1994; long enough for it to be able to make its way safely in the world.

But his arrival was literally a baptism of fire. If we wanted a big event in our lives, we got it. On Friday 20 November 1992 Windsor Castle was ablaze. My new Department was in charge of the Government's responsibilities for the Occupied Royal Palaces. In the afternoon I was telephoned by David Airlie, the Lord Chamberlain. I was in a meeting when he called and Heather explained that but said she would go and fetch me as a call from the Lord Chamberlain was a rare event and it had to imply something important. At that point he said to her, "Oh, no Heather, don't interrupt him. But if he could call back, might you tell him that Windsor Castle is on fire?" She tells me she yelped down the phone, "Please don't go away, Lord Airlie," and dashed to get me. He told me the fire was under control but there had been an enormous amount of damage. We agreed that Peter Brooke and I would go to Windsor on the following morning.

It was a damp grey day with a persistent drizzle and everything about the Castle looked and felt like the blackened remains of a past glory. We toured the most badly damaged parts of the Castle. Peter then had to meet the Press, all gathered below the Mound. He asked me who was responsible for paying for the restoration and I made the mistake of only telling him the truth, namely that Windsor Castle was owned by the State so the Government, i.e. the taxpayer, was responsible. He was duly asked that question and answered with the truth. The next day there was uproar – indeed even that evening the Treasury Permanent Secretary had asked me what on earth we thought we were doing. The press spent the weekend up in arms that the 'people' should be expected to pay to restore and refurbish a Castle in which a very rich woman lived.

The outcome, announced by the Prime Minister the following week, was that while there would be a Government contribution, the weight of the cost of restoration would be borne by income from the opening of Buckingham Palace to the public for the first time and, once the work had been completed, from the income from the opening of Windsor Castle. The Queen agreed to make a personal contribution but, underlining a moment of crisis for the monarchy, also agreed for the first time to pay income tax. I wondered at the time, and still do, whether these dramatic outcomes would have occurred if I had given different advice to Peter Brooke. I suppose that what I could have done was to have told him the truth but advised him to say in public no more than that he would discuss how the restoration would be paid for with the Chancellor of the Exchequer and the Palace authorities. But if he had said that would the substantive result have been any different? I doubt it, although the volume of noise would have been lower and my Secretary of State's reputation would not have been damaged to the extent which it was; thanks to my honest but unsubtle advice.

The restoration of Windsor Castle remained a part of my life for some time as I joined the Restoration Committee (which I preferred to refer to as the *Committee of Taste*) chaired by the Duke of Edinburgh, with the Prince of Wales as Deputy Chairman, plus David Airlie, Jocelyn Stevens[7], Frank Duffy[8] and me. It was a top class committee in that it met rarely, and when it met it met briefly. Discussion was succinct and the Chairman made it fun. The Duke was very clear that while a lot of the restoration should be just that, there should also be a 20th century contribution to a building which reflected so many styles over so many centuries. The seat of the fire had been in the Private Chapel which had been utterly destroyed. He persuaded the Committee, without any difficulty, that there should be a new architecturally modern Private Chapel flanked and lit from above by a new Lantern Lobby which was the first addition to the skyline of the Castle for 160 years.

One day I was a little late for his meeting and when I arrived the Duke took me over to the window looking down the Mall and asked me why there were new traffic arrangements being put in place around the Victoria Memorial. In his view they created chaos. I was not well briefed about the new planned arrangements and muttered something about two Japanese tourists being killed. This did not seem to work very well as a persuasive explanation so, in my rather flustered state, I added that he was not the only one to complain as, when my wife was late arriving for Covent Garden the week before and, agitatedly, I had asked her why, she said it was because of the new roadworks outside Buckingham Palace. He simply replied that if I was having trouble at home he would not add to my woes. He also much enjoyed one other minor disaster which could be laid at my door in relation to a Royal Park, St James's. There was terrible trouble (smell and mess) from the defecation of Canada geese on the grass surrounding the lake. I approved a plan whereby at dead of night while the geese were sleeping they would be drugged and put into trucks and driven to the Norfolk/Suffolk coast where they would be released. The geese arrived back in St James's Park before my staff returned from their outing to the seaside.

Around this time, in the autumn of 1992, I was asked if I would be prepared to move to the Department of Education as its Permanent Secretary. It was a very attractive suggestion but I said no on the grounds that would be wholly unfair on the new department for it to have to lose its first Secretary of State and then its Permanent Secretary within six months of its birth. I mentioned this to Peter Brooke who, I think, was both surprised and pleased at my decision.

Peter was wonderful to work with but there was one occasion on which I, briefly, did not feel quite so warm towards him. Central Television decided to give a dinner in honour of John Thaw[9] and the *Inspector Morse* series. Peter was asked to make the main speech. Two days before the event he told me that Parliamentary business meant he could not do it and I would have to stand in for him. I worked on a draft and, when the evening came I was ready to perform. After about half an hour into dinner Peter appeared and was placed on a side table. Everyone saw he

86

had arrived and was therefore able to speak. I shot round and asked him to do so but he said he really did not want to but I insisted it would look rude as he was there for him not to speak. So he said he would speak for a few minutes. He did so telling some brilliant and amusing stories that brought the house down. He ended by saying, "I will now ask the Permanent Secretary to give the official speech." As the rapturous applause died away and I stood up a voice said clearly, "Follow that then." I did, and I just about got away with it.

Our first public expenditure round in 1993 was memorable for one event. We had received a flat cash result which was disappointing. Peter and I had to explain this to our major dependent quangos. The Chairman of the Arts Council, Peter Palumbo, came in to see us and was told the bad news. He said that it was totally unacceptable and walked out without a further word. Unfortunately the door through which he walked was into a cupboard not into the corridor. There was no means of escape from inside the cupboard so I had to release him, to his embarrassment. He was however a great Chairman and I remember one occasion especially. He gave a dinner for the living former Chairs of the Arts Council of Great Britain and kindly invited me and my wife. I sat next to a very chatty Arnold Goodman[10]. After the second course Peter said we should pause for a moment and then Willard White[11] walked in and sang to us. Sheer magic. He had come to us in the interval of his Recital that evening at the Royal Festival Hall.

Having passed through the Windsor Castle crisis the strategic policy priority for the new Department and for me was the creation of the National Lottery. This was a big legislative task but we had a good team for that work so I could focus my personal contribution on putting the right people in place both to run the Lottery and to distribute the proceeds. After a competitive tender Camelot won the contract to run it and there was not too much controversy about that. We set up a regulator (Oflot – which sounded like a Russian airline) and then we had to appoint distributing bodies for "the good causes" - the Arts, Sport, the Heritage, the Millennium and Charities. The arts and sport already had their publicly funded sponsor bodies in the Arts Council and the Sports Council and there was no point in adding in new bureaucracies. The heritage was trickier as it covered the built and natural heritage as well as museums and galleries and a lot else beside. I did not want to set up a new quango unless I had to do so and fortunately I found the perfectly formed body in the shape of the National Heritage Memorial Fund (NHMF)[12]. But it was small and it was likely that lottery funds would completely transform its nature so I could only proceed by agreement. Lord Rothschild[13], whom I knew, had succeeded Sir Martin Charteris[14] as Chairman of the NHMF, so I needed to persuade him to take it on. I did this over a picnic lunch at a point-to-point at Barbury Castle near our home in Wiltshire. Lord and Lady Rothschild provided the picnic. However, as there were no existing structures to tackle grants to charities and plans for the Millennium the bodies to make these decisions had to be new creations.

The first Lottery Draw was on the 19th of November 1994. Peter Brooke and I had agreed we should buy tickets but that if we won we would give the money to charity. We did not win. (I was very faithful to the Lottery over the ten years in which I remained in the Civil Service always accepting that if I received a reasonably significant sum I would give it to a charity. Sadly that moral dilemma never occurred.)

During our preparations for the Lottery legislation we had taken independent professional commercial advice about how much money was likely to be raised. It turned out that, in practice, it realised three times as much as the best independent estimate that had been given to us. Why? My own view was and remains that, as so often in life, our clever consultants applied everything they knew technically and analytically about the modern gambling market but did not read the history books. Had they done so they would have known that lotteries had become increasingly popular in England from the 16th century onwards until they became a corrupted obsession for vast numbers of the population in the late 18th and early 19th century. Advertisements then appeared in classy broadsheets telling the reader that he or she could afford to buy a new carriage or a commission in the Army or Navy for a third son if they played the Lottery. It all got too big and as it was totally unregulated it became an easy victim of Victorian moralistic antipathy. Mrs Thatcher, perhaps unsurprisingly, inherited that very critical view. When I was in the Treasury and when she was Prime Minister I briefed against the introduction of a National Lottery. When John Major arrived I honed the arguments in its favour with care.

I realised early on in my tenure that John Major had put his finger on a continuing and chronic problem namely that the existing sectors he had in particular identified – the Arts, Sport and the Heritage – could never rely on the public subsidy they had and still did receive; partly because to some people the very existence of such public expenditure grants was anathema, and partly because they were never given a level of consistent support that enabled sensible planning. For example, in my first year, Mary Soames, whom I had known from Brussels days, asked me to visit her at the National Theatre where she, as Chairman, gave me an extensive tour of leaking roofs and ceilings. I asked her how much she needed for a temporary fix ahead of some serious refurbishment. She said £100,000. I saw to it that she got it. I then visited the Victoria & Albert Museum and was treated by my hosts to the delights of "six or twelve bucket galleries" where the water ingress was collected in that simple way on a regular basis. This degree of neglect was all a result of a familiar and predictable pattern of cutting expenditure on maintenance when times were hard only to find you had stored up major capital expenditure requirements and could often have a disaster on your hands. There was a lot of real pent-up and justified demand for help.

But these experiences, and others, made me realise we needed to build a firewall between the funds flowing from the Lottery to the "good causes" and the envious looks of politicians and the Treasury at this potential cornucopia of wealth flowing to sectors they did not think the electorate really cared about as much as, say, the NHS or schools. The National Lottery Charities Commission was probably safe from invasion but the rest of the distributing bodies were always at risk from a raid. So we developed and articulated the doctrine of "additionality" i.e. lottery funds had to be additional to and separate from those things which public expenditure had traditionally supported. In building the firewall I gained the support of the National Audit Office (NAO) and I insisted that all the Lottery bodies' rules on applications for money were cleared with the NAO. We held the line on this policy for long enough to achieve substantial success for the original good causes of the Lottery and prevented the policy of Lottery funds supporting only them being undermined too quickly.

One of the earliest big grants was £13.25 million from the Heritage Lottery Fund in April 1995 to enable the purchase of the Churchill Papers. The Cabinet Secretary (Robin Butler), Jacob Rothschild and I had congratulated ourselves on stopping the papers from being sold abroad and I felt that to have the first big grant having the name of Churchill on it would be highly evocative and welcomed; but, sadly, congratulations were not what the announcement of our securing the papers provoked. The purchase led to entirely adverse front-page news. Some expressed incredulity that the Papers were not already owned by the nation (actually some were, being official papers for which the Lottery did not pay). Others took the view that the lottery grant should not enrich "Young Winston"[15] who seemed to create some deep loathing in the Press. Others felt that the Churchill family should have handed them over for nothing. It was not a great public relations start for lottery grants but it was absolutely right to do it, and the storm blew away as quickly as its clouds had appeared in the sky.

Looking back over the first few years of the Lottery I believe it was a period of real success both in terms of creative investment and also in meeting long pent up needs for more resources. One of the most notable such investments I was closely involved with was the creation of Tate Modern. There were many voices, including mine, who said that our first national gallery of modern art should be housed in a wholly new architectural creation. But then Nick Serota[16] asked me to go with him to Bankside Power Station. We walked through the Turbine Hall, then full of turbines, and went up onto the roof, as if into a high place on a mountain and indeed it was rather biblical as we gazed across the Thames to St Paul's Cathedral. He converted me to his vision and I dropped my support of the idea of a wholly new creation as this new realisation would be more than enough of a new creation; and in the process we saved a great historic building for the nation.

The MCC wanted to apply for lottery funds. The Chairman at the time was Oliver Popplewell[17] and he and the MCC Secretary came to see me in my office in Cockspur Street. I told them bluntly that they could not apply until they admitted women members. This they eventually did in 1998.

The impact of the Lottery, of course, was not only in London but right across the country; the Eden Project in Cornwall and the Millennium Stadium in Cardiff are good examples. One of the things the

Millennium Commission did very well was to fund small local projects, like village halls and other types of local meeting or recreational places. I remember touring the West Country visiting a number of such small projects and I was welcomed like a cross between Father Christmas and Mother Theresa.

But there were also some disasters. I found myself as the Permanent Secretary with oversight of the plans to celebrate the Millennium, including the Dome. I had originally hoped that the Government might agree to a modern replay of the Great Exhibition of 1851 and indeed recreate a Crystal Palace for it in Hyde Park. My advice was taken on the substance of the idea of a modern Exhibition but its place was to be the Dome by the Thames and the content was to be less boring than my historical precedent had implied. Actually the Dome project was not all grief; as this remarkable architectural triumph by Richard Rogers[18] was brought in on time and on budget and that was achieved by the man I had hired to save me from the expensive misery of the Government's failed management of the construction of the British Library at St Pancras. In the early days of planning the Dome, things seemed to proceed quite smoothly. The Secretary of State of the day chaired the Millennium Commission, and the Deputy Prime Minister, Michael Heseltine, was in charge of the Dome project itself. Although I attended the meetings I was rarely asked to intervene. Then we suddenly had to find a new Chief Executive of the Commission and I asked Jennie Page[19], the very able and experienced head of English Heritage (EH), if she would do it and she agreed.

The next morning the Chairman of EH, Jocelyn Stevens, exploded into my office and told me in no uncertain terms what regime of torture would be visited on me for this abduction of his Chief Executive during the night. He then said that he resigned. I said I would not accept that and we talked further. He then resigned again and then once more. Each time I said I would not accept his resignation and he said he would go to see the Secretary of State, who at that point was Stephen Dorrell[20]. Jocelyn returned, beaming. I said that I assumed he had not resigned and he replied that I was right. He had told the Secretary of State that his price for continuing in office was twofold: first, he wanted my head in a Sainsbury's plastic bag and, second, he wanted £25 million extra for EH in compensation for the kidnapping of Jennie Page. Stephen Dorrell said he could not deliver the first, but he would deliver the second. I am still pondering on the reason for the specificity of a "Sainsbury's" plastic bag but I suppose Jocelyn was a loyal customer or shareholder. The late John Sainsbury[21] much enjoyed this story.

As we moved closer to the timing of big decisions on the Dome it became clear that a final judgement about whether it should go ahead as planned was likely to be made by a Labour Government. Labour's support of the plans was therefore necessary. Michael Heseltine, quite properly, had made sure that I was his Dome Permanent Secretary. He asked me to talk to Jack Cunningham[22], then my Shadow Secretary of State. I explained to Jack the level of investment already made and that if the Labour Party could not take it forward it would be a failure of ambition that might well be laid at their door. He told me that he did not have the authority to commit the leadership. I told Michael Heseltine who said I had done everything I could for him and he would now go to see Tony Blair himself. He did and Blair told him he was persuaded to support the Dome plan.

However, with the Blair Government in power it did not turn out to be that simple. Whatever my personal knowledge was of the exchanges between Blair and Heseltine before the Election, I was told to draft an entirely neutral paper for the Cabinet, without a recommendation; one of those mortifying "on the one hand and on the other but it's up to you" pieces of prose. In the new government Peter Mandelson[23] had taken over Michael Heseltine's role in relation to the Dome and the Millennium. In the subsequent discussion most of the Cabinet were against the Dome plan so the Prime Minister broke off the discussion and held a separate talk with a few key colleagues after which he announced that the Government would go ahead with the Dome.

On the night of 31st December 1999, after a drinks reception in the Royal Gallery of the House of Lords, my family and I joined the Government VIP group to take the underground to the Dome. As we walked from the station towards the Dome my 16 year old hunting and riding daughter, Louisa, spied an urban fox and called out "Kill the Fox" as we walked with the grandees of New Labour towards the disastrous opening night. Large numbers of important guests were seriously delayed by bungled security checks at Stratford. However that night I felt most keenly for the Archbishop of Canterbury who had to come on at midnight after the Corrs[24] had sung and therefore, in an entirely inappropriate atmosphere, to try to lift our eyes to a new and blessed future horizon. "The Corrs" then "Let us Pray." It was all truly awful. (Ironically my eldest daughter, Rachel, was in charge of public relations for the Dome, and spent a frantic few hours/days trying to put the pieces back together.) And it got worse for me and those of my family who were there that night. When we got off the tube at Waterloo to try to collect our car which was parked near the Houses of Parliament we found that the crush of people was so great that the police were preventing anyone leaving the station. One of my daughters (of "Kill the Fox" fame) sat down and refused to move and there we sat for two hours until we were allowed to leave.

Unfortunately, despite all our best efforts to try to ensure that the workings of the National Lottery were free from criticism, one issue of impropriety led to a high-profile departure following what I believe remains a unique decision in Whitehall's administrative history. This was at the National Heritage Lottery Fund which I had happily persuaded Lord Rothschild to chair. He took with him his Chief Executive at the NHMF, a much smaller but beautifully formed organisation of 'last resort' grants to save great heritage objects. It came to my attention from an audit report that the Chief Executive, an extremely able woman called Georgina Naylor[25], had given IT contracts to her partner without any competitive tender. My legal advice was that she had failed to fulfil her responsibilities as an Accounting Officer in terms of propriety and I should strip her of that responsibility. With a heavy heart I decided I should do so but it meant she would have to resign as Chief Executive, being unable to carry out a central part of her job. I understand this remains the only case in Whitehall history of such a decision. It led to a Public Accounts Committee (PAC) hearing in which I was congratulated on my decision. Only twice was I congratulated by the PAC – and on each occasion it was because I had sacked somebody. I appeared before the PAC very frequently and, no doubt, like many of my colleagues, I felt its approach and processes were mostly ones of destructive criticism and a search for blame rather than for how lessons should be learned. I exempt from this description of their work and approach the chairmanship of David Davis, who, in my experience, always tried to take a constructive approach and use the criticism the Committee had to make as a base for an outcome of positive change in a Department.

My years in charge of culture, media and sport, whether under the original DNH banner or its 1997 DCMS re-incarnation, were immensely rich in policy content and in events that needed to be managed; and it is difficult to select a narrative about that time that will best hold the attention of a reader.

So – not wholly arbitrarily – I will cover in more detail three issues: press regulation, the transformation of Horse Guards Parade, and the death and then funeral of Princess Diana. And I will touch on sport on the way. But there was also so much more I could write about – the successful disaster of the handling of Canova's *Three Graces*[26]; the future of the Royal Opera House as it bumped along the bottom of solvency when it was forced on to the road during its closure for restoration and refurbishment; and most importantly the gradual coming together of the different parts of the Department and a growing sense of their belonging to each other. So many critics said that the DCMS was an ephemeral creation – here today gone tomorrow – and it would be abolished at the 'next Election' but that has not happened so far. In 2022 it was 30 years old and had become, in addition to its original roles, the lead digital department in Government.

During the three years before the creation of the Department there had been a lot of criticism about the behaviour of the press. David Mellor, when at the Home Office had engaged Sir David Calcutt to inquire into press regulation. He had produced a critical report but recommended the Press Complaints Commission be given time to prove itself as an effective self-regulatory body. One of David's first acts as the new Secretary to State, my having secured responsibility for press regulation from the Home Office to be a part of our portfolio, was to ask David Calcutt to return and say whether he thought the PCC had done a good enough job in the time that had passed. He produced a report early in 1993 which said that self-regulation had not worked and that he had to recommend that the Government should introduce a statutory regulatory regime. The Government initially said that it agreed, but over the period of the following year, while the Conservative supporting press became increasingly critical of John Major's government more generally, Peter Brooke skilfully extracted the Government from any engagement with legislation on the press. Instead, I was sent off to Canary Wharf, where a powerful but, to the general public, obscure organisation called Pressbof (BoF stood for Board of Finance) had its being. Pressbof funded the PCC. There, high above the Thames and close to the future site of the Millennium Dome, I negotiated with them some strengthening amendments to the Editors' Code[27], sufficient for the Government to claim a substantive improvement in self-regulation. As I have already mentioned I found myself, post-Leveson in 2014, in the same territory, trying to solve some of the same issues, in setting up the Independent Press Standards Organisation, the reformed regulator.

Horse Guards Parade is a great London landmark. Neil MacGregor, then Director of the National Gallery, showed me a Canaletto of St James's Park and Horse Guards Parade as a delightfully integrated pedestrian space in the 18th century. In the 1990s, however, Horse Guards had become an unsightly car park, a 'parking perk' for senior people in the Civil Service, the military and the press who were quite grand but not grand enough to merit their own car and driver. The logic of the right nature of the space as revealed by Canaletto was endorsed by the Royal Parks Review Group, led by Dame Jennifer Jenkins. My problem then was how to achieve the elimination of the car park in the face of what I knew would be Establishment hostility. We (the Head of the Royal Parks and I) decided that Horse Guards badly needed to be resurfaced and that this would take six months. Existing car parking permit holders would be given temporary permits to park along the Mall. When the resurfacing work was completed no new parking permits for Horse Guards Parade would be issued. There was a great outcry in the Whitehall village. Simon Jenkins[28] took to *The Times* on 4 June 1994 to criticise the Cabinet Secretary and to support me in our confrontation on the issue. Robin Butler was indeed pretty cross at the way I had engineered this anti-parking coup, probably because it had worked, and he was inundated by powerful protestors. I have no doubt at all that what had been achieved was more in the public interest than a car park. As I drive or walk past Horse Guards Parade and see people strolling there I still have a little sense of pride that I had done something that added value to people's lives, without them knowing it or who had done it. Perhaps when I am dead and gone, some public spirited donor will put up a plaque naming me as the man who gave the space back to the people. But I am not counting on it.

The week following the death of Diana, Princess of Wales, in September 1997 was extraordinary and immensely demanding for a lot of people, including me and some of my staff. My department (by then renamed the Department for Culture, Media and Sport following the arrival in May of the new Labour Government) was in charge of relations with the media over the funeral arrangements and, by virtue of our responsibilities for the Royal Parks, for overseeing what happened on most of the processional route from Kensington Palace to Westminster Abbey. Every morning in that week there was a meeting at Buckingham Palace, chaired by the Lord Chamberlain, which I attended and which ensured the coordination of the variety of responsibilities around the table, including No 10 and the Metropolitan Police. I went to my office just off Trafalgar Square quite early each morning in order to see the build-up of the daily crowds that thronged the Mall. It was a week of magical Indian-Summer weather. People were sad but good humoured, carrying their flowers, cards and stuffed toys to lay at the gates of the Palace. In the evenings as dusk descended some carried candles to light their way.

There were two moments during the week that for me required attention and which I record as they carried some black humour with them. On, I think, the second or third morning I noticed that the queue to sign the Books of Condolence in St James's Palace was backed up around Trafalgar Square. So I telephoned the late Sir Malcolm Ross (then the Comptroller of the Royal Household) and said I thought we had to get people moving through faster. He was very responsive saying immediately that he had made the serious mistake, for a former senior military officer, of providing chairs to sit on for the people who were signing the Books of Condolence. One man, he said, had brought all his bank statements and was signing each page for the Princess. The chairs were removed. The queues speeded up.

In the middle of the week the Head of the Royal Parks came to see me. He explained that the enormous build-up of flowers at the gates of the Palaces, especially at Kensington Palace, was creating such a powerful central heat source that there was a real risk of explosion and fire. It was essential to embark on the removal of the tributes. I recognised that without a sensitive public explanation we would have a great row on our hands. So we announced that it was essential to remove the rotting flowers to prevent a conflagration but they would all be composted and that compost would be used for years on all the flower beds in the Royal Parks as the Princess Diana compost[29]. We said that all the stuffed animals (teddy bears, etc) would be sent to children's charities and all the written messages would be stored and retained. There was no criticism of these steps and each day more and more flowers and tributes arrived, and my staff progressively removed them every day.

In terms of the media we were able to agree two highly successful innovations with the BBC. There would be a giant screen in Hyde Park so people could watch the whole event from there and, even more importantly, in my view, there would be a radio commentary relay through loudspeakers all the way along the processional route to Westminster Abbey. It thus became the most public funeral service in our history. When the listening public applauded the address by Earl Spencer the Abbey congregation knew they had to follow suit.

I met Princess Diana only once. David Puttnam[30] rang to tell me that she wanted to make a TV programme in prisons talking to prisoners who had HIV Aids, that a number of her friends thought this was a bad idea but no-one had yet persuaded her against it. He asked me if I was willing to talk to her and told me she was willing to see me. I went to Kensington Palace and we had tea. I talked; about the process through which she would have to go not only with the Home Office but perhaps with No 10, and the bureaucratic hurdles she would have to jump to achieve what she wanted. And then there would be the controversy in the press. However strongly she felt about the issue of HIV Aids I said I did not think she needed all that potential grief. She listened. She did not pursue the idea.

1997 was my last year at DCMS. Chris Smith[31] had succeeded Virginia Bottomley[32] after the May General Election and he was to do the job for four years, which was wonderful for the Department's place in the world. In my six years as the Permanent Secretary I had had five Secretaries of State – David Mellor, Peter Brooke, Stephen Dorrell, Virginia Bottomley and Chris Smith – and whatever their individual qualities were, and each made a different but positive contribution, that rapidity of change is, of course, absolute nonsense from the point of view of building knowledge of the field you are in charge of, of accountability for the decisions you have taken and of relations with the bodies you sponsor. The handling by Prime Ministers of Departments that are not one of the three great Offices of State – the Treasury, the Home office and the Foreign Office – so that they are treated as stepping stones either up or down rather than substantive places to rest, and the speed of the up or down which is dictated by wholly extraneous factors, is a very damaging aspect of politics. That "churn" of Ministers is, I think, increasingly matched by that of their civil servants. The result is what I would describe as "reactive superficiality". But I know that is how things are and will remain.

One of the main risks for a department like DCMS is that it could be overshadowed by the relative grandness of many of the vast numbers of bodies it sponsors – the National Gallery, the British Museum, the BBC, the Royal Opera House and so on. Many of these institutions, with long and proud histories and international reputations for excellence, had always enjoyed a degree of independence from Government which most non-departmental public bodies would envy. In such circumstances a central task for a Department, especially a new creation, is to work hard at building good relations with all those bodies and, critically, with the people who lead them. That is one of the reasons why a very high turnover of Ministers is undesirable. But the rate of political churn I experienced also meant, and this happened in my case, that the Permanent Secretary inevitably became the senior person who had built the relationships with the Chairmen and/or Directors of all these great institutions on which the smooth working of the Department's role depended. I think some of my Secretaries of State found this rather irritating from time to time. But for me it meant that I was able to provide a continuity of leadership which is always welcomed by those with whom one is working.

Because of the contacts I made over the years, I also came to rely more and more on advice from people outside the Department to balance that which my officials prepared for me, especially in policy areas where there was no single dominant external institution. On film, and drama generally, Dickie Attenborough[33] became a reliable friend and mentor. I spent time with him on the set of *Shadowlands* at Magdalen College, Oxford, and then in his editorial suite at Twickenham. David Puttnam was also a great support on film and other things. I relied on Neil Macgregor for works of art, Richard Eyre for theatre and Peter Wright for dance. There were others and I thank them all; I was fortunate to enjoy a rich set of reliable and trusted relationships.

In a rather different context and away from the arts, during my time in charge of the 'Ministry of Sport' I began a personal engagement with one sport, horse racing, which still remains a part of my life. On Christmas Day 1995 I opened an envelope from 'Santa Claus' at breakfast only to find a photograph of a horse. I asked my wife what it was about and she told me it was my present as she had bought me half of a steeple-chaser. She was a keen and able rider and kept her horse at a stables run by a man who also trained race horses. I had told her I had always wanted to own a racehorse. The horse was not expensive as he was at the end of his career but it was an incredibly exciting Christmas present. We drove over to meet him. He was called Star Oats (his half-brother Master Oats had a significant chasing career). For the rest of the season we followed him avidly. In the first race he threw his jockey off at the first fence. In his second he bounded along so fast and so far in front of the rest of the field that he tired rapidly and walked in second. There were many such disasters but there was one triumph.

In March 1995 he went to race at Towcester on a wet Wednesday. My wife and a daughter went to watch. I slipped out from my Trafalgar Square office to the betting shop in Northumberland Avenue saying to my team that if the Secretary of State asked to see me they were to say that I would be back from the Cabinet Office shortly. I saw Star Oats win with my wife and daughter jumping up and down with excitement at the winning post. I (my horse) had won the *Empress Elizabeth of Austria Hunter Chase* and an enormous Gold Cup, which graced my study for a year. I gave the man on the counter at the betting shop a large tip and returned to the office only to be told that the Secretary of State (Virginia Bottomley) had asked for me and had rung the Cabinet Secretary to try to speak to me. I went in to confess my sin and was, I think, forgiven. I told this story of my surprising victory to the late Duke of Devonshire who, with his wife, had become a good friend, and he sent me a charming letter saying that I would now be forever addicted to the turf and enclosing his book on his great horse *Park Top*. (He was right: and I have gone on owning parts of racehorses, with friends, ever since.) The Devonshires were generous hosts, having insisted that whenever I went north to Yorkshire or Lancashire, I should stay at Chatsworth on the way. We did. On one trip I had forgotten to pack my black tie and appeared pre-dinner in my ordinary suit. The Duke disappeared and then returned dressed as I was. I know the rest of the black tie dressed guests realised they had witnessed the ultimate statement of good manners.

In the course of what turned out to be my last year at DCMS one of the other great - non-political - offices became vacant. The vacancy was that of Cabinet Secretary as Robin Butler was about to retire. Roy Jenkins, with Robin's agreement (and John Major's), gave a dinner at his flat for Tony Blair informally to meet some of the possible candidates to succeed Robin. Richard Wilson, Andrew Turnbull[34], Michael Bichard[35] and I were invited. Richard was eventually appointed and he was, in my view, the best at the dinner, as while the rest of us made statements when asked to speak, he challenged Tony with some questions. I was genuinely delighted at Richard's appointment. As a candidate I had at least one main disadvantage. I had not run one of the great grey battleships of Whitehall as Richard had done both at the Environment and the Home Office. Rather, had the candidates had to parade their experience as if in a Spithead review, I had only commanded a delightful frigate which brought up the rear of the convoy with music, dancing and singing. I imagine I was also not helped by an *Evening Standard* piece which said "New Labour loves Hayden". My friend Peter Mandelson continues to deny responsibility for this remark.

Richard Wilson's appointment left a vacancy at the Home Office. Curiously, I have a piece of paper in my records on which I had set out the pros and cons on whether I should apply for the job. Re-reading my notes at the time it was clearly not an easy decision but in the end I applied; the Home Office was where I had begun my professional life thirty years before and it was a place for which I held a deep affection and it dealt with such fundamentally important issues that I felt I could not avoid it. I was interviewed (this was a relatively new phenomenon and it was the first interview I had had since I applied to join the Civil Service in 1965), and was recommended for appointment, which was approved by the Prime Minister. The Home Secretary, Jack Straw[36], then interviewed me and took a different view. A Secretary of State has a veto and Jack exercised it in my case. Although he and I worked closely together in later years on the Funding of Political Parties we never discussed his opposition to my appointment. I imagine he felt I was too liberal a figure in an old Home Office tradition, for what he then believed the Home Office required. During the following years the Home Office gradually became more and more focussed on being a Ministry of the Interior which is not what I had joined in 1967, nor, what I continue to think, a seriously civilised country needs or deserves. I still believe that resolving conflicts between order and freedom, and between tight controls and human rights are better dealt with within a single command rather than through an argument between an Interior and a Justice Ministry.

My rejection from the leadership of the Home Office was at the time a personal blow, but, from my point of view, it turned out to be one of the best decisions Jack Straw ever made. When I was told the news I was asked what I would now want to do and I said I would carry on for a couple of years and then retire early. Robin Butler said he was not sure that was in the public interest and then rang me when I was on my way home to say that the Prime Minister would like me to go to the Lord Chancellor's Department. I said I did not see that was possible as there were statutory restrictions on who could be appointed as the Permanent Secretary and I did not meet them. He said that primary legislation was being introduced to remove those restrictions (these were having to have a legal qualification or at least five years' service in the Lord Chancellor's Department). He added that to try to avoid the personal chemistry problem (or whatever it was) that had occurred in relation to Jack Straw it had been arranged that I would go to see the Lord Chancellor at 8 am the following morning. He finally reported that the Prime Minister had said that my going to work with Derry Irvine[37] would be "a marriage made in heaven".

I duly appeared at 8 am and the Lord Chancellor, whom I had not met before, rather gruffly observed that the only person who had not rung him overnight to sing my praises was the Archbishop of Canterbury. He then asked me where I lived and I said we had a house at the end of the King's Road in Fulham. I then added that we also had a farm near Salisbury in Wiltshire. The forensic barrister in him spoke to ask me how I could possibly afford that on a public service salary. I said I couldn't but I had married an heiress. He grinned and I think he said: "You lucky bugger."

CHAPTER 7:
The Majesty of the Law

*The first non-lawyer at the LCD • an Honorary Bencher •
ceremonial dress • Clerk of the Crown in Chancery • the Archbishop's
legs • Prorogation • the abolition of the hereditary peers and the
arrival of organic pigs • changing the top team • suffering detaching
retinas • judicial and silk appointments • Nelson Mandela • Special
Advisers • the wit of Garry Hart • Home Office encroachment
resisted • new responsibilities • in China on 9/11 • in India with
Harry Woolf • last night of the proms in Cracow • Anglo-American
exchanges • a dangerous moment over Sark • Derry is sacked and
Charlie Falconer arrives • "Yes Minister" on stage • the Hutton Inquiry
• "The Concordat" • Review of the Honours System
• Good bye to the Civil Service.*

LEGISLATION WAS INDEED being passed to enable a non-lawyer or someone who had not spent five years in the Department to become its Permanent Secretary. But I still had to win the job and was interviewed for it. Michael Beloff QC[1] chaired the Appointment Panel. At one point he asked me what I thought the law was for; reaching back into my History degree memory I said that I recalled an observation of some 17th century jurist, whose name I said I had forgotten, which went, roughly, as follows: "The law is as hedges are set for men to walk in". I said I could not do better than that. The Panel recommended my appointment. The Prime Minister approved it. The Lord Chancellor did not object. Michael Beloff thanked me for interviewing the Panel.

I discovered quickly that this was no ordinary Permanent Secretary role, as I had moved into a world of values, behaviour, traditions and assumptions which was like no other in my experience than perhaps one that I got to know later, namely that of the upper echelons of the Church of England. When the Supreme Court (Offices) Bill 1997 (which removed the statutory restrictions on who could be qualified for appointment as the Permanent Secretary) was debated, Lord Woolf[2] had questioned whether someone with a background outside of the law and therefore perhaps without a deep knowledge of constitutional issues could satisfactorily be the Permanent Secretary to the Lord Chancellor. With great good grace, a year later, in a speech he gave at the Inner Temple, he said he withdrew any such doubt in my case and he courteously repeated the same in a speech at my Retirement in July 2004 in the Great Hall of the Royal Courts of Justice. The Inner Temple also featured quickly in my new life as the day before my appointment was announced, Elisabeth Butler-Sloss[3] (the Inner Temple Treasurer) rang to invite me to be an Honorary Bencher of the Inn. I agreed. The next day I received similar invitations from all the other Inns of Court. They were a day too late. And how could I have fairly decided such a beauty contest without irritating those who were not chosen.

The office of Permanent Secretary to the Lord Chancellor was over 100 years old and as, unlike any other Home Civil Service Department, it still had a range of ceremonial duties attached to it, a great deal of early attention had to be given to my wardrobe. The basic outfit was 19th century court dress – frock coat, silk jabot, lace cuffs, white gloves, breeches, black tights (German ballet tights which, I was told, were stronger in the crotch than their English counterpart), silver buckled shoes and a waistcoat with an aperture for the sword to go through . Unlike the Lord Chancellor I did not have to dress in this way every working day but only for a selection of grand events – the State Opening of Parliament, the Service to open the Legal Year, the appointment of the Lord Mayor of London, the swearing in of the most senior Judges, the annual Queen's Counsel ceremony and any other 'ad hoc' event at which the Lord Chancellor and I were required to be there and dressed up e.g. the Millennium Service in St Paul's.

The other role I had inherited – that of the Clerk of the Crown in Chancery[4] – required merely the addition of an academic gown and a wig to the underlying court dress (but crucially the removal of the sword and the gloves). This office was even more ancient dating from 1331 and once wielded considerable influence in the affairs of the state. In accepting it I was required to take a very long and complex oath of allegiance to The Queen. This was administered by the Lord Chancellor in the presence of my wife and my two guests, Roy and Jennifer Jenkins. The Crown Office[5], of which, in this capacity, I was nominally in charge, authorised writs on behalf of The Queen e.g. for the creation of Peers and for the calling of Elections. Election writs were summoned by The Queen in my name – Phillips – as the only commoner allowed to describe himself on formal documents by his surname only.

At the State Opening it turned out that I was the only person who had to change their clothes during the ceremony as I moved from being the Permanent Secretary, leading the Lord Chancellor's procession to greet The Queen, to being Clerk of the Crown sitting on the Clerks' Bench in the House of Lords behind the Law Lords. Sword and gloves had to be removed in the corridor outside the chamber and gown and wig donned instead. My briefing then said that as I entered the House, through a circle of the Gentlemen at Arms with their pikes: "Be careful not to trip over the Archbishop of Canterbury's legs as he sticks them out inconsiderately." (I sent that to the then Archbishop George Carey for his amusement and for use in a future sermon, if he was desperate).

The other main Clerk of the Crown event was Prorogation, a ceremony of infinite tricorn hat doffing in which The Queen formally gives her assent to Acts of Parliament through Her Commissioners seated on the Woolsack. My role was to read out the title of the Act – on my last occasion "The Ragwort Control Act", very apt for the owner of a farm – the Commissioners then doffed away. And the Clerk of the Parliaments[6] then intoned, in Norman French, "La Reine le veult" (The Queen wills it). During my time there was only one packed House for Prorogation, on the evening on which the abolition of the hereditary peers took effect, 11 November 1999. They came to say goodbye to the House in large numbers and at the moment I read out the final death-dealing words "The House of Lords Act", that was their end (save for those hereditary peers who had been reprieved and who were allowed to go on reproducing themselves under a cunningly bizarre electoral process we had invented). Then we all went to a jolly party in the Royal Gallery. The departure of the hereditary peers was a necessary sadness, but it slimmed the Chamber to a manageable and effective number before subsequent Prime Ministerial excesses of patronage made it a far too bloated assembly. However, in the course of all this delightful constitutional flummery, I was led accidentally into a farming partnership of great pleasure and fecundity.

During the discussions between Lord Cranborne (now the Marquess of Salisbury) and the Lord Chancellor, about the potential abolition of most of the hereditary peers, I mentioned to Lord Cranborne, whom I knew was a porcine lover, that our farm was near to his estate in Dorset and I had two Tamworth sows who needed servicing. "Send them to Buster" he said. His pig-man, Brian Card, who had opened the batting for Somerset, took charge, and from then on we had a most enjoyable commercial pig partnership; not just with Tamworths, but with Berkshires and Middle Whites as well. My porcine friends lost me money, hand over fist, but were utterly delightful. When they were about six months old they went off to Cranborne Manor to run in the woods there, eat acorns and so in due course qualify to be accredited as 'organic'. There will be more about our rural idyll later in this story but for now I must say that after a week in Whitehall what could be better on a Friday evening than a chat with the pigs before supper as the sun went down. These intelligent animals produced a great deal of sensible and supportive snuffling as I told them about my week's life in Government service.

In the Office I decided I had two central tasks: the first was to build and sustain good personal relations with the most senior Judiciary, particularly the Heads of Divisions. So I made sure I had monthly meetings with each of them to go through their concerns. The second was fundamentally to change the skills and leadership qualities of the senior staff of the Department. I have to say there was an incredibly 19th century feel to my new inheritance. When I arrived, apart from myself, there was only one other senior figure who had come from outside the LCD, with the exception of our Legal Adviser who, ironically, had been my Legal Adviser at the DCMS. All the rest were civil servant lawyers most of whom had spent their whole lives in the Department. Two years later, in my top team, there was only one lawyer, who had come from outside the LCD, and the rest were non-lawyer imports. This was a sharp but necessary change prompted by the fact that the Department had growing responsibilities and had a changing role among the great historic Departments of Whitehall; and there was also a pressing need to ensure that its political head, the Lord Chancellor, had a wider and more experienced base of advice on which to rely than he, and his predecessors, had been offered in the past.

The way the Department was run had two further changes to experience, one managerial, and the other financial. It was the financial one that made me realise rapidly that an iron of irritation had entered deeply into my soul. The Head of Finance asked me to approve a request to the Treasury for a Supplementary Estimate i.e. we were going to run out of money and wanted cover. This had never happened to me before and, as I had learned in my four Treasury years, it was a "bad thing" to have to ask for a Supplementary: much to be abhorred. So I refused to sign the request and waited for the house to fall down upon me. It did not. The Head of Finance humbly confessed that they had got it wrong, again, as I discovered they frequently had done this, often unnecessarily. I then resolved to bring in a finance director from the private sector to cut through the bureaucratic stew which my honest hard-working but non-professional staff had created. I reached out to my friends in the private sector for help and they responded fulsomely and recommended I talked to a man called Simon Ball. He appeared looking rather sceptical in the Pugin neo-Gothic splendour of my office to be offered the unusual challenge of becoming the Finance Director of the Lord Chancellor's Department. He surprisingly agreed. Within 18 months the whole financial management operation had changed for the better and instead of the Treasury putting the LCD at the bottom of the Whitehall financial competence league it was praised for its performance and raised on high.

The managerial issue grew and grew in importance. Our responsibility for the running of the Courts was a major one which needed urgent attention. I knew I could not handle both the policy and political advice that the Lord Chancellor needed and also pretend to run the whole of the Courts and the Tribunals system. I had to find a Chief Executive who could do that and who would also win the confidence of the Lord

Chancellor and the higher judiciary in doing so. I asked around and a reliable source told me that the best managerial leader in Whitehall was a man called Ian Magee[7]. He was persuaded to apply, was appointed, in due course became my Second Permanent Secretary and was made the cross-Whitehall "tsar" for operational management. I had now happily found my key leadership team and although to the external eye we were still covered in 19th century trappings the heart that beat within had become a much more modern one.

It turned out to be crucial that I had put such a strong top team in place for another very personal reason. During 2000 I was diagnosed with a serious retinal disease and underwent about ten eye operations from 2000 to 2002. Each operation needed a general anaesthetic and resulted in my having to take at least a week away from work after each procedure. My team held the fort admirably while I was away and both Derry Irvine and Richard Wilson behaved with typical personal generosity in accepting such an amount of time off and lightening other cross-departmental duties which I had. On one occasion I was in a meeting with the Cabinet Secretary and others when the retina in one eye detached itself and, apologising profusely, I had to ask to leave. Richard subsequently observed to me that you have to be made of stern stuff to manage that with apparent equanimity. I must say that had Jack Straw taken me into the Home Office I doubt whether the pressures of that role would have been as easily manageable given my eye problems.

There was one traditional policy responsibility strand which engaged me a great deal; judicial appointments (at every level from a Lord of Appeal in Ordinary and the Lord Chief Justice at the top, to a local District Judge) plus appointments to Silk i.e. to become a Queen's Counsel. Throughout my time in LCD these decisions were still very much the personal responsibility of the Lord Chancellor even if in many of the most senior roles he was making recommendations to the Prime Minister or to The Queen. When we were in the process of making appointments he received piles of personal files about the candidates, so did I and so did all the Heads of Divisions. We studied what we had been given conscientiously and assembled to discuss the merits of the different candidates. The meetings took hours. We were very diligent but the process was already much criticised as a closed system of "secret soundings"; and I knew in my bones it was doomed. On my advice the Lord Chancellor had already agreed that we should create a Judicial Appointments Advisory Commission which would oversee and comment on the processes we followed. The Lord Chief Justice, then Tom Bingham[8], told me that, by that means, I had temporarily plugged the dam against criticism but the water would soon overwhelm the old ways. He was right. It did so in 2003 when the Prime Minister announced the abolition of the office of Lord Chancellor and the creation of a Judicial Appointments Commission.

There were many interesting or indeed enjoyable appointments we made but the best of all was that of Nelson Mandela (a lawyer by profession) to be a QC. On the appointed day he arrived early in my room with the South African High Commissioner and I was fortunately already in my dressing-up clothes to receive him. My wife and I gave him coffee and conversation while we waited for the ceremony to begin. In that time, I told him that we had two South Africans living with us and helping us and would he sign a message to them. He readily agreed and asked me to whom he should address himself. I said: "Lionel and Margaret". He said, with a gentle reproving smile, "Hayden, I think you mean Margaret and Lionel". I knew this was not too presumptuous a thing for me to ask him to do as two years earlier I had sat next to him at a lunch and we had talked about our respective families and our children. As lunch was about to conclude he turned to me and said, "What is the name of your daughter who is doing her A Levels now?" I told him and, on the back of the Menu Card, he wrote "For Florence. You are the future. Best wishes. Nelson Mandela." It remains a cherished possession of hers.

There was one moment when the responsibility for judicial appointments arrived to attack the Lord Chancellor in his position as Chairman of the Society of Labour Lawyers. He had written to Society members to ask for donations, as is normal and reasonable, but was immediately criticised for doing so as involving potential corruption in appearing to imply offering judicial appointments for cash! Complete nonsense of course but difficult to rebut. I asked him why he had not told me he was doing this. He said it was a party political issue and therefore not a matter for me. I said he was precisely wrong in his view as advice on the task of policing the border between what was party political and what was governmental was what I was there for. I am not sure he understood. I have an original published cartoon from *The Times* on the incident show-ing Derry in his full robes riding on Tony Blair's shoulders as the latter negotiated a high wire cycle ride. The caption is "Judicial independence: a difficult act to swallow".

The other person in the Office most closely touched by this event, who did understand what I was saying, was Derry's Special Adviser, the late Garry Hart. I dealt with very many special advisers during my career but two stand out as being of the highest quality. The first was Anthony Lester during Roy Jenkins's second term as Home Secretary. Anthony, a brilliant human rights barrister, was a crucial creative influence on the reforming legislation from 1974 to 1976, especially on sex discrimination. He did not do this by simply commenting on papers from officials as they flowed up to Ministers but by sitting down with officials from the start and working with them on the detail. By the time proposals came to Roy for his approval he and I knew they were already agreed between Antho-ny and the civil servants.

The second was Garry. A distinguished and successful solicitor he was not making a career for himself in his Special Adviser role and he was wise and calm. He also had the most gently subtle sense of humour of almost anyone I ever worked with. In the speeches he wrote for Derry he was able to give the Lord Chancellor an uncharacteristic light touch and ready wit. I cannot resist an example of the slightly self-mocking irony he gives to the Lord Chancellor in the form of a pompous spoof programme for a visit to our farm one weekend in 1999. It ran as follows:

"SATURDAY 23 JANUARY

By train. Arrive Salisbury Railway Station. Inspect Salisbury City Silver Band on Platform 3. Speech to Mayor and Corporation. Receive the Freedom of the City.
Driven to Homington Farm, Homington (The Residence)
14.30 Time to change (gold-plated gumboots, waterproof wig). Process to cattle and pig barns. Speech on legal services in very remote rural areas. Q&A session (no briefing required as animals much like the House of Lords).

17.00 Hosing down in farmyard, followed by tea in Residence.
19.00 Time to change (Black Tie) to go to Longford Castle
Met by the Earl of Radnor, and villagers singing ancient melodies
View artistic masterpieces with customary knowledge, courtesy
and charm (Lady Irvine)
20.15 Dinner – Speech "The Future of the Hereditary Peer"
Return to Residence

SUNDAY 24 JANUARY

11.00 Bless Salisbury Cathedral; tour of the ecclesiastical facilities; present Millennium (Advance) Awards to the winners of "Adopt a Lawyer, They Need Love" scheme.
12.30 for 1 Lunch at Residence: with Lord Jenkins of Hillhead and Dame Jennifer; The Bishop of Salisbury and Mrs Stancliffe; Lady Bonham Carter and others.
Depart, thanking Trollope, The Common Agricultural Policy, Constable and New Labour, for making the weekend before a real joy".

Garry Hart, Lord Hart of Chilton, was a wonderful man, who went on to serve Charlie Falconer[9]. For all who knew him he died too soon.

As we approached the General Election in 2001 the Cabinet Secretary, Richard Wilson, told me that the Home Secretary (then David Blunkett[10]) wanted the responsibility for the criminal courts to be transferred to the Home Office and that the Prime Minister wished this to be seriously considered. So I had to produce a paper which proposed how we would separate the Lord Chancellor's responsibilities for the civil and the criminal courts. This was in managerial terms, in my view, an absurd idea, apart from the principal policy objection that you should not have the responsibility for the police and the courts in the same department. But when a Permanent Secretary is asked to advise on proposed machinery of government changes he/she must engage with the different ambitions of different Ministers and whatever your personal views may be you must try to handle the arguments objectively and fairly. This was a real challenge as in this particular case the proposal was, in my view, irrational (although to be fair the Home Office had once been in charge of the Magistrates' Courts in pre-rationality days). As we approached decision time, and in the light of the Election result, I decided to tell the Lord Chancellor of the nature of the threat to his department's coherence. Summoned to see the Prime Minister he suggested (forcefully) that before such a radical decision was taken it would be wise to consult the Senior Judiciary before just springing it on them. The Prime Minister agreed to see them, and so articulately determined was the opposition of the Judges to what was proposed, that the Prime Minister paused to reflect. The other machinery of Government changes which had been planned were announced but the changes to responsibility for the courts did not appear in the Press Notice. The moment for that had come and gone.

As a result the Lord Chancellor's Department became a net gainer, as among the other changes which were made were a series of absorbing and important new policy responsibilities which came to my Department from the Home Office and the Cabinet Office, originally intended by the Cabinet Secretary as some compensation for the potential loss of responsibility for the criminal courts. These responsibilities were all intrinsically interesting as well as important: devolution, and relations with the devolved administrations; human rights; freedom of information; elections and electoral law (including policy on the funding of political parties); and responsibility for the Channel Islands and the Isle of Man. Together with the Department's existing responsibility for relations between the Executive and the Judiciary this represented a package of constitutional issues brought together in Government for the first time. By a happy accident a logical, sensible and fundamental decision had been taken. These significant accretions led, later, to the Department being renamed the Department for Constitutional Affairs which is what it was called when I retired in 2004.

In the meantime as a result of these changes I found myself the Permanent Secretary to the Scotland Office (with Alastair Darling[11] as my Minister) and to the Wales Office (with Peter Hain[12] in charge). My accumulation of titles (I now had five) was becoming amusingly Ruritanian. But more seriously these changes provided, for a time, a good and efficient focus for a mechanism for regular discussion between the UK Government and the devolved administrations of Scotland, Wales and

Northern Ireland. It is a pity that the centrality of this crucial issue of how to manage the Union seems to have been lost. As I write I sense it is much needed.

As Lord Chancellor Derry was a disciplining taskmaster expecting the highest standards. It was therefore very important that I chose people who could withstand such forensic scrutiny. Most could but where they could not I had to find them somewhere else to go. He applied his stringency to his Ministers as well as officials. On one occasion in a meeting a Junior Minister in the Department, was clearly going on too long about something at which point Derry said: "Pause, a bad point does not become a good one by virtue of repetition." It was a sharp put-down but, to her credit or not, she pressed on.

Looking back I am surprised that such an apparently domestic department should involve so much foreign travel, which it did from 2001 onwards, but always at the request of those we visited. It began that year with a visit to China when I led a delegation to agree and sign a concordat on training exchanges for young Chinese lawyers coming to the UK. In addition to myself and my Legal Adviser, the late Paul Jenkins[13], I was accompanied by a Lord Justice of Appeal and a senior legal academic. There were lots of meetings and lots of speeches and lots of hospitality but the great joy was that our Chinese hosts stopped supper sharply just before 8 pm so there were none of those staggeringly boring late official nights.

On the evening of 11 September (9/11) we returned to our hotel and Paul rang me and told me to turn on the television. I watched, live, as the second plane flew into the second tower in New York. The next day, before we signed a Memorandum of Understanding in the Great Hall of the Ministry of Justice, the Minister made a lengthy speech about solidarity with the West in the face of terrorism; this was symbolised as far as our hosts were concerned by the arrest that day of large numbers of Uighur Muslims in Western China. Banquet followed banquet whether in Beijing, Xian or Guilin and my diary records a speciality of webbed duck feet in mustard sauce and forcing Paul Jenkins to try the squirrel in bamboo which I knew was rat. The degree to which our hosts had briefed themselves on our domestic preoccupations was most impressive. I held a seminar for postgraduate students at Peking University and I can honestly say it was the most demanding audience I had ever addressed. When I made the customary remarks about China's failings in the field of human rights my audience responded with detailed criticisms of the UK's own record with some very good examples and I was hard pressed to defend our alleged moral and political superiority.

The Lord Chancellor had declined to lead the delegation to China fearing the food (so I understood) and he applied the same criterion to a proposed visit to India, for which I was extremely grateful as, over many years, I had developed a great affection for and knowledge of that country. In January 2003, standing in for the Lord Chancellor, I went with the Lord Chief Justice (then Harry Woolf) to represent the UK at the 50th Anniversary of the creation of the Supreme Court of India (the one Indian institution reportedly free of any corruption). It was in many ways a most splendid occasion. Everyone took with them their best dressing-up clothes but we were all outshone by the two representatives of the Supreme Court of Bhutan. And they were only wearing their ordinary day-dress! There were formal visits to be made, speeches to be heard, and, as always, food and drink to be consumed.

For me there were two great highlights of that visit. First, I met the most senior female Judge in India who happened also to be the mother of a neighbour and friend in Wiltshire, the author Vikram Seth. I was some years later able to meet both his parents when they came to the Salisbury International Arts Festival of which my wife was the Chair. Second, the Lord Chief Justice and I were invited to the great ceremony of Beating the Retreat at Rashtrapati Bhavan, the great Lutyens architectural masterpiece rising up the hill past the Government Offices to the Presidential Palace, in the evening sunlight. We had to decline because of the timing of our return to England, so we were invited instead to the dress rehearsal on the evening before. We accepted and as our car arrived he and I stepped out to walk towards the guest seating area but were restrained by our hosts who pointed to two comfortable red armchairs looking up the hill to the Presidential Palace. We were being asked to take the salute from the places which, the next day, would be filled by the President and Prime Minister of India.

One after another, each immaculate regiment marched down the hill towards us from the Palace as the bands played and the camels and their riders gazed on impassively from their positions on the walls which separated one Government building from another. The drill was disciplined; the uniforms magnificent. I think we did our "taking the salute" duties competently enough, right fist clenched on heart and a quick nodded bow.

Another set of visits which this time Derry Irvine and I carried out together was to Eastern Europe. We went to Poland, Hungary and the Baltic states (Latvia, Lithuania and Estonia) which had asked the UK to advise them on their entry applications to the EU in relation to their arrangements for delivering justice. There was nothing particularly memorable or important to record in terms of the formal meetings we had to have or the endless lunches and dinners but there were some other highlights worth memorialisation. In the City Hall in Cracow we attended the Last Night of the Proms which was exactly the same as that in London save for the central piece being by a Polish composer. Our Ambassador, Michael Pakenham, introduced the evening in Polish to great laughter and lengthy applause. I did not understand a word but I could see that Michael was a hugely effective and popular Ambassador. We soon reached the point where, with the rest of the audience I could sing out lustily "Hearts of oak are our ships, jolly tars are our men," when Derry turned to me and said that he had not realised how decidedly English rather than British the Last Night of the Proms was. The concert had been preceded by an even more extraordinary show, of JCBs dancing to music "the Dancing Diggers"; a cutting-edge commercial event on behalf of British industry. In Budapest, Riga, Vilnius and Tallinn we had a tremendous reception. Our visit was one other small mark of their longed for return to the family of Western democracies. But there were constant reminders of the close neighbouring Russian presence. In Tallinn as we walked into the centre of the town from the Hotel I could hear stunning Russian singing of which I had powerful memories of my time in the Russian Chorus at Yale. It was a most compelling sound and so we went into the Russian Orthodox Church of St Nicholas and attended a Mass of great musical beauty. The bass singing of the priest was at the pinnacle of a magical tone.

I found I had also inherited another international responsibility, for organising the Anglo-American Legal Exchange, a high-level biennial meeting taking place alternately in the UK and in the USA. We had two of these during my tenure. Our team for the visit to Washington was led by Tom Bingham at a time when it was known that the UK was going to create a Supreme Court to replace the Law Lords. We went to the US Supreme Court for dinner in great early 19th century splendour, with music, and including tours of the offices of some of the Justices. As the evening ended and we climbed back onto the coach Tom said in his clear penetrating voice: "Well, Hayden, you have seen what we expect for our future accommodation." If only, I thought; although I hear that the present Justices are not displeased with their new accommodation in the old Middlesex Guildhall on Parliament Square.

I had to work rather harder when the Americans came to us. Apart from the working sessions it was traditional that the host arranged a day out. I had organised a trip to Oxford to visit the Library at Magdalen College and then to drive on to Waddesdon Manor for lunch. My organising partner on the American side was Associate Justice Stephen Breyer[14] who also happened to be a personal friend through my wife's family. As we drove along the M4 chatting away he suddenly said to me he had to stop talking because it was time for his 15 minutes of meditation. He fell silent and so did I. Precisely 15 minutes later he restarted our conversation at the very point it had been broken off. A real touch of class.

On our earlier visit to Washington there was some incredulity on the American side about the part I, a non-lawyer and civil servant, played in the management of the legal system and what my relations were with the higher judiciary. They asked if in one our working sessions I could explain what my role was. I did my best to explain the nature of the role of the Lord Chancellor from which my role stemmed and, in response, the American-side consensus was that they would have liked to have such a 'friend in Government.' As one American put it, "It would be quite useful if we could have a Hayden." But in 2003 the UK Government decided to ditch our own tradition and take more of an American route.

Travelling much nearer to home I did my pleasant duty and visited the Channel Islands and the Isle of Man. The last time I had done this was in 1970 when from the Home Office I was helping the Islands to clarify their future relationship with what was then known as the Common Market. In my time as 'their' Permanent Secretary there were no strained relations between the Islands and Her Majesty's Government: my task was to show real interest in the life of the Islands (which it was a pleasure to do), help them solve any external relations problems, but otherwise not to interfere. I pursued that policy with studied and enjoyable diligence.

One of the prizes for retiring senior military officers was the chance to be the Lieutenant Governor of one of the Islands. During my time there were two retired Air Chief Marshals (in Jersey and the Isle of Man) and one General (overseeing the Bailiwick of Guernsey, Alderney and Sark). On one visit General Sir John Foley, my wife, his Aide de Camp and I set off to tour the bailiwick. In a small aircraft we flew to Alderney where I addressed the States (or rather they addressed me) and I then walked along the famous Alderney breakwater. My wife and I had hoped to get to Sark but the sea was too rough and I asked if we could overfly the island instead and we were given permission to do so. I gave up the chance to sit beside the pilot and offered it to my wife. It was a bright clear day as we flew over this small magical-looking island. As we turned back to Guernsey the pilot banked sharply over the Northern tip of Sark so we could see the island more clearly and closely; then the right-hand door suddenly fell open and there was Laura hanging in her seat belt a thousand feet above the ocean. The General's Aide de Camp was fortunately very tall and from the back of the small plane reached right over Sir John and me, pulled her back firmly into her seat and tried to close the door but it would not shut. The pilot, having righted the plane, was calling Guernsey for urgent permission to land and we went there speedily while the door was held as near closed as possible.

We landed safely. Laura walked most unsteadily across the wing and on to the ground. The very nice pilot apologised and said the plane needed a service! The Lieutenant Governor observed laconically that I had clearly failed again to dispose of my wife. In retrospect we much enjoyed our visit and went back again, privately, when we were able to stay on Sark and had a delightful slow walking holiday over a long weekend.

At some point in 2002 Derry asked me if I would stay on beyond the normal retirement age of 60 which I would reach on 9 February 2003. His plan was that I should stay indefinitely on the grounds that Tony Blair had assured him that he would be Lord Chancellor for as long as Tony was Prime Minister. I was not against some extension but this proposal was for far too long. Unfortunately it appeared that the Prime

Minister was also content that I should stay on 'forever' so I had to appeal to Richard Wilson, the Cabinet Secretary, to save me. I proposed an extension of eighteen months to July 2004; and after lots of toing and froing, including letters between the PM and the Lord Chancellor, this was agreed. The deal was formally settled in a letter from Richard's successor, Andrew Turnbull, in February 2003.

However, the deal turned out quite differently from Derry's point of view. A few months later, on 12 June 2003, Derry was removed as Lord Chancellor. I was left and he had gone. Roughly a week before this happened, on 4th June, I was asked to go and see Andrew Turnbull in the Cabinet Office. He told me that it had been decided that the office of Lord Chancellor should be abolished, that a Judicial Appointments Commission should take over the Lord Chancellor's appointments role, and that the Law Lords would disappear and, in their stead, a Supreme Court would be created. Derry would be sacked. This would all be announced as a Machinery of Government change. I know I swallowed hard as it appeared to me that the Cabinet Office had done no adequate work on what was involved. I knew none of this could be achieved simply by announcing a 'so-called' Machinery of Government change but my immediate concern was more for Derry, given what the PM had promised him originally. So I said that while I would offer the Cabinet Office some detailed advice on the substance of their proposals, it was essential the Prime Minister should tell the Lord Chancellor of the plan, face to face. I added that I had worked for him for five years and he had become a friend and if the PM did not see him in the next 24 hours I would tell him what was planned myself. Tony Blair saw Derry the following afternoon.

This was a plan for a massive constitutional change, the magnitude and impact of which, so it appeared to me, the Cabinet Office had not fully grasped. Somehow over the next few days we had to try to get them to understand the implications of what the Prime Minister had decided to do. At one level I was dealing with important issues of substance; on another I was trying to support and encourage a rather stunned Lord Chancellor. I had long expected the arrival of an independent Judicial Appointments Commission and the plan for the creation of a Supreme Court was not a surprise; indeed I had, in a drawer of my desk, a paper setting out how the creation of a Supreme Court should be done, courtesy of my predecessor, Tom Legg. But the abolition of the office of Lord Chancellor was more of a surprise and I had done no planning for that. I understood the No 10 argument to go as follows – if you were modernising Government (that was the slogan then and it goes on and on because modernisation by definition is never finished) how can you continue to have a figure who is a Senior Cabinet Minister, the Speaker of the Upper House of Parliament and also the Head of the Judiciary. I could have tried to explain why this was a brilliant historical construct (Hegelian in its practical beauty) as a way of supporting a balanced and organic unwritten Constitution but I knew there was no point. Their minds were made up. The office of Lord Chancellor was an anachronism.

Over the next few days Derry and I talked a great deal and he decided, with my strong support, to offer to stay on and implement the planned changes. The result was a Minute from him to the Prime Minister of a slightly, I have to confess, didactic nature. I had already explained to the Cabinet Office that major legislation would be required to implement the changes proposed. There were thousands of statutory references to the Lord Chancellor that would have to be examined and amended. We (i.e. the Minute) said that the idea of appointing a non-lawyer member of the House of Commons as Lord Chancellor in the next few days, which was the Cabinet Office's plan, was both impossible and, indeed, would hold the Government up to ridicule. The Minute then set out a set of proposals for the way ahead and argued that Derry was the best qualified person to carry out the plan. All our proposals were accepted but that one.

On Thursday 12 June 2003 Derry was removed and Charlie Falconer arrived as Lord Chancellor. He, Charlie, was told very late because at noon on that day when I came out of my office in the House of Lords he was standing there in the corridor and asked me what was afoot as the news was that Derry was going. Did I know who was to take over? I said that if I did know I could not say. At 2 pm when he reappeared as Lord Chancellor I had been forgiven for not telling him two hours earlier. In the announcement of the changes I became the first Permanent Secretary of the newly named Department of Constitutional Affairs. This fitting title and the sensible decision to bring a range of constitutional issues together following the machinery of Government changes of 2000 turned out to be a brief moment of rationality in the ever-shifting process of moving bits of Government around.

I had known my new Lord Chancellor and Secretary of State for a number of years, in part as fellow actors at the annual "Westminster Palace of Varieties". At the instigation of Tom Chandos[15] I had agreed to play Sir Humphrey Appleby to his Bernard and Charlie's Jim Hacker. For the previous three years we had trodden the boards of St John's Smith Square every January with lots of MPs and Peers who were prepared to mob themselves up to raise money for Macmillan Cancer. The 2003 performance was reviewed in the *Daily Telegraph* which said: "Although Tony Blair could not attend, his close friend, Lord Falconer of Thoroton, did make an appearance, playing the role of Jim Hacker. He performed a sketch from *Yes Minister* accompanied by Sir Hayden Phillips (as Sir Humphrey) and Viscount Chandos (as his civil servant sidekick, Bernard). It was one of the highlights of the evening and all three were commended for their acting ability. But Lord Falconer is a Minister and Sir Hayden, as Permanent Secretary at the Lord Chancellor's Department, is a real Sir Humphrey, so perhaps acting did not come into it". At our last performance in 2004 Charlie was my Secretary of State so reality and fiction had completely merged.

Charlie's arrival as Lord Chancellor was itself like a scene from *Yes Minister*. I reminded him he would have to change into court dress, robes and wig to preside over the House from the Woolsack. He replied that as a first modernising step he would go to the House in the suit he was wearing. I said I didn't think that was possible as I understood that he had to have the Leave of the House to alter the traditional garb but, I added defensively, as this was something for the Clerk of the Parliaments to advise on and not for me, that Clerk should be summoned. He was and confirmed well and forcefully what I had said. The new Lord Chancellor then played what I think he thought was his trump card as, with a gentle smile, he said there was no alternative to what he had decided as he had no ceremonial clothes. I eyed his shape and told him that I thought with a pull here and a tuck there my ceremonial clothes would fit him admirably and I had a full-bottomed wig to offer him to boot. Bob Moy[16] and Norah Dobinson[17] attended rapidly to dress him in my offerings and he entered the House properly dressed and on time.

In the year I then had left before I retired from the Civil Service in July 2004 there were three events/issues that stand out to which I think I can claim to have made a significant contribution; significant of course is not necessarily a word of approval. They were: the Inquiry into the death of David Kelly by Lord Hutton[18]; constitutional reform, especially the Concordat between the Executive and the Judiciary; and a Review of the Honours System.

The death of the MOD scientist David Kelly and the furore that followed led the Prime Minister to decide on an Inquiry which would be led by a very senior Judge because this was no ordinary death. His suicide (which the Inquiry later confirmed) followed arguments between No 10 and the BBC over allegations by the journalist, Andrew Gilligan, about the alleged 'sexing up' of a dossier about the threat of weapons of mass destruction, and his (David Kelly's) appearance (probably a great mistake on his part and all those involved in advising him) before the relevant Select Committee. As the acknowledged source of the information which led to the great row, this highly intelligent, diffident and respected scientist found himself as a victim and then actually made himself one because he could not cope with the intense pressure that fell on him.

My immediate task, with the Lord Chancellor's approval, was to find the right judge to conduct the Inquiry. After consultation with the Lord Chief Justice and the Senior Law Lord I had three names in order of their recommendations. The first was Lord Hutton whom I rang and asked him to salute the flag. He did. Within the hour I had found him an able Secretary to the Inquiry whose job it was then to recruit the staff to run the whole thing and find the accommodation in which to hold the Inquiry. All this was done well and most speedily.

Next I needed to ensure that Mrs Kelly was assured that the Government would look after the cost of paying for the family's representation at the Inquiry. I knew that negotiating this would be delicate but luckily her solicitor turned out to be a friend through our sons having been at school together. The Kelly family he told me were very resistant to having anything to do with people from Government but he persuaded them to see me. I don't think it would have happened any other way. I drove to their house in Oxfordshire and met David Kelly's widow and their daughters. It was not an easy occasion for them or for me but I believed that by the time I left we had achieved an element of trust that would carry them into the Inquiry process.

Brian Hutton conducted the Inquiry brilliantly. The fairness of his hearing of all parties and all points of view could not be faulted which is why when he delivered his Report there was such a hostile outcry from some and such a triumphant shout of joy from others. The fallout from his decision that the Government was 'innocent' and the BBC 'guilty' was massive. My own view as a very involved observer was one of great surprise. Allowed into the Cabinet Office to read the Report on the morning before publication, I read it with growing consternation. While there was a bit of me that was pleased the Government had emerged unscathed there was another bit that felt that the result should not have been that simple given the complexity of the issues and arguments. As far as I could see, none of the parties had behaved particularly well and blame/responsibility should have been spread more widely, while still leaving the findings about the BBC's original errors and its responsibilities largely intact. However, that may be a too balanced a view; after all to find one party guilty and the other innocent is what happens in a criminal trial. But this was not a criminal trial. The late Brian Hutton's professional reputation should not rest on the controversy around this Inquiry. He was a good and noble man and, on the whole, a fine Judge.

The other major preoccupation of my last year was to draft, and agree with the Lord Chief Justice, the "Concordat" which would govern the new relationship between the Judiciary and the Government (i.e. with the 'new' Lord Chancellor and the Prime Minister) following the abolition of the role of the 'old' Lord Chancellor. Harry Woolf and I spent hours on this work. It was tricky at my end as it meant establishing in the consciousness of the department that the senior figure in all judicial matters would in future be the Lord Chief Justice not the Lord Chancellor. This meant an unwinding of assumptions sunk deep in the Department's culture about the role of the Lord Chancellor (put more crudely, explaining that what some politicians now wished they had not agreed to do was actually going to happen) and equipping the Lord Chief Justice with the proper support to carry out his new role. At my leaving Party in July 2004 Harry Woolf was generous in his thanks for my contribution. "The Concordat" was, in my view, a great State Paper and a watershed of a change in our constitution but, when published in January 2004 it was modestly titled "The Lord Chancellor's judiciary related functions: Proposals."

My farewell to my Civil Service life in terms of policy development was the publication of a Review of the Honours System. I had been involved with the Honours process, like many other Permanent Secretaries, for a very long time. The task of overseeing it had always fallen to the Cabinet Secretary but it was an onerous and distracting part of an already overloaded role and when Andrew Turnbull succeeded Richard Wilson we agreed that I would run the system on his behalf. For years there had been criticisms of the system's lack of independence and its archaic nature. In 2003 the House of Commons Public Administration Committee studied the same issues and came out with an interesting and very radical report which welcomed the value of Honours but recommended a 'slash and burn' exercise on the existing system. In the meantime the Prime Minister had asked me to review the system. With the considerable help of Mark Ormerod[19], I produced a less radical but nonetheless reforming report which removed Permanent Secretaries from chairing the various advisory Committees in favour of independent people. While the Select Committee wanted to say goodbye to the titles of Empire, Bath and St Michael and St George, I saw those as historical connections with our past which simply needed a good explanation, and suggested we leave iconoclasm alone and adopt a policy of "retain but explain", a forerunner of the Government's response to the current 'contested heritage' debate and the toppling of statues. However, if asked to do another report now I would recommend the abolition of the Order to the British Empire

In my Report I produced two unconventional recommendations. The first was that we should do what the French and the Italians did and encourage Honours' recipients to wear a "boutonnière" in public to advertise their recognition by the State. I have worn one ever since for marketing purposes but I fear we British are too shy/modest/mean/(you have to buy it) to make this continental import a part of our culture. However, the Government accepted this and, indeed, all but one of my 31 recommendations. The one it declined was my suggestion that the apparent automaticity of Knighthoods/Damehoods for Permanent Secretaries should be seen to cease. I understand why this was a bridge too far for the rest of the Establishment other than me. I could hear the Mandarin Chorus saying, "it's fine for him as he has passed through the gate and collected all his Honours but why should he slam the gate shut on those still waiting outside." After I had retired, I was, in April 2005, conducting the interviews to choose the new independent Chairs of the various Honours Committees. So far, this seems to have been a lasting reform.

On 13th July 2004 in the Great Hall of the Royal Courts of Justice I bade farewell to my Civil Service career. It was a good party in a wonderful space but there were too many speakers and the microphones were only intermittently successful. The crowd grew restless and by the time I had to respond they were talking to themselves at a good hubbub level. All I could do was to ditch the microphone and shout. It sort of worked and most of the audience listened for long enough. I told the gathering that Tony Blair had said that my going to work with Derry Irvine was a "marriage made in heaven". I then quoted Dr Johnson who said: "I believe marriages would in general be as happy, and often more so, if they were all made by the Lord Chancellor, upon a due consideration of characters and circumstances without the parties having any choice in the matter."

By then I had been appointed as the Chairman of the National Theatre so I was able to conclude my farewell speech with the words: "Hello Darlings, I'm back."

CHAPTER 8:
The Theatre, the City and the Prince

*I learn to use a computer • become Chairman of the National Theatre •
transfers to the West End • NT Live in cinemas across the nation • the
building refurbished • Lord Cottesloe • Vivien Duffield • the Chairman
is like The Queen • a velvet smoking cloak • James Hanson • corporate
finance and private equity • working for The Prince of Wales.*

BEFORE I LEFT the Civil Service I had been appointed Chairman
of the National Theatre, had agreed to work with Lord Hanson and
had accepted a role as a consultant to HRH the Prince of Wales. But I
could do none of these things for three months – the minimum furlough
period in those days before taking up new jobs for a Permanent Secretary
on leaving office, so during that time I taught myself how to use a computer. Looking back it is extraordinary to recall that, while all around me
in the 1990s and early 2000s people were working on screen, I still worked
on paper with a fountain pen or dictated memoranda to a member of my
staff. So after three months in the country learning new technical skills,
reading books and driving a tractor, I was ready and able to return to
London just about fit for a modern working life.

When I gave a dinner for a retiring friend a few years later he said
in reply to my little speech: "Unlike Hayden I am going to do the most
difficult thing and actually retire, so each morning I will have to decide
how to spend my day. Hayden has done the easier thing and just carried

on working." But if I needed any compensation for going on working I found it happily in the immense variety of things that came my way over the ensuing years; from farming to the theatre, from the City to press regulation, from Salisbury Cathedral to the funding of political parties, and from the world of advertising to becoming a film actor (sadly not 'star') late in life.

In the autumn of 2003 I had seen an advertisement for a new Chairman of the National Theatre and I knew how much I would like to do it. But I had almost a year still to serve as a Permanent Secretary and I felt I could not apply. Then in March 2004 I received a call from a friend who was on the National Theatre Board who said that the Board was split over whom to appoint and the then Chairman, Christopher Hogg[1], wanted a decision by consensus and not by a vote. He had asked whether I could offer suggestions for other people whom they might look at. I rang my friend back, after a weekend of serious pondering and asking for my wife's advice, and said I had thought of only one name, namely my own. She did not seem put out by this and I was told that if I was interested then I had to meet the head-hunters, then attend a small interviewing panel and then be interviewed by the whole Board. The small Panel of Board members was supplemented by Joan Bakewell[2] who told me that everyone knew how fond I was of music, opera and ballet but could I persuade them that theatre was my first love? I did my best. Confronting the whole Board later was a bit daunting but I survived, was appointed, and the Chairman invited me back in to the meeting to a courteous round of applause. He had achieved the consensus he wanted. I have never sought to probe into whether the first call I took from my friend on the Board was a genuine question to ask my views on other possible candidates or whether Chris Hogg had already decided I would be an acceptable consensus candidate and he simply needed to lure me in.

Mary Soames, a previous Chair, wrote me a congratulatory letter and told me to make sure they did not take my office away. She had created the office and she was right about my hanging on to it. It was a small but comfortable room with a separate loo and shower. During my time as Chairman I went to the Theatre every Monday and could use the office as a base to which to invite staff in to talk but more often I used the time to wander round the vastness of the NT, meeting and talking to people.

The National Theatre's screen says "Farewell to Hayden" on the author's retirement as Chairman.

Sir Hayden Phillips, Chairman of the Reviewing Committee on the Export of Works of Art

The Chairman channelling the spirit of Mr Toad

Behind the wheel of a Rolls Royce Silver Ghost – before a hearing on it by the RCEWA.

The River Ebble at the bottom of the author's garden, complete with swan and sheep.

Kingfishers on the river at Homington Farm. Husband and wife.

A longhorn cow emerging from the undergrowth.

In masked conversation with The King (then the Prince of Wales)
at Salisbury Cathedral's 800th Anniversary.

It did not take me long to discover that the theatre was extremely well run by the duumvirate of Nick Hytner[3] and Nick Starr[4] with the able assistance of Lisa Burger. Chairing Board meetings was not too onerous as on the whole people were well behaved and quite succinct. The Finance Committee (which I attended) did excellent due diligence. What went on to the stage was a decision for the Director not the Board. It was not always thus. When Laurence Olivier was leading the theatre decisions on which plays to stage were taken by a sub-committee of the Board. He protested and it was decided the decisions should be by the main Board. Why the Great Man put up with this is beyond me but Peter Hall[5] put a stop to the nonsense of interested amateurs deciding on a professional artistic programme. There is an argument for Board involvement as it is the Board which is legally responsible for what goes on stage. But that is procedurally and properly satisfied if the Board formally delegates to the Artistic Director the necessary decisions, without removing the Board's ultimate legal responsibility. (I recall only one occasion when I was called on to make a decision about a play and it was over a section of a David Hare play. I said I thought we should cut the relevant bit which was in dispute and which I said I would find difficult to defend if challenged. The author said he saw the point of my concern and thankfully the deletion was agreed without argument or rancour.)

However, I felt it was a gap in the life of the Board if it did not have any chance to discuss the Theatre's artistic successes or failures. Nick Hytner generously responded to the idea that, once a year, he would talk to the Board about what had gone well or less well in the previous year. This retrospective assessment was a good thing. Nick did it openly and not in any way defensively; it engaged the Board in the impact of the theatrical programme without interfering in the Director's freedom of artistic decision-making.

There were three Board decisions in my time which helped shape the future of the National Theatre in strategic terms.

The first was the decision to take the risk ourselves of transferring plays into the West End rather than just passing a play over for a fee for someone else to make money, or not. Three blockbusters subsequently underlined the good sense of this decision: *The History Boys, War Horse* and *One Man, Two Guvnors.* Sitting next to Nick Hytner on Broadway at the opening night of *History Boys* we wondered whether a New York audience would get the dramatic point of a story set in a Yorkshire grammar school. Within five minutes it was clear that the audience was lapping it up and a nightly standing ovation became the order of the day.

The second was the creation of "NT Live", the streaming of live theatre, and not just from the NT, to cinemas all over the country. This is now an established and highly successful phenomenon, with a tremendous outreach. An older friend living near a market town told me she went to its Town Hall regularly to see the shows, and with a glass of wine to purchase and regular familiar company, it was a wonderful evening out.

The third big issue was to decide to refurbish and reorganise the NT's building complex, a major project which would cost millions of pounds. It did cost millions and it was successfully completed but not under my leadership. Having done six years as Chairman by 2010, and although I would have liked to stay on, and I made that quite clear to anyone who would listen, the Board decided I was not the fund-raising type (whatever that means), and that was what they thought they needed, so they wanted to make a change. Maybe they were right; we shall never know. But, like Mrs Thatcher, I could have happily gone on and on and on. It was one of the most interesting and absorbing jobs I had had, although being in charge of anti-terrorism and riots, and chairing the Reviewing Committee on the Export of Works of Art (which came later), run it fairly close. But let the National Theatre win. It was a very happy place.

While I was still Chairman, Lloyd Dorfman[6] generously agreed to fund the refurbishment of the Cottesloe Theatre and Vivien Duffield[7] agreed to fund an education centre. In each case I was able to play a small part in enabling this to happen. In relation to the Cottesloe my task was to persuade Lord Cottesloe[8] that it was fine that his father's name (and therefore his) was to be removed from the Theatre; and Dorfman was put in its place. I did this by explaining that his father's bust would go into a Cottesloe Room, which was what was originally intended, as part of the new education area of the Theatre. I set this out in a letter to him but no reply came so I telephoned him. He apologised for not replying but he said my letter had worried him because he could not afford to make a donation. I reassured him that was not the point of my letter and his father would still be properly memorialised in the theatre. He then said he was happy.

We also wanted an education centre and the Clore-Duffield Foundation had already invested a great deal in the creation of such centres across the country, usually in museums and galleries. But Vivien Duffield had never done one in and for a theatre. Nick Hytner and I invited her out to lunch. After a half hour of jolly chat and gossip she "OK boys, it's nice to see you but what do you want, what do you want it for, and how much are you asking for?" We told her we wanted £5 million. She said, she thought half of our request would be enough but she would send her adviser to investigate our plan. Having got the advice she gave us precisely half of our request and half was enough to achieve enough of our education centre ambition.

At my farewell dinner I was presented with the velvet smoking cloak worn by Simon Russell Beale[9] as Sir Harcourt Courtly in *London Assurance*. (It has since been worn only once theatrically, when I played the part of the Narrator — an attempt to emulate Richard Burton — in *Under Milk Wood* in a beautiful church in the village of Farley, east of Salisbury built by Stephen Fox.) My other great farewell treats on my departure evening were being serenaded at dinner by some of the cast of *The History Boys* and seeing the NT screens on the river front of the theatre advertising *For One Night only; Goodbye to Hayden*.

What is the role of the Chairman of the National Theatre? Forget all the normal clichés about leadership, financial discipline, strategic thinking and crisis management. They are of course necessary requirements but they are not sufficient ones and the quality that made one's performance sufficient was to be the Theatre's constitutional monarch. One afternoon I was having a chat with Nick Hytner in his office when he said he had to go to a 'meet and greet' (meeting all those involved in a new play) and would I like to come? I agreed and as we went along he said he hoped I would speak to those assembled. I said yes. We went into a very large room full of people. Nick spoke to them and then turned to me. I spoke and cannot remember what I said but it had the effect of producing some resounding applause. As we left I asked Nick what had occurred and why they had been so nice to me. He said that they saw him all the time but I was a rare grand moment in their lives, like a visit from

The Queen. He sustained that light-hearted but perceptive view of the role he wanted me to perform. But it had a downside. One afternoon I attended a rehearsal for *Henry IV Part 2* directed by Nick. It was the garden scene in Gloucestershire. There was one actor missing who was to play Pistol, a choleric bombast. I said I knew the part well from my English O Levels and volunteered to read it to the amused acclaim of the distinguished cast, including Michael Gambon as Falstaff. Nick turned a whiter shade of pale and prompted a young understudy forward to read the part. I imagine he did not want the Chairman, as the constitutional monarch, to make a fool of himself.

I once found one other and more humble role. One afternoon in 2005 I was outside the Stage Door chatting to Frances de la Tour[10], and smoking a small cigar, when a taxi drew up and out of it emerged the substantial form of the late Richard Griffiths[11]. He then dropped everything he was carrying and was, understandably, unable to reach down to pick it all up. I knelt before him gathering up his possessions as Michael Gambon walked up to ask what was afoot. I explained that it was the normal role of the Chairman of the Theatre to abase himself before the stars who arrived and needed help.

On Mondays, as I have said, I worked at the theatre, while on Tuesdays and Wednesdays I moved into my new financial services life due, in large part, to my friendship with Mrs Thatcher's favourite businessman, James Hanson[12]. It was an unlikely pairing. We had met in the 1980s when I was running the Top Management Programme. Tall, handsome and superbly dressed he was a star performer. We stayed in touch both when I was at the Treasury and at DCMS particularly then as he owned a radio station (Melody Radio) and was interested in the policy issues for which I had responsibility. When I was at the LCD he said that he hoped that when I came to leave the Civil Service I would go to work with him. And from time to time we'd meet for lunch and he would remind me of his request. He had become a loyal friend. An example of this occurred in 2003 when an article about me by Andrew Gimson appeared in *The Spectator* titled "Charming wit or oily Welshman?". It was not intended as a flattering piece but was, in my view, entertaining and well based on good gossip. Why Gimson bothered to write it is still beyond me (but it was August). Out of the blue Lord Hanson wrote to the Editor as follows:

UNDESERVED INSULT

From Lord Hanson

Sir: What personal grudge against Sir Hayden Phillips causes Andrew Gimson to write his spiteful piece (16 August) about one of the finest examples of our much envied British Civil Service? Your headline – 'Charming wit or oily Welshman?' – was just insulting.

The timing of the piece was especially unsympathetic. Sir Hayden's current workload on the reorganisation of his department is absolutely vital to us all and must be heavier than at any other time in his career – even for his experienced shoulders. He will doubtless handle it with his customary aplomb, but he and we certainly can do without such sneering, unhelpful pieces.

Nul Points, Gimson.

Hanson

London SW7

Some parts of the article were friendly but the headline came out of this passage: "A high Tory said, 'He's an oily little Welshman who thought he was going to be Cabinet Secretary by oiling up to the Labour Party .... He is not a man I would be happy to go tiger-shooting with'." The article concluded by saying: "He is variously described as the Vicar of Bray and the original Sir Humphrey – this latter a joke he has taken in good part. If anyone can give a falsely reassuring feel to Labour's wild constitutional experiments, it is Sir Hayden Phillips."

I had a mixed press over the years. A regular commentator on my Parliamentary Committee appearances was Quentin Letts whose sketches in *The Times* I continue to enjoy. I include only one piece from the selection he has kindly offered me over the years, from the *Daily Mail* of May 17 2006 when I was appearing to answer questions on Party Funding. While waiting outside the Committee room I met and greeted him. He then wrote: "Normally I try to avoid witnesses. Like a certain type of dentist I prefer not to make too much eye contact with victims beforehand. But retired Whitehall grandee Sir Hayden, oh, he's a piece of work. 'The mandarins' ex-mandarin. A champion schmoozer. The Ronaldinho of greasing."

During my last year at the Lord Chancellor's Department I learnt that James Hanson had serious cancer and I did not feel I should ring up and say he had offered me a job. But he rang me instead and when we met I agreed to join him to help oversee his family investment interests. We agreed a salary and he gave me his office and his secretary. I was to start on 4 November 2004 – sadly the morning on which he died. His son Robert honoured his father's commitments to me and over the next ten years I remained a non-executive Director of a succession of Hanson companies including the original founding company, Hanson Transport, based in Huddersfield. For a long time in this context I was happily a part of a small corporate finance stockbroking company, created by Bill Staple[13], variously named Hanson Westhouse (of which I was Chairman) and then Westhouse, when Robert sold his holding and others took over. The business was hit hard by the 2008 financial crash.

By a quite separate route I found myself in the world of private equity, invited by Dominic Shorthouse[14] on to the Advisory Board of Englefield Capital, a very successful private equity investment boutique. The Advisory Board dined and debated issues at Mosimann's. I became a non-executive director of one of the companies they had bought, an out-sourcing service provider working in part for the Home Office on which it was thought I had some historic expertise. My association lasted seven years.

On Thursdays I worked from St James's Palace, one day a week, for the next five years. This role, as Charities Consultant to the Prince of Wales, happened quite accidentally. The plan had been that I would work with Jacob Rothschild for a day a week on his cultural rather than invest-ment interests. Jacob mentioned this to the Prince of Wales who said that he would welcome it if I came to Clarence House instead. So it was decided. Essentially I helped out in two ways: where there were cultural or heritage projects to pursue I became involved; and I also dealt with the ap-pointments of Trustees to his vast portfolio of charities, trying to bring in a more systematic and disciplined process. The former was interesting and fun; the latter was dull but essential in order to produce proper and defen-sible accountability about the way appointments were made. I had helped His Royal Highness set up a buildings heritage charity in the 1990s and had boldly arranged for him to give presentations to Cabinet Ministers in the Cabinet Office on its planned work. So I imagine, as Civil Servants went, I was thought by him, in Wodehousian terms, to be a reasonably 'good egg'. One year, at the staff Christmas Party in St James's Palace, a voice said to me, "would you like a canape, Sir?" and I turned round to find my daughter Louisa who was working temporarily in the holidays for the catering company which was organising the event. I immediately introduced her to the Duchess of Cornwall. She (my daughter) was not best pleased as she was in her Father Christmas elf costume. But the Duchess was her usual brilliant self and put Louisa completely at her ease.

CHAPTER 9:
Party Funding — A Farewell to Westminster

The agreement of the Party leaders is secured • meetings with all parties • Alex Salmond • Dover House (Lord Melbourne, Lord Byron and Lady Caroline Lamb) • the principles for an agreement are settled • the optimism of July 2007 • the issue of the affiliation fees of Trade Union members brings us down • a Times *cartoon • I suspend the inter-party talks • Matthew Parris and Peter Riddell on the "project" • Francis Maude and Civil Service reform.*

THE AGREEABLE PATTERN of professional life into which I had fallen after I left the Civil Service was disrupted in March 2006 when the Prime Minister asked me to conduct a review of Party political funding following a noisy controversy about 'cash for peerages.' I looked at the draft Terms of Reference I was offered and said I would agree to do it provided the Leaders of the Conservative and Liberal Democrat Parties approved of my appointment as well. I think it was Jonathan Powell who rang me to say that David Cameron and Ming Campbell were so effusive in their praise for my doing the review that the Prime Minister thought he may have chosen the wrong man.

I took the task on because it wasn't just the conventional 'review and report' process handed to ex-Mandarins but because I was asked to find as much common ground between the Parties as I could. It was the politics of handling this, rather than the necessary analytical work, that really interested me. After almost a year's work of research and discussion (in which I was most ably assisted by the late Andrew McDonald[1] and Ian Gambles[2]) I produced a report which was genuinely optimistic about the chances of getting an agreement. On the basis of some very good analytical work, and lots of separate bilateral discussions with the three main parties, there seemed to be an emerging consensus that the size of donations to political parties should be capped; that expenditure should be limited and reduced; and that a stable future system probably required an increase in public funding to the parties.

I should add that I did not confine my discussions to the Labour, Conservative and Liberal Democratic parties. I held talks with all the parties with representation at Westminster or with representatives in the devolved assemblies. And I made sure that I went to Edinburgh, Cardiff and Belfast for those discussions rather than making them come to me in London. The main person who could not see me in Edinburgh but in London was Alex Salmond. We met in the House of Commons for an immensely surprising conversation. He led it with a small but ferocious harangue in which he described me as "Blair's poodle." He then stopped abruptly, grinned and said that what he had said was simply his Press hand-out of our meeting, and then we talked about the real issues at stake.

I was then asked to chair negotiations between the parties to try to find an agreement for reform based on the proposals in my initial report. I managed to arrange for the talks to be held in Dover House, the Grade 1 listed neo-classical mansion at 70 Whitehall which I came across when I found myself the Permanent Secretary at the Scotland Office which had its London home there. In my view it is one of the most beautiful 18th century houses in the whole of central London – home to Lord Melbourne when Prime Minister to the young Queen Victoria. The ropes to help you up the central staircase were, I was told, there for Lord Byron to haul himself up with his club foot when visiting his mistress, Lady Caroline Lamb. I hoped some of the elegance and ambience of the house would helpfully rub off on my political colleagues and mellow their approach to the talks!

We agreed three principles for the conduct of these talks. The first was that nothing could be agreed until everything was agreed (with hindsight that was a counsel of perfection which, in the end, proved too high a hurdle for everyone to jump but it seemed a necessary condition when the talks began). The second was that a new and fairer system need not initially be uniform but should become so progressively over time – this was to enable the adaptation of agreed changes to the different cultures and histories of the different Parties. The third was that we would only proceed by consensus. We had three sets of talks between May and July in 2007 and one more in October. On 24 July I put out a rather bullish press notice. It said: "Significant progress has been made in the inter-party talks, and I believe we are nearer to a comprehensive agreement on a range of measures to reform party political funding. Some outstanding issues remain to be resolved. The parties themselves deserve credit for the way they have engaged with the talks and I believe there is a greater under-standing between them on the key issues." The sun was shining but when we met again after the summer break the political weather had changed and my summer optimism was proved to be mistaken.

The substantive issue on which the talks foundered was the treat-ment of the affiliation fees paid by individual trade union members to the Labour Party. There was no apparent objection to my proposals that these should not be aggregated and then capped under our new proposals for limits on major donations but should be treated as small individual donations. However, the Conservatives had never really moved from their original preference that since a significant minority of union members voted either Tory or Lib-Dem these individual donations should be vol-untary and sent to a political party of the individual's choice. On the face of it that looked like a reasonable and defensible argument. However, even though it was proposed that this change need only be implemented after a long transitional period I knew that for the Labour Party, given the history and culture of their relationship with the Trade Union move-ment, to take a decision of principle on this basis was likely to be a bridge too far. A cartoon in *The Times* captured the issue well. I am portrayed as a gardener putting plants into pots. I have potted the yellow Lib-Dem plant and the green Conservative one but I am struggling with the task of lifting the Labour red rose because of the resistance of its extensive root system, labelled the Trade Unions. I did not think we could get round this rock on the road and I suspended the talks. The blame game began immediately. The Conservatives said that the Labour Party had lost interest in a compromise when Gordon Brown succeeded Tony Blair. The Labour Party accused the Conservatives on insisting on a condition to advance the talks which they knew the Labour Party could not deliver. I was asked by the parties to continue the talks but judged it would have been pointless.

Looking back, I think there is some truth in both of those opposing points of view but more importantly I believe that during the summer and into the autumn of 2007 the underlying general political position had begun to move, culminating in the much heralded general election that Gordon Brown did not call. After some really good and positive meetings earlier in the year when we met again in the autumn it felt as though the two main parties had reverted to their default positions of tribal introspection. It turned out it had been better to travel hopefully than to arrive, as when we were in sight of the originally agreed destination, the passengers started to argue about where they wanted to go. As we were on a democratic trip I could not insist, as Captain, that we stuck to the itinerary to which the parties had initially responded so positively. There was a glimmer of hope that the talks might be revived (after all they had only been 'suspended' not closed) when the Coalition Government was formed. Indeed Nick Clegg's[3] list of 'red lines' for negotiation with David Cameron, photographed through a taxi-cab window, showed one item as "Hayden Phillips." The Committee on Standards of Conduct in Public Life was asked to have a further look at the issues. They made some adjustments to my detailed proposals but nothing came of their involvement. If the Parties ever want to solve their funding problem then all I can say is that the Report I produced and the discussions I had held still hold the solution. (I know I am right because Matthew Parris[4] said so in *The Times* describing my report as the "lodestar" on the subject.) There is really no need for more enquiries and reports other than that a new generation must have the credit for finding a solution; and if they can unearth my report and breathe life into it they deserve the credit.

I think the most charming epitaph on my failure to solve this chronic problem came from Peter Riddell[5] writing in *The Times* in March 2007:

"Sir Hayden Phillips still has one potential winning card .... as he is also Chairman of the National Theatre. Taking up Tony Blair's offer to chair further talks between the parties, he should break the habit of a lifetime and move from behind the scenes to the front of the stage. He should host the talks in the full spotlight of the Lyttelton or the Olivier. That, I am sure, would produce agreement within a few hours."

There was, later, a sort of attached codicil to this story. The talks had been led on the Conservative side by Francis Maude[6] with whom I had worked briefly when I was in the Treasury and he was Financial Secretary – we shared grim memories of the length of submissions from the Inland Revenue. In the Coalition Government he was the Minister in the Cabinet Office and in charge of Civil Service Reform. We had stayed in touch and I had offered him advice when he asked for it. He consulted me about two particular propositions: fixed terms for Permanent Secretaries and the creation of a more mixed-team of civil servants and special advisers as the Private Office for Ministers. I thought both of these were timely changes and I agreed to say so publicly. So on July 11 2013 I produced a piece in *The Times* headed "It's not the thin end of the wedge, Sir Humphrey" which supported his proposals. It had long been my view that those who claimed that appointments were being 'politicised' had missed the point that they could always, and reasonably, be 'personalised'. Ministers should be allowed to choose the people, following an 'on merit' process, with whom they felt most comfortable. After all, that is the way I became Roy Jenkins's Principal Private Secretary and it was the way in which I did not become Jack Straw's Permanent Secretary. And I also supported a broadening of the composition of the Private Office so it could become, if a Minister so chose, more like a continental-style *Cabinet,* the strengths of which I had experienced in my time in Brussels. I now regret somewhat my support of the first of these as I have noticed in the last few years the fixed-term (5 years) appointment has been used to remove people who appeared to me very able and entitled on merit to a further term or job. 'Churn' in the Civil Service has become almost as much of a problem as lack of knowledge and expertise has always been among some Ministerial appointments.

CHAPTER 10:
A Professional After-Life — Advertising, Art and the Movies

The value of succinct writing and good listening • an 18th century process to become the Independent Reviewer of the Rulings of the ASA • in the High Court • the case of a "chair leg" • the most tasteless ad I had to consider • setting up IPSO post Leveson in 2014 • I become Chairman of Marlborough College • the behaviour of parents on the touchline • the Holbourne Museum, a good home for great works of art • I chair the Reviewing Committee on the Export of Works of Art • Portrait of a Young Man in a Red Cap • Lady Chatterley's Lover • how the RCEWA works • The Wellington Collection at Apsley House • my life in movies • Colonel Dent in Jane Eyre (2011) and Spectre Agent No 4 in No Time to Die (2021).

O VER THE NEXT DECADE, I was offered, or succeeded in getting, a series of different but absorbing roles. I have tried to discern whether they tell a reasonably consistent story as to why people would want to continue to employ ex-Mandarins well after their normal retirement date. I think I can identify a couple. My generation of civil servants could still summarise the heart of an issue in a single page rather than five; and a very distinguished senior banker once said to me that he would always pay good money for that skill. In addition, our customary day-today life in the Civil Service was a constant process of analysing and balancing conflicting arguments which often meant we made good chairmen, provided the capacity to listen was also there accompanied by the right personality and temperament. But at the end of the day, whatever walk of life one came from, what mattered was character and experience. Two roles came my way in the world of regulation which made use of the two particular characteristics I have mentioned.

In 2010 my former Secretary of State, Chris Smith, then Chairman of the Advertising Standards Authority (ASA), asked if I had a day a week free and might be interested in the role as the Independent Reviewer of the decisions and rulings of the Council of the ASA; a sort of Judge-like/Ombudsman position. As the National Theatre and Clarence House had by then fallen away I thought I would investigate. It turned out that the retiring office holder was a former colleague, John Caines[1]. I agreed to meet the Chairman of the appointing body which was the Advertising Standards Board of Finance (ASBOF). He (Winston Fletcher[2]) invited me to lunch at the Garrick and we had a most engaging time discussing everything but the role. I asked a bit about it towards the end but he did not seem to want to discuss it very much and said he knew I would do it with ease. I said I was interested and he said he would be back in touch. Three months of silence passed. Then the phone rang and he said that the Selection Panel would meet the following day and was I still interested? I used the clichéd response that silence had made the heart grow fonder and we put the phones down.

The next day he rang around noon and said the job was mine but there had been a slight glitch as two of the Panel members thought they ought to meet me. I told them, he said, that was quite unnecessary as the present Chairman of the ASA and his two predecessors had said I was perfectly qualified: all in all this had been a very 18th century process of 'a tap on the shoulder'.

The work turned out to be intrinsically interesting as advertising holds up a mirror to contemporary society; the work is varied and some of the cases are intellectually demanding. In competitive arguments between big companies about the advertising of their products they reached for their lawyers and I had to reach for mine. In process terms my task was simple. If I thought the ASA Council had got it right I wrote back to say so, with carefully explained reasons, given the risk of judicial review. If I thought the case had gone wrong I returned it to the ASA Council and invited them either to reverse their decision or to amend their rationale for it. My decisions (grandly titled as Determinations) have so far been challenged only once via judicial review in the High Court and the Court found in my favour. The case was a commercial battle between Sainsbury's and Tesco. Each company was represented by Counsel as was I. I sat in court for two and a half days listening to the arguments. It was like being at one's own Memorial Service as each of the three Counsel referred to my arguments and views in the past tense as though I had died.

I have dealt with hundreds of cases over the years but it might illustrate the nature of the task to describe one of which I am particularly fond as it produced a charming but cumbersome present for the ASA Chairman when he retired. It concerned a TV ad for the company Oak Furniture Land. The contentious issues were two statements in the advertisement: first, the claim that there was "no veneer in 'ere" and, second, the claim "100% solid hardwood". The complainant argued that the company's 'oak wrap' technique – a thin layer of oak around pieces of oak glued together – would be understood as a veneer and that it was therefore misleading to describe the result as "100% solid". The ASA Council agreed and upheld the complaint. The advertiser appealed to me partly on the grounds that the Council had not adopted the commonly understood meaning of a veneer which was a layer of good quality wood covering a core of less good material. The company sent me a table leg of theirs and one, veneered, from a rival. Theirs looked and felt entirely solid; the other was much inferior. I told the Council that in my view they had got it wrong but offered them two draft decisions, one consistent with their original ruling but rewritten and one which reversed it. By a narrow majority the Council voted to agree with my recommendation. The very solid chair leg was engraved with the names of all the Council members, of the senior staff and mine and presented to the Chairman, Chris Smith, when he stepped down. At the time of writing it lives in his study as Master of Pembroke College, Cambridge.

The range of types of cases is vast. Taking just TV and radio advertising, in 2021 I reviewed decisions on ads by Toyota, Kentucky Fried Chicken, cider, Starbucks, Cinch cars, erectile dysfunction, baldness, petcare, mask wearing, vaccines and many more. In 2021 I dealt with an ad which wins a prize for being the most tasteless ad I had dealt with in a long time. It was a TV ad by Highways England about moving to the left on smart motorways if your car is in trouble. An overweight driver sees his warning light is on then sees two humanoid flies arrive on his windscreen singing "Go Left." They keep singing while he moves over and can park. The flies are then knocked to the ground when the windscreen wipers are turned on. The ad was silly and lacked any dignity given the subject of safety on smart motorways was a highly emotive issue. Some of the people who wrote to me to complain had suffered death in their families on these roads. But the ad was not in breach of the rules in the advertising Code.

My next entrance into the world of regulation concerned the Press after the publication of the Leveson Report in November 2012. All the major newspaper and magazine publishers were hostile to any form of regulation which was touched by Government or by Parliament. This was true even of those who decided to go their own way rather than sign up to the self-regulatory Independent Press Standards Organisation (IPSO) namely *The Guardian, The Financial Times* and the *Independent*. Those in the industry who had worked up their proposals for a new self-regulatory body to replace the discredited Press Complaints Commission decided to ask Nick Phillips, Lord Phillips of Worth Matravers, former Lord Chief Justice and President of the Supreme Court, to gather together a group of people, known as the Foundation Group, which would select and appoint someone to Chair a Panel to appoint a Chairman of the new regulator and its Board. I was asked to take this on and I said yes, because, despite the controversy then surrounding the issue of self-regulation versus statutory regulation, it seemed to me that IPSO was most likely to become the principal regulatory body, as it has proved to be, and one should therefore do ones best to make it as effective as possible. I also knew the press would never willingly accept statutory regulation and having been involved in helping to sustain self-regulation of the Press in the mid-1990s (see Chapter 6) and as I was now involved in the self-regulation of advertising, I felt I also had some relevant expertise to offer. The whole process of IPSO's creation was very carefully distanced from those who would fund the system.

I was joined in the task of setting up IPSO by a national newspaper Editor, a regional Editor, a former Supreme Court Justice and a senior academic. There were many applicants for all the advertised roles and it took us many meetings/weeks to work through the lists. We decided to appoint Sir Alan Moses[3] as the first Chairman and, once appointed, he joined us in the selection of Board members. I then joined him in the selection process for membership of the Complaints Committee, appointments to which were reserved to the Board rather than the Appointments Panel. I continued in this role as Chair of the IPSO Appointments Panel until the autumn of 2021, having appointed Lord (Edward) Faulks QC[4] as the new Chairman of IPSO in the year before.

There are some people and groups who will never be reconciled to self-regulation, believing that the regulator is controlled, or at least heavily influenced, by a cabal of 'press barons'. I was closely involved with all those concerned for eight years and I have to say that that rationale is based on "fake views" inherited from a bitter past controversy which I recognise still involves passionate engagement and deeply held beliefs.

At the time I was beginning this work (2013) I was retiring after seven years as the Chairman of the Council of Marlborough College, the school's governing body. During my time in office we opened a Marlborough College in Malaysia, and a new girls' House, and appointed a new Master. We had a serious falling out with Radley over cricket and one with Wellington over rugby.

There is something dangerously infectious to parents about school sport when they are on the touchline. Why do some parents make a practice of embarrassing their children? I do not have a great track-record. Indeed, I was responsible for three bad performances of parental over-exuberance. The worst was when my youngest son was about 10 or 11 and playing in a hockey match against another school. Whichever school won that particular game would top the League. With about two or three minutes to go the score was 1-1. My son Tom then skipped into the circle and slammed the ball into the back of the net. Total triumph; and I shouted "That's my boy". He ran towards me; I assumed he was coming for a congratulatory hug; not at all, as he said very clearly for all to hear: "If you do that again I don't want you ever to come to my matches."

Some years earlier I had gone to see my daughter, Louisa, play in a netball match against another school in Battersea Park. She must have been about 7 or 8 years old. When I arrived I asked another parent what the score was and she explained that 'we' were well in the lead. Then Louisa scored a goal and I shouted congratulations; at which point the referee, one of my daughter's teachers, ran across to me and said: "Mr Phillips please don't cheer when we score; it demoralises the other side." I muttered to myself that I thought that was the point.

My final parental disaster was when my other daughter, Flo, was playing in the English Schools Lacrosse Final. I, and another father, both passionate supporters, cheered so loudly that the girls could not hear the whistle and the other side were awarded a goal, making the score 1 – 1. Sufficiently chastised by the coach who basically told us to shut up we then kept quiet. In the end our side won 2 – 1 and lifted the trophy. My daughter went on to play for England and to captain Cambridge University. I did not disgrace myself or embarrass her when attending any of those matches. I had learned my lesson.

To the best of my knowledge I am the only Chairman of Marlborough so far who has not been an old Marlburian; the other two candidates when I was elected were both 'old boys'. Indeed, in electing a former State schoolboy to the Chair, the Council of the day was being more revolutionary than it probably realised. However, with the support of the Bishop of Salisbury[5] and a Field-Marshal[6], I had become the 'establishment' candidate.

I had originally joined the Council in 1997 because the then Chairman was looking for someone who had been involved with the art market. Years before, the College had been given a Gainsborough portrait of *The Byam Family* which was seen only by inky-fingered schoolboys and the odd art-historian. With the agreement of the donor family, we sold it to provide a number of improvements to the school facilities. The anonymous buyer/donor enabled it to become part of the collection at the Holburne Museum in Bath. A very convincing copy was placed in the Adderley, the room where the original had hung.

When, subsequently, I was at the National Theatre I further developed this penchant for disposing of great art. The Theatre owned a collection of theatrical pictures given to it by Somerset Maugham. They could not be hung easily in a Theatre of such architectural modernity and they languished unseen in the care of the Victoria & Albert Museum. I visited the collection in a warehouse in Battersea, decided that the two best Zoffanys, of David Garrick, should be hung in my office at the Theatre and pondered what to do about the rest. I knew they should be on public display (beyond the two being seen by visitors to my office), so I consulted Neil MacGregor, who was on the National Theatre Board and who thought the Holburne in Bath would be a good home. I explained the plan to Maugham's family and sought their agreement, which they gave most willingly, and now the collection is on display in Bath both at the Museum and at the Theatre Royal. When I go to the Holburne I can see "my" Gainsborough and "my" Zoffanys in the same room.

The culmination of these passing engagements with the visual arts was something more substantial and enduring. In 2013 I applied to be the Chairman of the Reviewing Committee on the Export of Works of Art and Objects of Cultural Interest. This lengthily-titled national quango, serviced by the Arts Council, with its members appointed by the Culture Secretary, had been in existence since the report of Viscount Waverley in 1952. When export licences are applied for works of art over 50 years old the job of the Committee is to make a judgement whether to allow the licence to be issued or whether the export is not in the national interest. When an application is made the Export Licensing Unit at the Arts Council consults one of a great number of Expert Advisers to the Secretary of State as to whether the object – painting, sculpture, manuscript, etc – fulfils one or more of the three criteria which Waverley had laid down for holding up the grant of an export licence in order to see whether an institution or person could raise the money to keep it in the UK. It is the Committee's task to apply these criteria. However, before turning to some of the works of art we considered under my chairmanship, I have to comment on the appointments process for the role of Chairman. This was deeply frustrating.

The advertisement for a Chairman came out in August and applicants were told that there was a target of October for a decision. October came and went so I enquired what was going on. I was told that the Secretary of State had found an all-male shortlist unacceptable so there would have to be a re-advertisement. More time passed and I was told that three women had applied, which was good news, but the only trouble was that each one of them, it turned out, was personally connected either to the art market or to a museum or gallery and they were therefore disqualified. This extra process had been a complete waste of time in a good cause the need for which should have been clarified right from the start. The now very frustrated all-male shortlist of three was interviewed in February. Four Panel members each asked me a question, the last one of which was: "What is your view of the underlying weaknesses in the legislation governing the export of works of art"? My reply was something like: "I think I once knew the answer to that question but this process has taken so long that I was too exhausted to re-read all the papers." There was laughter. The interview ended. It had been scheduled for 45 minutes and had lasted for 18. As I left I said to the young man who was escorting me that it had been so quick they must have been quite uninterested in my candidature. He said he did not think that was the case. He was right and I was appointed and began the job in March 2014.

Over the following years the Reviewing Committee considered some of the most beautiful and extraordinary things. Many were retained but many were lost, usually because the amount of funds that needed to be raised to save them was too large. One of the most controversial cases during my Chairmanship was a Pontormo – *Portrait of a Young Man in a Red Cap* – the matching price for which was over £30 million. Following tremendous efforts, the National Gallery raised the funds only for the owner then to decline to accept their offer on the grounds that he needed to be compensated for the losses he had incurred on the changes in the exchange rate between the £ and the $ after the Brexit vote in 2016. However, in my Committee hearing of the case, his agents had agreed to accept a matching offer with no qualifications. In my view this was a disgraceful reneging by someone who had pledged their word but neither I nor the Government had any sanctions we could apply. I wrote a letter saying, in effect, that in our country our word was our bond but I knew that even if the letter made me feel better I was just whistling in the wind. The picture cannot leave the country, except temporarily, but no one wins in these circumstances. Partly as a result of that case, and some others, the Government has announced the introduction of legally binding offers from 1 January 2022, so this sort of thing can no longer occur.

But there were other more successful moments in a wonderful flow of objects which came before us or which we had to visit because they were either too large or too fragile to travel to us. The National Gallery managed to raise another substantial sum to secure a Bellotto – *The Fortress of Königstein from the North;* Queen Victoria's Coronet, designed by Prince Albert, is now in the V&A, thanks to the generosity of a private donor; and nearby in a different V&A gallery is Salvador Dalí's *Lips Sofa*. Also, in the exotic realm we considered an Arab Jambaya dagger and robes given to TE Lawrence after he had captured Aqaba from the Turks (now in the National Army Museum); a Rolls Royce Silver Ghost from 1907, said to be the only car in which Mr Rolls and Mr Royce had been driven together; and a sledge and flag from Shackleton's 1906 Nimrod expedition.

One of my personal favourites was a piece of Martinware pottery of an *Anthropomorphic Crab.* We decided that this met the criterion of being of outstanding aesthetic importance. As the piece was pretty ugly we had concluded that the criterion we had to apply did not mean an object had to be beautiful! Another favourite of mine was the Judge's copy of *Lady Chatterley's Lover,* from one of the most important criminal trials of the 20th century. It had been annotated by him and by his wife (she underlined for him, in advance of the hearing, the more erotic sentences), and the book may have been the last surviving contemporary 'witness' who had taken part in the proceedings. I wrote in the Press Notice announcing the decision to pause its export:

"Picture the scene: the High Court Judge presiding in his red robes, his wife beside him on the Bench (as was allowed in those days) as a succession of singular and distinguished witnesses for the Defence were cross examined day by day. I was 17 at the time and studying a D H Lawrence as a set text for A Levels – it was not Lady Chatterley's Lover - but at least I could follow the riveting course of the trial in the daily papers. It would be more than sad, it would be a misfortune, if this last surviving 'witness' of the trial left our shores."

It did not and is now housed in Bristol University.

Sadly, however, there were many things which could not be secured for the nation, often simply because of their cost. But one was lost because the Expert Adviser system failed to spot its uniqueness and it never came before the Committee, it was given an Export Licence and went to be sold in New York. This was Alan Turing's[7] 1942 notebook. A national treasure lost by an unusual accident of a lack of available qualified expertise on the day.

In my view the Reviewing Committee has stood the test of time because it was founded on the basis of the sort of detailed work, with added wisdom, on which Governments used regularly to draw and rely. I feel a real historic affinity with Viscount Waverley as he had been the Permanent Secretary at the Home Office, which I was denied, before becoming the wartime Home Secretary. He then, like me, moved in part into the world of culture. As a result of his work I, like some Chairmen before me, became the only amateur among a group of professionals of deep expertise, great charm and with a good sense of humour, liking a proper lunch with a glass or two of good wine (which I hasten to add was paid for each month by a member of the Committee not by the taxpayer). The Committee operates rather like a court of law. The Expert Adviser presents the case for why the object should remain in the UK, while the applicant for the licence usually (but not always) argues against and in favour of its export. The Committee, supplemented by two or three Independent Assessors (experts on the particular object or artist) question the parties. Then I invite the prosecution and defence to leave while we debate the merits of the arguments. We then vote and, when the parties have returned, I announce our verdict and the nature of the sentence – a delayed execution for three or more months but then, if a serious interest to purchase is made by a museum or gallery in the UK, some more months to raise the funds. In my view it is a pretty well balanced and fair system trusted both by the art market and by the museum and gallery world.

My last big case as Chairman was *Portrait of Omai* by Sir Joshua Reynolds. Omai (really called Mai), a young Pacific Islander, travelled with Captain Cook to London in 1774 and became an instant celebrity, meeting King George III, attending the State Opening of Parliament and touring the country. My Committee decided that the picture was of outstanding importance under all three of the Waverley criteria[8] and recommended that the grant of an export licence should be deferred for four months and then, if a serious expression of interest in purchasing it was made, a further eight months should be allowed to raise the funds required. The Secretary of State accepted that and also agreed to an independent valuation of the picture. This endorsed the value of £50 million.

I also took the further step of writing to the Secretary of State advising her to seek a special Exchequer grant to help to keep the painting in the UK. This was a highly unusual step as, since the advent of Lottery funds in the early 1990's, the Treasury had made it clear that it expected funds to come from Lottery and other sources rather than the taxpayer. However my Committee's terms of reference entitled me to make that request and although I felt that some lottery and other funds might be forthcoming I did not see, unless some billionaire was persuaded to intervene, how enough money could be raised without Government help.

During this period, and indeed for some time before, I was fortunate to be involved in helping to run an actual museum and Gallery, namely The Wellington Collection at Apsley House. This is a stunning grouping of pictures, furniture and other objects associated with the 1st Duke, and open for the public to see in the House where he lived, No1 London. The House and its contents were given to the nation by the present Duke's grandfather and the gift was enshrined in the Wellington Museum Act 1947. Since 2004 the Collection has been managed by English Heritage on behalf of the Government which is responsible for the care and maintenance of the building and the Collection. I was appointed by DCMS as the Chairman of the Wellington Collection Management Committee with the present Duke representing the Wellesley family, with the late Lord Leicester, but now Sir Laurie Magnus, representing English Heritage/Historic England, and Sir Hugh Roberts, former Director of the Royal Collection as our expert independent member.

Apart from the aesthetic quality of the Collection the unique feature of this "national museum" is that the family live in the private apartments and, through the present Duke, personify the engagement of the 1st Duke in the creation and care of the Collection. The number of loans from the family to the Collection are significant and the most beautiful of those, in recent years, is *Danaë* by Titian. However, the most striking object is a monumental sculpture of a naked Napoleon, by Canova, at the bottom of the main staircase – Napoleon has a fig-leaf which fell off from the effects of vibration during the bombing of London in the

War. Napoleon was, apparently, horrified by Canova's effort and it was put in a basement in the Louvre until the British Government bought it as a thank you present for Wellington. The Collection is too little visited, despite its quality and our best efforts. Once it was No 1 London but now, although it hasn't moved, it is on the Hyde Park Corner roundabout – not a good location to attract passing trade as the trade just passes, very fast!

Alongside my engagement with the world of art I also found myself during this time in yet another cultural world, the world of film, and, surprisingly as an actor in a movie. It came about by yet another happy accident. In December 2009 a dust cloud over Iceland closed down all transatlantic flights and my daughter Flo rang to ask if an American friend of hers, who could not get back to New York to be with his family, could come to us for Christmas. I of course said yes. He turned out to be a young film Director called Cary Fukanaga[9] who was in England looking at locations for the shooting of a new film version of *Jane Eyre.* Over a glass of wine or two, I told him that I had a great latent acting talent which had never been given a chance to flower and I hoped he would have a part for me in the movie. His excellent good manners towards his Christmas host meant he said 'yes'. We enjoyed ourselves and I forgot all about it.

But he did not forget. Six weeks later I received an email from his Casting Director saying he was offering me the part of Colonel Dent, a speaking part for an old soldier who had served under Wellington at Waterloo, with thirteen lines, and if I wanted to do it they were shooting for a week at the end of March 2010 at Haddon Hall in Derbyshire. I cleared my diary immediately and said yes. They replied asking me if I was a member of Equity. I wrote back saying I was not but that I was the Chairman of the National Theatre and I hoped that was good enough. The reply apologised and said that if I was not in Equity they could not pay me as much as they would like. The email added that if my wife wished to come up for the shooting the Director would like to cast her as my wife, Mrs Dent, albeit as an 'extra', a non-speaking part. She accepted. There has been a good deal of family teasing since then over who has 'speaking' and 'non-speaking' parts in real life.

Our filming week had the most beautiful spring weather of sun, blue sky and growing warmth, to accompany it in a stunning location. We were booked in to a comfortable hotel with most of the young actors and Judi Dench, whose part played a crucial and mysterious role in the book and therefore in the film. My lines were slipped under my bedroom door each evening and early in the morning a car arrived to take me to the location, and to my trailer, with my stage name on it. When I saw it I knew I was really "in the movies." I graciously allowed my wife to have the car to take her on to where the 'extras' were gathered. Each morning the first knock on my trailer door heralded a request for what coffee I wanted. The next knock meant that make-up was ready. This mostly involved my hair, which I had been asked not to cut for two months and which was turned into ringlets all over my head. Returning to my trailer, the next knock was from my dresser. I was then driven, in morning or evening dress, to Haddon Hall itself. Rehearsals for scenes were fine. I remembered my lines and was not overawed by doing my scene with Michael Fassbender as Rochester. (Indeed we both enjoyed the fine Havana cigars with which we were provided while we waited for action.)

But when it came to the shooting itself it was a nightmare. We had one easy scene when my wife and I and other house-party guests arriving for the weekend had to walk across the courtyard to enter the house. However, in 'my' big drawing room scene, I was required to walk across the room while complaining to Rochester, who was standing by the fireplace, about the quality of the carriage he had sent to collect us. The rehearsal was fine but when it came actually to shooting the scene the trouble was that the floor was now covered in railway tracks with cameras on them and, bent, scurrying cameramen. I thought I was managing to get by but there were many shouts of "cut" and then: "Sir Hayden, you must not lift your legs like a horse when walking across the room." In between takes we took our cigars to the Green Room and read novels. I had one more garden scene before I left in which I had no lines but was told to sit still and look distinguished.

On my last day the cast and crew applauded my departure, either as a great relief to say goodbye to a bumbling amateur or as a genuine thank you for my stumbling but friendly efforts. On returning to my trailer the charming hairdresser who had fashioned my ringlets every day offered to take them out. I said she should leave them, as I wanted to show my family what I had looked like on set, and I travelled home on the trains from Derby via London stations to Salisbury; for the other passengers, of whose looks at me I was very conscious, they saw a spectacle of an elderly, and no doubt gay, actor who had failed to take off his make-up. At the end of the day my 13 lines were reduced to two with the rest on the cutting room floor: the main line I had left was simply, "Hear Hear!" Such is the fleeting fame of showbiz.

In 2019 Cary Fukunaga took over as Director of the latest Bond film, *No Time to Die*. My wife wrote to congratulate him. All he said in reply was that he had to take it on as he had promised me a cameo role in his next film in England and Bond was perfect for me. So my second on-set experience was a week in October 2019 at Pinewood Studios. Early in the morning, at about 5.30 am, a car collected me from my house at the end of the King's Road and dropped me back about 8.30 pm in the evening. Each day was a long one of intensive takes and boring waits. I was cast as a real 'baddy'; a Spectre Agent. There were twelve of us, and I was Agent No 4. Again as 'Cast', I had my own trailer with my stage name on it. Our main scene was a big party in Havana so we were all in black tie, or evening dresses for the female agents. We were there to celebrate Blofeld's birthday and the expected execution of Bond but, as it turned out, it was our deaths that occurred as the poison falling from the ceiling we thought was intended for him took us out and left him alive.

Rehearsing death, an exhausting process, took a whole day with two bodyguards dragging me off the set to die, possibly off-camera, which I didn't feel I liked. However, on death-filming day itself (after one and a half hours in make-up to produce a face covered in blood and poisoned pustules), the Director came on set and said to me, in front of everyone, "Sir Hayden (this was not clever as for three days I had carefully hidden my title) I don't want you to die like the others, writhing and screaming; I want you to die the perfect English stiff-upper-lip death. Just fall backwards staring at Bond." I did as I was told and, happily, I had a bodyguard to catch me as I fell. I had great confidence in my catcher but there is a tiny squeak of panic inside you when you fall back before you are caught.

I had one other scene which was nothing to do with death but with the party atmosphere. The Director placed me in an elegant easy chair in a room filled with men in black tie wearing animal masks and animal heads, immensely elegant women some in evening dress and others scantily clad, and some 'shorter people' as it said in the cast list. I was given two tall elegant women who were draped over me and a scantily clad 'shorter' female person who was instructed to kiss my Spectre ring. I was told to tell them jokes and we were all told to laugh and laugh and laugh; it was meant to be a really good party moment. And it was.

On set one day those who were about to die were waiting around and I noticed that Daniel Craig was standing by the stage, where the band played, on his own, looking a bit glum. I don't think other people dared to approach him but I decided that I would like to meet him and marched over. I said that my name was Hayden Phillips, that I was in the film but I was not an actor. He smiled and said that there were moments when he felt the same. We continued chatting about the filming they had done in Southern Italy including at the railway station at Sapri, which is near our family house there, until Barbara Broccoli took him away. I hoped a little of his stardust had been sprinkled on me and perhaps it was as, after my death, when he had to leap over my body to escape and the bullets (blanks but very noisy) whizzed over our heads, I was walking back to my trailer for a rest, I passed him and as I did so he said, looking at my bloodied face, "Darling, you look just as beautiful as you did this morning." This was a good epitaph on my film career. My death on-screen was greatly delayed, as far as the public were concerned, by Covid-19. But my wife and I were at the Royal Albert Hall premiere in the Autumn of 2021 and I then did interviews for the BBC and we were photographed on the red carpet. How many ex-civil servants can claim that? When the credits rolled I saw I had been given a name, Sir Sebastian De Ath, in addition to being Spectre Agent No 4.

CHAPTER 11:
Government Service in Retrospect

Why did I join? • policy advice versus management and "delivery" • an interview with a psychologist • the wartime generation of politicians • the centrality of the EU • the 2016 Referendum result in our house in Southern Italy • 1967 compared to 2004 • relations with Ministers like arranged marriages • Willie Whitelaw on Special Advisers • political appointees and civil servants briefly analysed • being in charge of what Britain does best.

A BOOK I MUCH enjoyed was Gwen Raverat's *Period Piece,* about growing up in Cambridge in the 1920s. Apart from its obvious personal link with the city of my childhood, there is a settled completeness and steadiness about the world it describes and, when I reflected on what I have written here, the main story, of my life in public service, much of the early part of that seems equally frozen in time. Indeed perhaps to a younger generation of public servants most of my story does.

I joined the Civil Service to give policy advice to Ministers and, in the words of that elegant and well known phrase, "to speak truth unto power". And that is what I was able to try to do for 37 years, from 1967 to 2004. Along the way as the years rolled by, I had also learned to become as much of a manager and leader as an analyst and writer, to be more financially literate than certainly I was at the beginning, and to know how to set realistic objectives and produce measurable results both for myself and for my staff. These 'modernising' demands, through the 1980s and 1990s were actually a very distinctive part of what made my generation different in our range of skills from our predecessors. Whatever other criticisms of Mrs Thatcher as Prime Minister may be made, her determination to sharpen up the Civil Service was a good and necessary legacy of those years. I have to say that adapting to those new demands I found quite natural. From my point of view, at the time and in retrospect, the trickier and more absorbing part of the work was always the giving of policy advice, and handling the interface between the pressures of politics and the discipline of objective independent analysis.

Whatever Ministers, Cabinet Secretaries and Permanent Secretaries might say about the need for the Civil Service to be better qualified at "service delivery" (which was true but always sounded like producing 'take-away' food), what the Ministers I worked with seemed most to value was one's ability to help them sort out the policy choices and political dilemmas they faced. (Running the Department well was a necessary condition for being an effective Permanent Secretary but the sufficient condition which added value was the advice one gave on the policy/political interface.) So because of that, right to the end of my career, this led to a rather traditional, some might say old-fashioned, relationship with the Ministers with whom I worked. For them I was not a semi-detached figure who "ran the Department" and was pre-occupied with issues of process. And, as I have already explained, I made sure that, in my last post, when the pressures for more reform and more modernisation further increased under Tony Blair (and the sheer size of my department grew and grew), I made sure I had senior colleagues who were really expert at "delivery" and at "finance", so I could concentrate on what I knew I was best at doing and what my Secretary of State/Lord Chancellor appeared most to value.

What other characteristics did my generation of Mandarins exhibit? I was, as were many of my colleagues, part of a post-war generation which had benefitted from Rab Butler's 1944 Education Act[1] and the social mobility which the creation of grammar schools had enabled, for those children who had been able to pass the 11 Plus exam. For those of us brought up successfully in that meritocratic world, taking the Civil Service exams was an entirely natural thing to do; there was nothing infra-dig about public service then, quite the opposite. And we were either told, or self-regardingly assumed, that the Civil Service exams were the crème de la crème of competitive examinations in the whole country. My cohort did them in Savile Row. I remember vividly my interview with the psychologist. It was a rainy day and while on the underground I had managed to put my umbrella through a trouser leg. I also had flu. All this trauma I explained to the courteous shrink. He simply reached into a drawer, handed me some pills and told me to go home to bed. He had no immediate remedy for the trousers. I assume he reported that I appeared normal and not deranged.

The Ministers with whom I worked in my early years had all fought in the Second World War and whatever political differences they may have had, one with another, they had a mature sense of common perspective and shared experience which was very reassuring: whether that experience was Willie Whitelaw's in the Scots Guards fighting into Germany or Roy Jenkins at Bletchley Park. That shared life, a confident quality of leadership, and also in many of them a sharp and critical intelligence, helped reinforce in my generation a sense of optimism and an expectation, which I think we already had, of our own capacity for individual and collective progress. After all, this was, in my case, the 1960s; the music was cool; our clothes were cool; drugs and free love abounded. My generation was not backward-looking, nostalgically hanging on to a lost empire, but ready for the next phase of our non-imperial leadership internationally, the best example of which, in my view, was our membership of the European Union.

To many of my generation this was our obvious new destiny in global terms – to be leaders in and of a new Europe, united, and free of the internecine warfare of the past. It had an economic core but it was more than that. The resounding victory for those who felt that way in the 1975 Referendum seemed to underpin a new sense of certainty, commitment and vision. The turn-around in the 2016 Referendum represented, in my view, a total failure on the part of my generation to articulate with conviction to at least half of our fellow citizens how we felt about the best place for Britain to be in the post-war world, and also a failure on our part to realise how alienated a majority of the electorate felt from what we (the London-based Establishment) were doing, or not doing in relation, for example, to immigration. This was something of which, as a former Head of the Immigration Department, I should have been much more aware. The simple power of a single slogan - 'taking back control' - I had failed to grasp. I had, and have, the view that in the modern world sovereignty is always shared unless you are North Korea (but even that degree of isolation is not true sovereignty, given the dependent relationship with China). I would still have preferred us to be the leaders of Europe (in the union) but that I recognise is probably a lost cause during my lifetime. On the morning when the 2016 Referendum result was declared we were on holiday in our family house in southern Italy. When we went into the kitchen to say good morning to the staff who looked after us, they burst into tears at the news. I think they thought we might sell the house and never come back.

One aspect of our departure from the EU has received little attention and that is the way in which the UK sowed the seeds of its departure through its determination to push for the enlargement of the EU which moved from nine to twenty-eight member states. Following from the political reasons for opening our arms to embrace the new democracies of 'old Europe' (Greece, Spain and Portugal) there was then the political need to welcome the return to Europe of the former soviet satellites. Britain strongly supported these developments because, inter alia, I assume it felt it was a good way of diluting the risk of a federal Europe. But in doing so we increased its bureaucratic red tape and created a greater sense of alienation from it of the British public.

In terms of relations with Ministers, throughout my Civil Service career I felt part of a shared enterprise with them, working together confidently and having good personal relations. My relations with Roy Jenkins, at the beginning of my career, as a Private Secretary, and with Derry Irvine, towards the end, as a Permanent Secretary, were, in some respects very similar. They certainly had a similar context as they were two highly intelligent liberals of the Labour persuasion. But in other respects they were sharply different. Roy was a politician to his fingertips. Derry was not and once told me how much he disliked politics (he had a crushing logicality which left little room for compromise – not usually a political skill). Roy had a real creative sense of long term strategy (much needed if you are Chancellor of the Exchequer) which Derry had to some degree as a constitutional reformer. But each became a real friend and that personal relationship worked to help produce such professional success as we secured. But this was also true of many others on the other side of the political divide; with Willie Whitelaw (especially – he was a man of enormously intelligent intuition) and Leon Brittan in the Home Office; with John Major in the Treasury and as Prime Minister; and with the great raft of Culture Ministers I got through from 1992 to 1998, especially Peter Brooke, Virginia Bottomley and Chris Smith. Peter Mandelson and Charlie Falconer concluded the litany of Ministers who became personal friends.

But the past before all that was another country. I started work in 1967 in the Home Office in a room with coal fires and a visiting tea lady who rang a bell as she arrived with her trolley. Each morning I had coffee (pretty grim stuff in those days) and a cheese roll. My Civil Service career ended with my having an office which was one of the largest and most beautiful rooms, by Pugin, in the House of Lords looking across Victoria Gardens and the Thames to Lambeth Palace – but by then we were also surrounded by computer screens. In 1967 the Civil Service felt an enclosed and comfortable world. Special advisers had not really been invented (save at No 10 under Harold Wilson) and there were few external think tanks from which Ministers could draw advice independent of the Civil Service. There was a sort of monastic sense of purity and also one of confident mission. I remember suggesting to my first Head of Division (a nice man, one T A Critchley[2]) when I was involved in research on policing that I might usefully visit a police force which was enthusiastic for one of the projects on which I was then working. "I wouldn't do that if I were you," he said, "it will prevent you from being properly detached." I sensed then that his world was not going to be mine.

Life in politics and Government has been utterly transformed from the late 1960s. Active membership of political parties has largely collapsed except for intermittent bouts of enthusiasm, usually from some rather extreme position. Cabinet Government has been gradually undermined. Rising cohorts of Special Advisers have arrived making the role of the permanent official not what it was. The statute book has got fatter and fatter every year as if more and more new laws were the right or only answer to all of our real problems. And above all, there is now the round the clock seven days a week intensive media commentary which has progressively changed the nature of politics. When I joined there was just enough time to think properly about what it might be best to do about an issue or problem. When I left that was no longer true and that was 18 years ago. And I therefore imagine that the pressure for instant and apparently authoritative comment is even more difficult now.

The classic TV programmes, *Yes Minister* and *Yes, Prime Minister,* remain brilliant caricatures of a clever manipulative mandarin and a not too clever Minister: it was compulsory viewing for senior civil servants when Mrs Thatcher was in charge in case she questioned you about some aspect of the most recent episode. Its cartoon antithesis would have been of an overbearing Minister and a supine civil servant. (I can see why that TV series has not been attempted!) But it does not have to be like that either way round and it is best for the citizen and the taxpayer if it is neither. In my experience relations between Ministers and civil servants should be like successful arranged marriages; immensely strong if each party works hard and openly at the relationship, and really wants it to work. It also helps if the parties share some real common interests in life beyond the professional routine of Government and politics: books, music, fishing, art, and cricket – especially cricket. I enjoyed all of these in different measure with many of the Ministers with whom I worked. The result can then be a professional relationship based on personal and professional, not political, rapport. I wonder whether the present generation of Permanent Secretaries would be able to write about their relationship with Ministers in the way that, happily, I can. I do hope so.

An extreme example of the culture of the distant past comes out of a conversation I once had with Willie Whitelaw while he and I were driving back from the scenes of riots in 1981 in Toxteth and Moss Side. I asked him why, unlike his Cabinet colleagues with the exception of Peter Carrington, he had no Special Adviser. "Why Hayden," he replied, "would I want one of those? I don't need some young man from Central Office telling me what political advice I need to give myself; nor, above all, do I want someone standing between me and my civil servants." That is a singular message from a world which has long gone and, I expect, will never return. But its passing should not necessarily mean that the building of successful personal relationships between politicians and civil servants has to be a sepia-tinted and forgotten piece of history; just another period piece.

Is the balance between the role and influence of the political appointee and the civil servant now a sensible one? I find it very difficult to judge after so many years away from life in Government. Had I been working in the American Federal Government every job I had for 30 of the 37 years I served would have been as a political appointee. Indeed in Brussels I was a political appointee. I have discovered a contrapuntal academic critique of the difference between the special adviser (political) and the civil servant, in which the contrast is between the political appointee as an opportunistic courtier compared to the civic (community) minded mandarin. The political appointee magnifies the difference between the political parties, while the mandarin seeks the common ground of what he/she believes is the public interest. The thesis then runs on as follows: "The mandarin is an amateur to the professional; a statist to the libertarian; and an elitist to the populist. What possibly could be worse than a society run by such people?" I would like to believe that the answer is a society without them. In my so-called 'retirement' I find that a comforting argument, albeit for some of my friends, it is a tendentious one.

Reflecting on my life in Government service I know I was immensely lucky to find myself over my last twelve years in charge of two Departments which dealt with and oversaw parts of our national life in which the United Kingdom had a pre-eminent international reputation; first the world of culture - the performing arts, our heritage, in museums and galleries and elsewhere, and the quality of our broadcasting; and then, second, our legal and judicial system which was and remains of the most outstanding quality, and the leadership of which is acknowledged globally in all common law countries. There was a real sense of buoyancy in my day to day professional life as I knew I was part of a national and international success story. Generally there was no defensiveness required. In principle we were always on the front foot. Of course some things went wrong; some of our decisions were criticised as sometimes were our lack of decisions. But to be in charge of two parts of Government from which the world was always willing to hear and to listen to what we had to say, was both inspirational and a great comfort in times of difficulty.

Would I advise a 20 year old contemplating a career choice to apply to be a fast-stream civil servant? I have thought a lot about this as I am sure my eldest grand-children's contemporary expectation and motivation is very different from mine all those years ago. And, of course, they do not think, as my generation tended to do, of a career in one hierarchical or professional context but of gaining knowledge and experience that will carry them along a more varied route from one entity or role to another. But my answer to my own question is an unequivocal 'yes'; public service remains a vital calling whether you choose to pursue it through the political or the non-political route. The continuing buoyancy in the number of applications to join the fast stream of the Civil Service is, I hope, an enduring testimony to the value which my grand-children's generation place on public service.

CHAPTER 12:
A Sense of Place

Glebe House on the Kennet • A "Wind in the Willows" place • fishing, hunting and swimming • St John the Baptist, Mildenhall, a Georgian gem • Homington Farm • Lord Radnor and Ted Heath at Christmas • Salisbury Cathedral in 1963 • the West Front • the Fabric Advisory Committee • a great new stained glass window? • a ledger stone for a Prime Minister • Bill Pye's font • dressing up as a Lay Canon (in the cathedral) and as a GCB (in Westminster Abbey) • the drama of a Bishop's farewell with a scallop shell • an intervention by Vikram Seth • Under Milk Wood in Farley Church • Desmond Tutu dances in The Close • vaccinations in the Cathedral • my wife as High Sheriff • our farming life • the naming of Longhorn calves • Wiltshire horn sheep • the River Ebble • fish, birds, other animals and flowers.

MY PROFESSIONAL LIFE had been based in London although we had always been able to go to Wiltshire at weekends and during the school holidays. After three years of renting, we managed to buy a most delightful house in the village of Mildenhall (pronounced Mynal) just outside Marlborough. The house, the Glebe House, across from the church, was owned by Barbara Brooke[1], whose husband Henry[2] had died the year before. My wife and I went to visit it with our baby daughter and when I explained to her I was then running the Immigration Department of the Home Office she and I were engaged in serious reminiscences about Home Office issues. The sale of the house was a sealed bids auction. Our bid was chosen but I know it was not the highest. Barbara Brooke liked the fact that we had a serious connection and she wanted the house to be one in which a new growing family lived. She moved up the lane to Roman's Halt.

It was a "Wind in The Willows" place for my children. The garden ran down to the River Kennet. Lady Brooke had left us a canoe and a rowing boat and oars and life jackets. Another daughter arrived and then a son and we all lived in the garden and on the river for year after year in sunshine or in rain. My wife bought me a fishing rod of great quality and I went down to the river and caught my first brown trout, weighing 4lbs 8oz. I was hooked. A local friend, Andrew Caldecott, taught me how properly to fish. Tragically he drowned while fishing on the Spey. His widow asked the Littlecote fishing syndicate of which he was a member if I could replace him without having to go on the waiting list. This was, she said, what he would have wanted. It was agreed.

From May to September I went fishing, accompanied by our black Labrador, Sweep. This most intelligent animal could spot a rise before I could. She would then lie down pointing her nose towards the fish. From October to March, however, was when my wife took to the hunting field and my role was to drive the horsebox and look after the children. I don't think they minded as every Saturday we went to Ducks Toy Shop in Marlborough High Street to spend their pocket money. Sadly that old-fashioned and much loved emporium is no more. Our final weekend ritual was swimming on a Sunday at the municipal pool from noon to one o'clock. Because of the differing ages of the children I think I spent something like 10 years in the shallow end teaching one of them how to swim.

Our parish church, across the lane from our house, had an impressive late Georgian interior. High box pews with children's benches in them meant that, provided the children were not heard, they could play throughout the sermon. There were twin pulpits (labelled 'Peace' and 'Grace') and over the chancel arch the royal arms of George III. It is one of the grandest village churches in England. On one occasion as I was crossing the lane to go to the morning service I met my neighbour, Miss Pat Courtman, hurrying back to her cottage. I asked her what the problem was and she told me that a woman priest was going to take the service and she could not possibly attend. Pat was the daughter of the former Rector who had been in post for so many years that it was said that when he retired the congregation had been reduced to one, his daughter. Glebe House, Mildenhall, was and is a magical place.

But in 1997 our life took on a rather different dimension when my wife decided to buy a farm about three miles south-west of Salisbury. This came about because she had, with her two Grenfell half-sisters, sold their family home, Wilbury Park in Wiltshire, Grade 1 listed, and the first neo-Palladian house in England, designed by William Benson in 1710. The farm and house she then bought in the hamlet of Homington[3] was built in 1763 and had been cleverly extended by our predecessor owners, Tertius and Clare Murray-Threipland, to take in a range of 19th century barns so the house ran round three sides of a large courtyard. The farm-land was, indeed is, a wonderful mixture of chalk down-land and a river and water meadows.

In our first week we were warmly welcomed by one of our neighbours, the late Earl Radnor[4]. He rang and asked us to dinner, reminding us that they changed (i.e. into black tie) every night. There was a personal history here as my wife used to be taken by her grand-mother to the Radnor seat at Longford Castle for tea. So began a most enjoyable relationship of a delightful old fashioned and courteous sort. Every Christmas Eve, for example, Lord Radnor gave a reception for guests, and for staff on the estate. There was an enormous Christmas tree with real candles which men, positioned on the first floor balcony above with long candle-snuffers, prevented the candles from setting the Castle on fire. There were carols accompanied by the Salisbury Salvation Army band, whose sharps and flats did not always mingle harmoniously. Lord Radnor said he particularly welcomed my arrival on the Christmas Eve scene as my future task on his behalf was to talk to Ted Heath, something which other guests, so he said, had proved not to be very good at doing. We could not have asked for a warmer welcome. On one occasion we had guests staying with us in mid-week and I thought we would take them to supper at a local pub with very good food, the Radnor Arms in Nunton. I telephoned and asked for a table for six at 8 pm. A familiar voice replied saying that it would be lovely to see us and our friends but she thought we should tell our guests that they should be in black tie. I had rung the Castle and Lady Radnor had dealt with me beautifully; a good joke against me ever after.

From the top of our farm, over two hills, you can see the spire of Salisbury Cathedral. The first time I had visited Salisbury Cathedral was in 1963 when I was 20. There was then a new Bishop for the diocese, Joe Fison[5], who had been Vicar at Great St Mary's (the University Church) in Cambridge. It so happened that I went into that church on the day his new appointment (of which I knew nothing) had been announced and asked to see him. I was told he was in the organ loft and when I asked why I was told that I would find out when I went there. I climbed up and there he was sitting on the floor with his head in his hands. I asked him what the problem was and he explained he was to be made a Bishop and he wasn't sure he could cope with that. I think I understood his apprehension as he was a gentle pastoral academic theologian not a managerial Prince of the Church.

However, he succumbed to the honour of the appointment, and, at his invitation, in the summer of 1963 (at the end of my first year at Cambridge) I climbed onto my beautiful white Vespa scooter and drove to the Bishop's house, the South Canonry, in Salisbury Cathedral Close. After some evening discussion of St John's Gospel (I thought I was a world expert on the other, three, synoptic gospels because of my O Level scripture pass, but I needed tutoring on John) and then supper, he said we would spend the next two days travelling round the Diocese. In a rather ancient but elegant Bentley we were driven through the lanes of Wiltshire and Dorset making surprise visits to the clergy in various towns and villages. This safari of visitation rather tickled his sense of fun. What the surprised clerics thought I can only guess at. Our visit to Sherborne Abbey most sticks in my mind. It has, in my view, the finest fan-vaulted ceiling in Western Christendom. We re-visit it from time to time.

Salisbury Cathedral is remarkable. It is set in the largest Close in the country beside the gently flowing river Avon. The highest spire in the realm rises above the body of the Cathedral and it has a West Front of confused and puzzling beauty. Sir Nikolaus Pevsner passed a rather harsh judgement on it: "The façade of Salisbury Cathedral is a headache. There is so much in it that is perversely unbeautiful. There are also far too many motifs, and they are distributed without a comprehensible system." However, in the gentle light of a summer evening, I think it can be forgiven its trespasses on Pevsner's taste.

I engaged in the life of the Cathedral not just as a member of the congregation but also through my membership of the Cathedral Council (a legally required "talking shop" but now to be abolished) and then through becoming Chairman of the Fabric Advisory Committee (FAC), which has statutory duties to advise on, or decide, important issues about the building and all its treasures. For example, the Committee was much involved when our original copy of Magna Carta had to travel to the House of Lords to be exhibited with the other three originals, from the British Library and Lincoln Cathedral respectively.

The most difficult issue I faced as Chairman (at the time of writing) was whether or not to support a proposal for a major new stained glass window in the North Transept. The Dean and Chapter had welcomed a donor's commission to Brian Clarke[6] to create the design. It embraced 44 windows, so it was massive. The supporters of the plan felt that the Cathedral was too cool and lacked vibrancy and colour, as they argued it would originally have had in medieval times, and that it should now be re-enlivened and warmed up. The critics felt that such a major intervention would interrupt the clear vision of the West to East axis and the sense of space and grand distance which had, in their view, become over time, the essence of the Cathedral's ethos, impact and liturgy (in processional terms). The majority of my Committee were against the proposal, taking the view that the existing clear glass in the North Transept's western elevation enabled us to see, as one Committee member, Ptolemy Dean[7], put it "God's own stained glass," of blue sky and white scudding clouds.

This conflict required me to walk a tricky diplomatic tightrope between the artist, who became a friend in the process, the commissioning Chapter, and the sceptics on my Committee to whom I had to report, represent and try to lead. The Cathedral Fabric Commission for England (CFCE), when consulted at a meeting I had to attend, asked questions about the theological and liturgical justification for any change; to which I do not think we had persuasive answers. This saga began under one Dean, June Osborne[8], and ended under another, Nick Papadopoulos[9]. In the end the critics of the proposed window won the argument and it was decided not to go ahead. The then Bishop, Nicholas Holtam[10] and I went to see Brian Clarke to explain the basis of the decision. Before we could say a word he said, with a smile, when I heard you were coming together to see me I knew the answer was "no."

Early in my term of office we dealt with a most singular and peculiar issue. On the death of Sir Edward Heath, who had lived in a most charming 18th century house in the Close, Arundells, it was decided to honour him with a ledger stone[11] in the floor of the Nave. My committee approved a wording which, after referring to his name and the fact he had been Prime Minister added the words "Statesman, Musician, Sailor." As this was a material change to the fabric we had to submit an application for the agreement of the CFCE in London. After an appropriate – i.e. long - pause for thought they told us that they were happy with word "Sailor" which was factual but that "Statesman" was a questionable subjective value judgement and, while he loved music and performed occasionally, to say he was a "Musician" was to give him a professional status which could be challenged. We felt we could not be left with a stone that described a former Prime Minister as simply a 'sailor'. And so with the help of Robert Armstrong (Ted's former Private Secretary, close friend and executor of his estate) and the common sense of Frank Field[12] (the then Chairman of the CFCE) the original inscription was finally endorsed.

We may have decided against a new stained glass window but during my time in charge of the FAC we managed to achieve a stunning 21st century addition to the Cathedral in the shape of William Pye's[13] water sculpture font. And there was also the great achievement of the completion of the Major Repair Programme after thirty years of skilled toil by the masons of the Cathedral workshop. The last part of this work – the East end – was the hardest of all as it was the earliest part of the building to be built and therefore more subject to decay than much of the rest. But it will now be adorned by the addition of the stone that commemorates the 800th anniversary of the re-founding of the Cathedral at New Sarum in 1220. This was consecrated at a socially distanced ceremony on 7 December 2020 in the presence of The Prince of Wales and the Duchess of Cornwall. High up on the side of the South Transept there is another new stone which bears my initials and those of my wife: HP and LP. This is the result of our taking part in 'Sponsor a Stone.' I hope we will be sitting up there for some hundreds of years.

The Fabric Advisory Committee, is full of architectural and heritage expertise and is great fun. It has two external clerical members whose task, with mine, is to remind us all what the building is for; namely worship. We need constantly to have that and its supporting liturgy in mind.

As a thank you for my work in support of the Cathedral I was appointed a Lay Canon. This added to my wardrobe of dressing-up clothes with a dark green cloak rather like that of a Knight Templar with the Cathedral badge embossed upon it. The real knightly robes I have, in the Order of the Bath[14] are actually salmon pink or rose and covered in white ribbons. I was installed i.e. put into my stall, in the Henry VII Chapel in Westminster Abbey in a simple ceremony shared with General Sir Mike Jackson[15], a Wiltshire friend. My banner of three golden Longhorn bulls' heads on the blue ground of a river spanned by the bridge over the Cam at Clare is raised above my stall. The Order of the Bath, has a grand service in Westminster Abbey every four years, but both there and in Salisbury, the trick to learn, so I have discovered, is that 'processing' is an art-form and that if you don't quite know what you are doing on any particular occasion then always do what you think you should do slowly.

This was brought home to me forcibly at the Service of Evensong to mark the departure of David Stancliffe as Bishop of Salisbury. In a packed Cathedral, five minutes before the service began, the Canon Precentor, Jeremy Davies[16], told me that he would like me to make the presentation to the departing Bishop of a scallop shell; a traditional symbol wishing good fortune to someone going on a journey. He added that he was sorry there was no time for a rehearsal but when the moment came he would collect me from my stall in the Quire and explain the process as we processed. He came. We gave each other the accustomed mutual bow and walked together towards the temporary High Altar under the Spire Crossing. He said I should go down the steps to the left and he would go to the right and collect the presentation object and bring it to me. So far so good. I stood and waited and as a Hymn was coming to a close he walked to me carrying a cushion on which the scallop shell rested. My final whispered instruction was to walk up the steps and make the presentation. I did so, only to be told by the Bishop that he did not need the cushion but only the shell. All this was done sotto voce while I struggled to extract the shell and its anchorage from the cushion. This achieved, I descended the steps and suddenly realised I was marooned with an empty cushion and had run out of instructions. The Bishop's procession was clearly about to leave for the real High Altar so I moved up to join it muttering to the Bishop's Verger that I promised I would peel off when I reached my stall. I processed with due solemnity holding my empty cushion.

My role as a Canon was delightfully mocked on one occasion by my neighbour and friend Vikram Seth, who bought the charming house in Bemerton which had been owned by the priest and poet George Herbert. The church in our village, Homington, needed to raise money and I agreed to give a talk there for which people had to pay to attend. There was a good turnout fortunately and before I began I was introduced at too great length, by a kindly neighbour who laid my whole career before the audience. When the speaker, going on and on, referred to the fact that I was a Canon, Vikram shouted "loose cannon" which helped me start my talk in an atmosphere of fun and laughter. General Sir Mike Jackson gave the next talk (at my request) and he was not treated with such contumely.

My friend Jeremy Davies, as a choreographer, always tended to leave his instructions to his actors to the last minute. He persuaded me and a number of other local Salisbury folk who were Welsh or had some Welsh blood to perform a dramatic reading (which meant we could have the text with us on stage) of *Under Milk Wood,* in the beautiful Wren church in the village of Farley, east of Salisbury. I had agreed to be the Narrator – the "Richard Burton" part – which fills the first few pages. I had learnt all the early lines, and thank God I had, as on the night of the performance my friend the Director changed the plan. He said he wanted me to walk in total darkness through the Nave while delivering all the opening lines and when I came to the Chancel steps the lights would come on. I was given a small torch and I set off needing the torch not to read the text as I walked but simply to see where I was going. I survived, avoided walking into the font, and it worked. After the lights came on I climbed up into the pulpit, wearing Simon Russell Beale's velvet smoking cloak, to deliver the rest of my lines in the rest of the play. All my colleague performers were wonderful and there was a full audience of paying customers, from which the church benefitted. At the end of the show as we were taking our 'non-curtain call' someone walked up the nave towards me with a great bouquet of flowers. I tried to give it to one of the female cast members but the carrier explained it was for me; from my children.

On Sunday 8 June 2008 Archbishop Desmond Tutu[17] preached

at the Eucharist at which he was made a Canon of the Cathedral. In his sermon he said "I have a magic wand which I now wave to turn you restrained English people into South Africans who know how to applaud themselves". The congregation released from its natural bondage erupted in applause. But on the evening before he had starred in a different and even more spontaneous performance. It was the last night of the Salisbury International Arts Festival, of which my wife was the Chairman. He was our guest at the closing open-air concert in the Cathedral Close because we had engaged a visiting South African school choir from a township near Cape Town; but we had not let on to them that the Archbishop was coming. When the choir finished their performance and came down the steps from the stage they were greeted by him, each one getting a big hug amidst immense happiness and laughter. A band then struck up with dance music and Desmond Tutu turned to us and said we had too much British reserve and we should dance; so my wife and I and a friend, Maureen, who was from South Africa, joined in. Suddenly the rest of the audience saw who was leading the dance and in a few minutes there were about three hundred people on their feet and moving cheerfully. It was a living example of the line in the hymn – "I'll lead you all in the dance said he". When it was about 8.15 in the evening we asked him if, in addition to a glass of wine, he would like to share our supper. He declined, adding that he was to have supper with the Dean. I asked when that was and he said he was meant to be there by 7.30. My wife and I walked him over to the Deanery with some speed.

On another celebratory occasion after a Service we were having drinks in the Dean's garden on a beautiful summer evening. I was sitting next to Lord Carrington when Sir David Willcocks[18], a former organist and choirmaster at Salisbury, came towards us. I was about to ask Peter Carrington whether he knew David when the latter stopped before him, saluted and said "Major Carrington, Captain Willcocks reporting". The great musician and the distinguished statesman had not seen each other since they were on the beach on D-Day. They settled down to reminisce and my wife and I slipped quietly away.

The finale on the story of the Cathedral in my life has to be its transformation into a vaccination centre in 2021. I was asked to approve this 'change of use' in my Fabric Committee capacity but it was a brilliant decision by the Dean and Chapter. Around 36,000 people had their jabs in the South Transept while listening to an organ recital on the recently restored Father Willis organ. An American friend emailed to give us the story which took up the front page of the *New York Times*. For many of the most elderly who came to be vaccinated it was their first outing for a long time and many had never been into the building before. They were blown away by its beauty. My wife and I were jabbed there to the sound of music. The whole thing was the best modern shop window to show how the Church is there for hope and healing. You do not have to have faith to be awakened by a stunning atmosphere and a reality of great grand beauty. But it may come to you because of that experience.

Our life in Wiltshire had and still has many dimensions. While London remains our cultural centre we are fortunate to enjoy two art galleries – Roche Court, a sculpture park, presided over imaginatively and graciously by Madeleine Bessborough, and Messums, at the great Tithe Barn at Tisbury. And then we have the Grange Festival Opera, a feast of great music in June and July which is run elegantly and informedly by Michael Chance; and, in no way least, the Chalke Valley History Festival, with its succulent menu of brilliant speakers and outdoor events for young and, in my case, old. Jane Pleydell-Bouverie runs it with efficient panache – even when it rains day after day producing a sea of mud or there is a train strike (as happened in 2022).

My wife ran our farm, advised by a local farmer and friend, Will Dickson; I was allowed to drive a tractor and top (i.e. cut) the grass on the verges and tracks while listening to music or cricket commentary. I also did some harrowing in the spring. She was High Sheriff of Wiltshire for a year and I was a Deputy Lieutenant for a decade. During her year in office, 2011/12, we were able to do some events together, but when merely present as a consort I dutifully walked two paces behind. On those occasions she was wearing the dressing-up clothes and I was not. But I had been given this beautiful Victorian smoking cloak which I regretted was getting too few outings. I mentioned this to Nick Hytner who sent me an email saying he had found the following quotation from one of Shakespeare's less well known history plays which set a good precedent for my wearing the cloak when walking behind my wife: "And, Lo, the High Sheriff comes, He of Wiltshire. And there within his train, his spouse, sporting her velvet cloak."

During the infliction of foot and mouth disease in 2001 we had to wear a very different uniform, of personal protection, like a space outfit just as in the Covid-19 pandemic, and walk or drive through a disinfectant trough when going into or out of the farmyard. Public rights of way had to be shut down. I write this when that is exactly 21 years ago and the threat to rural life and all the animals with whom we lived and loved were then in danger as people were by Covid-19. Our livestock survived. But we had one friend in Somerset whose great pride was his Aberdeen Angus herd which he had built up over very many years. The whole herd had to be slaughtered. He stopped farming his estate directly, and simply rented out his land. The General Election was delayed. More than six million pigs, cattle and sheep were slaughtered on more than 10,000 farms.

Our farm's profits - it was a commercial enterprise not a hobby - came, when profits could be made, from about 500 acres of combinable crops, normally wheat, barley and oilseed rape, and sometimes peas. The whole arable operation was contracted out to a knowledgeable local farmer called Marcus Light. In the early days when the time for harvesting came, the grain was tipped into the receiving pit in the farmyard, went through the drier if needed and was sucked through a series of augers on to the floor of the main barn. But year on year the combine harvesters got bigger and bigger and the work of reaping was done faster and faster so we had to dump the grain on the floor overnight and buy drying and storage facilities from an external company. (The receiving pit hadn't done badly: 1948-2005).

The terrain which we had bought with the farm, down-land, pasture and water meadows enabled us to have an old-fashioned mixed farm, with both arable crops and livestock. And we ran it in an environmentally sensitive way; even before there were grants to incentivise us to do so. In our early days the fields were ploughed and I always wondered how the seagulls living on the Dorset coast knew when we were ploughing as I watched them following the plough in their hundreds. This now rarely occurs as we know that direct tilling is better for the soil. There is nothing, to my mind, to trump the beauty of a field of barley turning from pale green to gold and moving, like the waves of the sea, in a gentle breeze.

But farming is not always an idyll. If you have livestock, as we did, cattle, pigs and sheep, there is no day off. And at some times of year it is really hard-pounding. In winter it is no fun in the early morning breaking the ice in the troughs so the animals can drink or using a blow torch to melt the ice in the pipes. Nor is there much fun in plodding through the mud to make sure the cattle can get to the hay or silage they need. You also have to be very nimble when giving the young cattle their food. Ours were fast and had horns. Pigs are a different experience. When you appear in the pen with their food there is screaming and rushing and you are at risk of being bowled over in the stampede. But peace and calm rapidly arrive.

Let me develop this part of the story. When we bought the farm we also bought from our predecessors a small herd of Longhorn cattle, fierce-looking but docile, and producing the most delicious meat, and a bull called Rousham Monty. (When we began our farming life the English Longhorn was a rare-breed and at risk; when we ended it was one of the most successful and well established native breeds.) Gradually we grew the herd, either hiring or buying new bulls as each one ran out of time so as not to be allowed to run with his own offspring. Every Spring, it was a delight when calving began and these small slightly tottering children played in the evening light. My main task, a sedentary academic one, was the naming of the calves and as they were all to be called after characters from opera I turned each year to *Kobbé's Complete Opera Book* and trawled through as many operas as I needed to in order to find enough male and female names.

Some initial letters were easier than others; as a result some calves, usually steers, ended up being called such names as *Homington Idiot* or *Homington Innkeeper,* both characters from opera, of course. But there were many more delightful traditional names such as Fiordiligi, Manon, Tosca, Violetta and Valkyrie. When we decided to come out of farming in 2021 and sold most of the grazing land, the initial letter for naming the new-born calves was V and I could not resist breaking from tradition and naming two steers *Virus* and *Vaccine* respectively. Sadly after 24 years we had to sell the herd which we much miss as it had been an integral part of our life for such a long time; but all of the herd went to three good homes. We had a wonderful cattle man called David Thick. David could handle cattle in a way that made them calm and if not he could leap over a five bar gate in his early eighties.

There had always been sheep on the farm but Mark Eyres, who looked after the livestock, introduced a new line of rare-breed Wiltshire Horn sheep. They have the great advantage of shearing themselves i.e. their coats fall off; so there were many fences across the farm with a good covering of white wool. The adult rams have immensely impressive horns. On the announcement of Nick Holtam's appointment as the Bishop of Salisbury we were able to offer him and the Dean a farming photo opportunity of each holding a large ram by a horn on each side. The photo made the caption competition in the *Church Times*.

Some of the sheep have remained, for part of the year, on the land we have retained by the River Ebble[19], which is the smallest of the chalk streams which flow into the River Avon. Although a small river, it remains a good home for wild brown trout and grayling (fishing is tricky but rewarding); kingfishers flash by and otters have returned. If, when walking along the river bank you close your eyes and shut out the electricity wires, which power the intensive care unit in Salisbury District Hospital, you still have an 18th century landscape which Constable would have recognised and indeed which he painted. On the down-land above, wild flowers abound and my wife returned one arable field to chalk down-land grass with a wild flower mix. Each summer it is a sea of large white daisies and below them many other species including orchids, the common purple orchid and the charming looking bee orchid. There is an abundance of roe-deer and hares; fieldfares in the winter; egrets in the water meadows and skylarks on the downs in the summer; and swallows and house-martins nesting in the stables. It is a small paradise for us and our children and grandchildren. It is our present place on earth; for which we are the temporary and grateful stewards. At Harvest Festival in the village church, when we are all singing "We plough the fields and scatter the good seed on the land," I can look out of the window on to one of our fields, Church Hill, and say: "Thank you".

CHAPTER 13:
Boy on a Bicycle – A Cambridge Childhood

Choosing a name • the fate of HMS Puckeridge • my maternal grandparents • watching Luton Town at Kenilworth Road • my father's family (a different story) • we move to Cambridge • I have scarlet fever and meet Nurse Darling • my parents • Sedley Taylor Primary School (music and maypoles) • Romsey County Junior School • stuttering then singing • my chorister's world • a report on my singing • the public library and the radio were vital • Cambridgeshire High School • cricket at Fenners • being caned and Pink Floyd • a Latin Reading Prize • playing Crocker Harris in The Browning Version.

IWAS BORN ON 9 February 1943 in a nursing home in Luton. The week before, the Soviet Union had retaken Stalingrad after 462 days of fighting. My father was in the navy on convoy duty off the coast of Africa in a destroyer called HMS Puckeridge. A few days before I was born, so my mother told me, my father's mother came to see her to say she was convinced my father would be killed and so the baby (it would certainly be a boy) should be called Gerald, as my father was. My mother called Dorothy Florence but always known as 'Babs' – managed to get hold of a book of names, with their alleged meanings, and scoured it for something more mellifluous and attractive. She lighted on Hayden, which meant 'lover of fields and woods'. Happily my father returned from the war alive, and early, because of injury. I was baptised Gerald Hayden but Gerald was never used as my name. My first initial G hung about for years but was gradually abolished in practice and even removed from my passport. Only three institutions still know me as Gerald H Phillips – Her Majesty's Revenue and Customs, the NHS and the DVLA. I have never been able to face the bureaucratic challenge of trying to persuade them to change my name.

My father was invalided out of the navy having received a serious arm injury. His ship put into Freetown, in the then Gold Coast, now Sierra Leone, and he went into hospital there. The ship went back on duty escorting a convoy without him, was torpedoed off Gibraltar and was sunk with all hands. He came home when I was about six months old and the three of us lived with my maternal grandparents for about a year in a village called Leagrave, which has now been swallowed up by an expanding Luton.

As I grew up and got to know my grandparents it is no exaggeration to say that I adored them. He was called Alfred Joyner and she was called Kate Biggs. When they met he was a baker delivering bread and cakes to the great house at which she was in service. He was a clever man and eventually became an accountant. My grandmother was a most wonderful cook and always smelt delicious, of cinnamon, oranges and other good things. In later years if my mother was ill she would come to stay and look after us which was always a great treat. Sadly she died when I was 14. Over many preceding years I had stayed many times with my grandparents. She loved theatre and opera, a gene which I inherited from her. My grandfather, however, was more into gardening and football. He grew prize chrysanthemums. They needed a lot of watering and he let me use his large (enormous to me aged 7) brass syringe to water them. I would suck the water out of the water-butt which was taller than I was then and I had to stand on a stool to do it. When I plunged in the handle of the syringe I could create the most wonderful high arc of water over the garden in the evening sun.

As to football, during the season my father and I would go with my grandfather to all of Luton Town's home games. It was, of course, all standing in those days, and boys like me were passed down hand by hand over men's shoulders to the front, right by the pitch. Luton were then in the First Division (now the Premier League), Syd Owen was our captain and centre half and, under his leadership Luton went to the Cup Final. From my perch right beside the pitch I saw a host of great players of that age – Stanley Matthews, Tom Finney, Nat Lofthouse, Stan Mortenson and many others – right close up. After the match my grandmother produced an enormous and delicious early supper and then my father drove us back to Cambridge. This was a singular ritual in the football season. But I inherited neither the gardening nor the football genes.

My father's family had a less happy history. He was the youngest of five children, three of whom, all girls, died in infancy from diphtheria. My Father's brother, Cyril, was very much older. My paternal grandmother, born Daisy Sutton, was a very handsome woman and had a certain style about her even in later life when I knew her. But by then she was both rather miserable and a bit crabby. However, perhaps that was hardly surprising as her husband had suddenly disappeared when my father was a child. We never referred to my paternal grandfather or why he had run off. But she had to fend for herself and her two boys alone and she bought and ran a small grocery shop. My much older cousin, Peter, alleged that his father, Cyril, had spotted his father from the top of a bus in St James's Street. But I am not sure that buses were then allowed to pass Brooks's and Whites! My one regret is that I did not try to find out what had happened to my paternal grandfather.

In 1944 my parents moved to Cambridge where my father had been offered a job. I was a year old. We started in a rented flat in a house off the Cherry Hinton Road owned by Mrs Mowl, who seemed quite old to me when I was young, but lived for very many years and used to enjoy my visits for tea with her after school when I was older. Her house had a large garden and an air-raid shelter. At the age of three both the garden and the shelter were very exciting (and I had a Mickey Mouse gas-mask to add to the sense of brave adventure). We then moved into a rented house of our own in a neighbouring road, semi-detached with a small garden at the front and a large one at the back. After a couple of years my parents bought the house. Although I could have been no more than five or six I can clearly remember some anxious discussions between them about whether this big decision was affordable. I lived in that house in Lichfield Road until I went to university.

My most traumatic recollected experience as a child was the impact of contracting scarlet fever aged six. I remember the ambulance arriving and taking me off to the Mill Road isolation hospital. There I was for six weeks. My parents visited and could see me through a window, but I was not allowed see them or touch them. My immediate support was Nurse Darling with whom I fell in love. She used to inject me in the bottom on a daily basis. When I eventually came home my parents had produced a mass of presents for my 7th birthday but I was not at all interested in them. My parents had invested a lot of money and love in order to celebrate my return and I now know I was then being a rather tricky child to handle. But that immediate reaction did not last for too long. Shopping in the town a few weeks later I squeezed my mother's hand as I said "Hello" to a very large lady passing by beside us. It was Nurse Darling and I blushed a deep red so much had I loved her; albeit briefly.

I spoke at the funerals of both my parents, who died within a relatively short time of each other. On each of those occasions I was happy to recall my memories of my Cambridge childhood with them: the sun was always shining; we were always cycling, my sister on the back of my father's bike; we rode down to the river either at Newnham or Grantchester, with cucumber sandwiches and orange squash: idyllic memories of a very happy childhood. Sometimes we took a motorboat as far as Ely, visiting the Cathedral and having a rather grand tea.

My father was kind, modest and quiet; he was not ambitious and seemed happy with his lot. My mother was different: busy, energetic, clever, curious and very keen on her children's education. Before and during the war she had worked; first as a hat-maker (unsurprising in Luton), then putting engines into fighter aircraft, even while she was pregnant with me. When I was growing up, however, she was a typical 1950s housewife and mother, but she took an untypical interest in news and current affairs and we greatly enjoyed arguing our different points of view on the issues of the day. She decided to defend the Government over Suez; I did not. That was a rich confrontation. My father used to look at us with a sort of bemused tolerance and affection. Neither of my parents were at school beyond the age of 13. My mother was offered the chance of going further but her parents decided they could not afford it. Had she been able to do so, and had School Certificates in 'arguing' existed, she would have taken those exams and passed with flying colours.

I started my formal education when I was five, at Sedley Taylor Primary School. My mother took me to school in the morning, collected me and took me home for lunch, returned me afterwards and collected me at the end of the day. I was happy there. I remember conducting the school band – a no doubt ghastly cacophony of triangles, cymbals, drums and tambourines - and dancing round a maypole (I have photos to prove both of these statements). Two years later I moved on to Romsey County Junior School to which I cycled at the start of the day, cycled home for lunch and back again for afternoon classes, and then cycled back when school was over. In my first year there I developed quite a severe stutter. (Only when writing this memoir have I thought about how this might have occurred and have decided that the trauma of six weeks isolation in hospital produced a delayed nervous lack of confidence, of which the stutter was the outward and hearable sign.) However, we had an excellent GP called Dr Silberstein who first arranged for me to go one afternoon a week to Addenbrooke's Hospital for occupational therapy to help tackle the stutter. This did not reduce it at all, but it produced a number of useful things for the home like wastepaper baskets and straw bags. The nurses said that I was very helpful with the other patients. His next pre-scription was much more successful. As I could sing he first tried to get me into King's College Chapel Choir but there was either no room or we missed the application date. However, he found out that next door, at Clare College, they took in boy choristers from the town, and I audi-tioned successfully.

My next six years of singing not only gradually controlled the stuttering but were immensely rewarding in themselves and gave me a deep and enduring love of high quality church music. We sang Evensong on Tuesdays and Fridays and the Eucharist on Sunday mornings. (Roger Norrington[1] was then a Choral Scholar). The settings for the Responses and Psalms, the hymns and the anthems for each of the services changed constantly so I gradually learnt a vast repertoire, which remains a cher-ished part of my life. During my time as a chorister I was sent to the Roy-al School of Church Music at Addington Palace in Surrey for a week's course – a sort of reward for singing well. Not long ago my wife found a report on my performance there in a box in a barn at our farm with some other historic papers. I had last read that report in 1956. The rediscovered report is in sections such as – "Voice - Well produced, a good round tone; Breathing - sometimes lacks control; Enunciation - Very careful and intelligent; and finally, the extract I enjoy the most – "Chanting - Excellent"– not only good himself but an able leader." I was 13.

After school and homework, I would cycle into town, sing, and cycle back. When I was not at school (which included after-school sport, which I enjoyed and at which I was proficient rather than brilliant) or singing, my other principal preoccupations were reading and listening to the radio. The most important building in my life other than home, school and Clare College Chapel was the nearby Rock Road Public Library. I got through two to three library books a week and when I was frustrated by the limits of the Junior Collection (I must have read every Biggles novel twice), I made my parents sign up to the Library and dragged them with me so I could borrow from the adult department. My parents gave me *The Children's Newspaper* every week and tolerated one comic, the *Eagle*. The radio, or 'wireless' as it was called in the 1950s, was a crucial part of life. As I went home for lunch I then listened to *Workers' Playtime* and I remember listening to the first edition of *The Archers* in 1951. My parents refused to buy a TV until both I and my sister had left school so as to prevent anything getting in the way of our homework.

The 11 Plus came and I passed into the Cambridgeshire High School for Boys. Looking back, I know it was a remarkably good school, full of highly qualified and highly committed teachers. I also now know, having become later in life the Chairman of Marlborough College, that it modelled its day-today life on that of a public school. We had Houses and a very full extra-curricular programme. There I discovered, over time, that if I applied myself I was intelligent enough to do quite well, especially at exams. I usually came first in History and English but a friend, Richard Norman[2] did better in most other subjects. (He made his career as an academic and became Professor of Moral Philosophy at the University of Kent). During the late spring and early summer he and I would cycle to Fenners after school to watch the cricket. In those days there were first class county matches at the ground and the touring teams also came to play the University. I watched Lock[3] and Laker[4] bowl for Surrey in tandem and was there when Ray Lindwall[5] made an unexpected century in the match against Australia. Hero worship in sunshine and collecting autographs is a good way to pass the time when you are 13 years old; better than train-spotting (although I did some of that at Cambridge railway station).

Normally I was a well-behaved boy but when I was 14 and in the Remove, I had occasional outbursts of minor protest, managing to rack up three hours of detention at one point. That amount of stored punishment meant the detention took place on a Saturday morning. It was a bright sunny day and after about 40 minutes I felt I couldn't take any more of the destruction of my free time so I raised my hand: "I need to go to the loo, Sir." "All right, Phillips, but don't be long." When I reached the lavatory I realized that with a bit of a squeeze I could get out of the small window. Out I went, grabbed my bicycle and rode away home.

Corporal punishment was normal in those days and mid-morning on the following Monday I was summoned to the Headmaster's study. He did not say "This is going to hurt me more than it hurts you", a Victorian paternalistic myth, but he did say, "I did not expect this of you, Phillips, and I am going to have to beat you." I bent over his desk; he selected a thin and flexible cane and, six strokes later, said I could leave. The pain was agonising; and when I got back to my class I asked if I could stand for the rest of the lesson as it was too painful to sit down. Years later when I visited the Pink Floyd exhibition at the V&A I was amazed and irritated to find that the Headmaster's cane was in the exhibition as was his punishment book, open at the page recording that Roger Waters[6], one of my contemporaries at school, had received three strokes. Only three; pathetic to make such a thing of it, I thought. But I suppose if you are a celebrity rock-star who merits an Exhibition at the V&A rather than a retired mandarin different rules apply and his three were therefore bound to be more glamorous than my six.

The time for O Level exams came and went; at exam time, and on the cricket pitch in the summer, I was plagued for years with hay-fever, sneezing my way through. Despite this, the exams went well enough (other than failing O Level Art, an almost impossible thing to do) and I was asked what I wanted to do for A Levels. History, English and Biology, I replied. This led to another summons to see the Headmaster who told me that I couldn't mix Arts and Science, and my third subject would be Latin and he would teach me. How lucky the modern pupil is who would have been allowed, indeed possibly encouraged, to combine Arts and Science.

Sixth form went well enough at A and S Level. Medieval History was taught by Mr Warne but in a most curious way. Each lesson was a lecture delivered at dictation speed so we could write it all down in longhand. Beyond these set pieces we were given book lists and told to fend for ourselves. It was a good preparation for university. My English Literature master was Mr Walker who taught us with a dramatic emotional engagement with his subject and a melodramatic waving of his arms. He was brilliant when we were on to 20th century poetry. It was a struggle to decide whether to read History or English at University. In the end I went for History. This academic conflict between peaks to conquer, did not include the Classics in which I was an also-ran, despite the Headmaster's best didactic efforts, save for winning the Cambridge University Latin Reading Prize for which Cambridge schools competed. I had to recite the death of Dido: *"sic, sic iuvat ire sub umbras"*. The prize competition was judged by Sir Denys Page, the Regius Professor of Greek and Master of Jesus College. His other claim to fame, from my point of view, is that he subsequently turned out to be the father of my first serious girlfriend.

I had had a good deal of enjoyment from drama at school. As a relatively good looking young man I was cast early on as the Princess of Egypt (Anath Bithia) in *Moses*, in which the title role was played by Tony Palmer. I declined to play Lady Macbeth, but played Noah in André Obey's play of the same name. My last school performance was as Crocker-Harris in *The Browning Version.* I did not tread the boards again until the year 2000 when I played Sir Humphrey Appleby in a *Yes Minister* sketch at St John's Smith Square in London.

I stayed on for a 7th term to take the scholarship exams at Oxford and Cambridge. I remember that term as a delightful time; no formal lessons and I set my own curriculum, reading widely beyond the Medieval History I had been taught and plunging into Shakespeare plays I had not read, Milton, other poets and 20th century novels. I was a conventional success at school (which I am sure is unfashionable to admit to), becoming Head Boy and Head of the Combined Cadet Force (I was Head of the Royal Air Force section). The only drawback to this was that, as Head Boy, I had to supervise school dinners (i.e. lunch which, in terms of quality, was as bad as I had always expected and which meant I could not go home for lunch any more – a serious deprivation). On one occasion I heard laughter developing in the Dining Hall only to see that some boys had removed the square pink puddings from their plates and had stuck them on the wall. The puddings walked down the wall like metal spiral toys going down the stairs. It was a brilliant and funny moment but I had to produce some cosmetic fury and a bit of gentle punishment. The pink puddings were never served again. My other duty was to read the lesson in Assembly. After the Hymn, Reading and Prayer – in the Anglican tradition - I can still see in my mind's eye the Roman Catholic and Jewish pupils being admitted for school notices and sporting results.

CHAPTER 14:
University Life — Cambridge and Yale

A scholarship at Clare arrives • teaching in an awful school in Norfolk • Professor CMW Moule and books • my life in Cambridge • the University Church and its vicar • a Mellon Fellowship to Yale • the Statue of Liberty • asking Paul Mellon for more money • I join the Yale Russian Chorus • singing to the US Navy and the Navajo • my one and only game of American football ends on crutches • I collect my Draft Card for Vietnam and an MA • I am made to have a hair cut.

I HAD APPLIED TO go to Clare College in Cambridge (unsurprisingly given my connection there) and to St John's College in Oxford. St John's had already offered me a place on the strength of my A and S Levels; Clare had not. The Cambridge scholarship exams were before Christmas; the Oxford ones in January. I went to the Engineering Labs in Cambridge to take the scholarship exam. Next to me was a boy called Alastair Goodlad[1] who had been at Marlborough, and we later worked together in Government and became friends. On Christmas Eve 1961 my father received a telegram from Clare saying I had been awarded an Exhibition in History. That was good enough for me and not to have to take the Oxford exams was a relief at the time, though possibly a long-term error of judgement. I then found myself a teaching job – English, RE and cricket - for two terms at a very poor quality boys' boarding school near Aylsham in Norfolk. This was my *Decline and Fall* period but I cannot write about the extraordinary characters who taught at the school and the bizarre events which occurred because of the litigation that would ensue from those who may still be alive or their descendants. The boys were fine. Some of the staff were weird. That the parents were prepared to pay for this doubtful educational experience amazed me. My state education, free at the point of delivery like the NHS, was of an infinitely higher quality. But I at least got myself two games for the Norfolk 2nd XI cricket team while I was there.

To be able to go as an undergraduate to the College where I had been a boy chorister was a privilege. In my first week I was invited for a drink with the Revd Professor CMW Moule, a Fellow and Professor of Divinity, who had known me in my younger chorister days. (He was a man of high intelligence and the greatest gentle diffident charm.) He told me that he was the sole Trustee of the Clare Choristers Fund and as I was the first, and probably, the only former chorister to come to Clare as an undergraduate, he was going to give me the £80 remaining in the Fund, provided I spent it on books relevant to my studies. At 1962 prices this produced a great literary windfall. As I was being supervised by Geoffrey Elton[2] one of the books I bought was his *Tudor Revolution in Government* in which he "discovered" Thomas Cromwell. That very copy is still in my library; as are all the other books I bought with the Fund money in 1962.

Over my three undergraduate years I did not attend any lectures in my own subject but went to lectures in others: Divinity, English and Greek (particularly to listen to my girlfriend's father). I did my research work in the University Library, close to my rooms in Clare Memorial Court, in the mornings, and wrote my essays in the evenings. At Clare I was supervised by Geoffrey Elton, which was mildly terrifying and by Duncan Forbes who was a sheer delight. My best exam result was in Political Thought and the question on Hegel, on which he had guided me. In my last year my special subject was Pope Pius II, Aeneas Silvius Piccolomini and my supervisor, RF Bennett at Magdalene, turned out to be my publisher's father. In the afternoons I repaired to the sports field: hockey in autumn and winter and coxing some rather desultory rowing crews in spring and summer. However, I made it into the University 1st Hockey team for two matches and into the College 1st Boat when its cox was ill.

The bicycle kept going through my first two years but was then replaced by a smart white Vespa scooter.

Cambridge in the 1950s and early 60s was a wonderful place to live. It was full of green spaces and bicycles; it had the architectural charm of much of the University, and lots and lots of music. Its surrounding countryside was not exciting but it was enjoyably comfortable. And it had a river running through it, in two parts – Granta to the west and Cam to the east. There were rich teas to be had at Grantchester and further afield at Ely. For me personally in those years it also had a wonderful Anglican thread beyond my life as a chorister. My parents and I attended the University Church of Great St Mary's. It had a series of brilliant vicars – Mervyn Stockwood (who prepared me for confirmation and became Bishop of Southwark); Joe Fison – a wonderful modest man who became Bishop of Salisbury and reappears in another chapter; and Hugh Montefiore – later Bishop of Birmingham, who officiated at my first marriage and who also appears again in another chapter in this book. Cambridge also had then and has now the Fitzwilliam Museum. This was and is a cavern of national treasures. From the age of eight I cycled there, climbed up to its forbidding entrance, and enjoyed everything within it (especially the mummies in the Egyptian section).

In my last year at Clare I was concerned that however delightful my life in Cambridge had been that was all I had ever known as a place in which to live, and I wondered whether I should have gone to Oxford after all. So, certain in my mind that a real break with the past was required, I went to Yale instead. There was a Mellon Fellowship for two Clare graduates to go to Yale each year and two from Yale to come the other way. I had applied for other scholarships to the USA and this came to the attention of the Master, Sir Eric Ashby. He stopped me in Old Court one day and told me that there was no need for me to accept interviews for the other scholarships as it had been decided I would be awarded a Mellon Fellowship. So in September 1965, accompanied by my Mellon Colleague, Duncan Robinson[3], I set off on the *Queen Elizabeth* for New York. We decided to go by sea rather than air to provide a greater sense of distance and a touch of adventure. And there is nothing to beat the sight of New York as you steam up the Hudson past the Statue of Liberty as millions of Old World immigrants had done before. To have the right sort of bookends to our time at Yale we returned two years later on the *SS France*, and by then Duncan had found an American wife, Lisa, to take home with him.

After about a month at Yale Duncan and I realised that although the Fellowship was worth $10,000 a year we could not see how this could support us for the whole year. Unlike many previous recipients of the Fellowship we did not have any private means and, in my case, I had used a large part of the first tranche I had received in May 1965 to pay off my Cambridge debts. Our research revealed that the Fellowship had not been increased for some years (I think about twelve) so we had a double-barrelled argument for change (no private means and no uplift for years). We wrote to Paul Mellon setting out our case and when he replied he said he understood our position and asked how much more would we like. This put us on our mettle to propose something reasonable rather than something greedy. We made a sensible proposal. He paid up. He was a generous and gracious man.

One evening in early November in my first year at Yale I was walking along Elm Street towards my college, Saybrook. Snow was gently falling when, out of a lighted window, I heard some wonderful Russian choral singing. Keen to know more I mounted the three flights of stairs and knocked on the door. "Come in," said a voice with a heavy Russian accent. "What you want"? I explained that what I had heard from the street was so beautiful I just had to come to listen. He (the conductor/pianist) asked if I could sight-read and I said yes. He beckoned me towards the piano. "You will not understand the Russian so just sing La la la to what you see of the notes on the page." I did as he said and, after a short time, he said, "Good. First tenors," and pointed to the front row. I had joined the Yale Russian Chorus, a polyglot and delightful group of singers from a number of different countries. In term-time we sang concerts in New England but in the Easter vacation each year we climbed into a bus and toured the USA from East to West and North to South. We sang to some extraordinary audiences – to the US Navy in San Diego (I think the large audience must have been ordered to attend) and to Native Americans on a Navajo reservation in Arizona. We normally sang concerts with roughly a half of ecclesiastical music and a half of folk songs. Our Native American audience looked very glum as we worked through a couple of pieces of church music. There was no applause. Our conductor told us to switch to the second half plan and we began with a song about Cossacks riding across the steppes. Their faces changed as it gradually dawned on them that here were sounds and rhythms to which they could relate. The applause began to ring out and by the time we had finished a most rousing rendering of *Kalinka* they were almost standing on their chairs.

I have always much enjoyed watching American football. One American friend who had been at school with me in Cambridge played for Harvard and another, an American Mellon Fellow at Clare with me, had played for Yale. I longed to have a go, despite not having the bulky physique normally required, so I asked the captain of my College team whether I could have a chance. He agreed and so, dressed in the full kit, helmet and shoulder pads, I appeared. He said I would not be allowed on the field until he was quite sure that our team could not lose. When he was certain of that I joined the "huddle" and listened to an incomprehensible litany of various numbers and words. Asking what it meant I was told to run down the right hand touchline for 20 yards and turn and catch the ball. I duly ran and jumped. The ball hit me in the chest and went to ground. We returned to the huddle. The captain said that we would repeat the move as the opposition would not believe we would try it again. So I ran down again and this time I caught the ball when, suddenly, a very large body felled me with considerable force. I tried to get up but could not. I looked down at a painful ankle and saw it had swelled and spilled over the outside of the boot. I spent the next six weeks on crutches limping around the campus. But I had achieved my goal of having played in an American football game.

In my time at Yale it was the height of the Vietnam War (which I marched against) and of drugs on Haight Ashbury[4] (which I visited, with my Russian Chorus friends, and inhaled). I had grown my hair long and wore a black leather jacket. (At Cambridge it had been a tweed jacket, short hair and a pipe, which you could smoke while in town and wearing a gown. King George VI had been fined 6s 8d for doing so; so was I.) I joined a Yale Secret Society – St Anthony Hall, the Sigma chapter of the Delta Psi Fraternity, which had not too many silly rituals but was a very good place for breakfast; and the Elizabethan Club, very English and a good place for tea (I think they offered the best cucumber sandwiches in the Western World). Not long before I was due to return to England, in mid-1967, I received a Draft Card telling me to turn up at the New Haven Army Depot to report for service in Vietnam. When I appeared the Sergeant looked at me beadily and said that while I was a student I was OK but if I stayed in the USA and got a job then I would be on my way much further East than the UK. I collected a Master's Degree and returned to England.

My two years at Yale had helped me grow beyond my delightful Cambridge background which had been both enjoyable and quite successful but entirely conventional, and very English. Yale broke that mould, quite gently but cleverly, and made me feel much more open to new ideas, to new and different friends and to new and different experiences. I owe the USA a big thank you, not just for Yale but for lots of other things which followed over many years after my time there – including my future American family.

In July 1967 I returned from the USA to England. My father took one look at the length of my hair and made it very clear that I could not start my working life like that. I was hauled off to the barbers, though I was 24 not 12, and given a 'short back and sides'. Thus trimmed, and in a new suit, I walked across Whitehall into the Home Office in sunshine and into whatever the future would hold.

FOOTNOTES

PROLOGUE

1. AR Bunker. Arthur Bunker was the Principal Establishment Officer (or in more modern terms the Personnel or HR Director). He had served in the RAF in the War. He kept in touch as my career developed and, from time to time, took me to lunch at the RAF Club in Piccadilly.

2. Mellon Fellowship – An academic exchange programme between Cambridge and Yale established in 1932 by Clare College alumnus Paul Mellon. Two Mellon Fellows are selected each year from Clare College and another two from Yale. The exchange lasts two years. The award covers the cost of accommodation, tuition and university fees, and pays a quarterly living allowance.

CHAPTER 1:
London – The Private Office

1 PD James - I met her again in the 1990s when I was in charge of government policy towards the BBC and she was a BBC governor.

2 David Ennals - He subsequently went on to become Minister of State for Health and Social Services. He served first as MP for Dover and later for Norwich North.

3 Fulton Report – Delivered in 1968, Lord Fulton's report into the civil service found it to be too much based on the philosophy of the 'generalist' or 'all-rounder', and that scientists, engineers and other specialists were not being given the responsibilities, opportunities and authority they should have.

4 Sir Robert Mark - Chief Constable of Leicester City Police, and later Commissioner of the Metropolitan Police from 1972 to 1977. Probably the most outstanding Commissioner of the second half of the 20th century.

5 Syd Norris - described by Roy Jenkins as "an able assistant secretary, but not in my view a natural private secretary". On retiring he sadly died too young.

6 Anthony Lester – a very distinguished human rights QC and committed Liberal Democrat. Decided to resign from the House of Lords under a personal cloud.

7 Shirley Summerskill – Labour MP for Halifax from 1964-1983. She had the great

bad fortune of being in charge of animal welfare at the Home Office when beagles were made to smoke cigarettes to test their impact on the human population.

8 Sir Arthur Peterson - Became Permanent Secretary at the Home Office after having served as Director General of the Greater London council. He and his wife owned a pub in Lincolnshire, where at the weekend he pulled the pints.

9 Chuter Ede - He served as Home Secretary under Prime Minister Clement Attlee from 1945 to 1951, becoming the longest-serving Home Secretary of the 20th century. He subsequently became Leader of the House of Commons.

10 Nico Henderson - One of the most distinguished Ambassadors of the 20th century; Poland, West Germany, Paris, and Washington. He was very kindly disposed towards me and wrote in his memoir *Mandarin* "He should go far, despite his sense of humour".

11 Bill Rodgers – Secretary of State for Transport from 1976-1979. Defected from the Labour Party forming the SDP 'Gang of Four' with Roy Jenkins, David Owen and Shirley Williams. He subsequently helped to lead the SDP into the merger that formed the Liberal Democrats in 1988, and later served as that party's leader in the House of Lords between 1997 and 2001.

12 Philip Allen – Permanent Secretary at the Home office. He was created a life peer as Baron Allen of Abbeydale in the year after the 1975 Referendum.

13. Ian Gilmour – Shadow Home Secretary 1975-1976, Shadow Secretary for Defence 1976-79 and Lord Keeper of the Privy Seal in Margaret Thatcher's first government. I got to know him very well and we remained friends until the end of his life.

14 William Whitelaw – Margaret Thatcher's Deputy Prime Minister from 1979-1988. He was a natural leader and one of the most delightful people one could wish to work for.

15 Shirley Williams – Baroness Williams of Crosby. Having served in the Labour cabinet from 1974-1979, she broke away in 1981 as one of the "Gang of Four" to found the Social Democratic Party (SDP). She served as President of the SDP from 1982-1987 and supported the SDP's merger with the Liberal Party that formed the Liberal Democrats.

16 Helmut Schmidt – Chancellor of West Germany from 1974-1982. He was an energetic diplomat who sought European co-operation and international economic co-ordination and was the leading force in creating the European Monetary System in 1978.

17 Giscard D'Estaing – President of France from 1974-1981. His tenure was marked by a more liberal attitude on social issues, such as divorce, contraception and abortion, and attempts to modernise the country and the office of the presidency, notably overseeing such far-reaching infrastructure projects as the TGV and the turn towards reliance on nuclear power as France's main energy source.

18 Nigel Lawson – Chancellor of the Exchequer 1983-1989. Lawson was a key proponent of Margaret Thatcher's policies of privatisation of several key industries, and oversaw the sudden deregulation of financial markets in 1986, commonly referred to as the 'Big Bang'.

19 Robert Armstrong - Principal Private Secretary to Ted Heath and Harold Wilson, then Cabinet Secretary under Margaret Thatcher. He was a great mentor and became a firm friend until he died in 2020 aged 93.

20 Michael Palliser - Permanent Representative to the European Communities and later Permanent Under-Secretary at the Foreign Office from 1975-1982. He was extremely helpful to me in advice about going to Brussels.

21 Crispin Tickell - Chef de Cabinet to the President of the European Commission (1977–1980), Ambassador to Mexico (1981-1983) and British Ambassador to the United Nations. He later became Warden of Green College, Oxford and was an internationally-acknowledged expert on climate change.

CHAPTER 2:
Brussels – The *Cabinet*

1 Emile Noel - Secretary-General of the European Commission, 1967-1987. An extremely subtle and highly experienced operator, whose French I found quite difficult to understand because of his use of the subjunctive.

2 Nick Stuart – A Private Secretary in No 10 he then spent two years in Brussels in Roy Jenkins' cabinet in 1979-1981. After Brussels he returned to the Department for Education, from which he retired as a Director General.

3 General Gordon - Major-General Charles George Gordon, or 'Chinese Gordon, was placed in command of the "Ever Victorious Army", a force of Chinese soldiers led by European officers which was instrumental in putting down the Taiping Rebellion, regularly defeating much larger forces.

CHAPTER 3:
Terrorism and Riots – Promotion on the Field of Battle

1 Condé Nast – My wife's grandfather. He purchased *Vogue* magazine in 1909, incorporating Condé Nast Publications in 1922. Eventually the portfolio expanded to include *House & Garden*, *Vanity Fair*, *Glamour* and *The New Yorker*, amongst many others. He is largely considered to be the originator of the "class publication", focusing on a

particular social group or interest instead of targeting the largest possible readership. In my view the best book about him is by Susan Ronald and was published in 2019.

2 John Dellow – The police Commander at the Iranian Embassy Siege and subsequently Deputy Commissioner of the Metropolitan Police. A lifelong friend. He, Michael Rose and I from time to time meet for lunch, mainly to reminisce about this extraordinary moment in our lives.

3 Michael Rose – As well as Special Air Service Regiment commanding officer, General Sir Michael Rose was Commander UNPROFOR Bosnia in 1994 during the Yugoslav Wars. As with John Dellow, a lifelong friend.

4 Bishops - The Anglican Bishop was the Rt Reverend David Sheppard (an England Test Cricketer) and the Roman Catholic Bishop Derek Worlock. Two great spiritual leaders, they had a personal relationship which was deeply respected by the people of Liverpool. They co-authored *Better Together* and *With Hope in our Hearts*.

5 Clive Whitmore - Principal Private Secretary to Margaret Thatcher from 1979-1982, then Permanent Secretary of the Ministry of Defence until 1988 and Permanent Under-Secretary of State at the Home Office until 1994.

6 Christopher Soames - Shadow Foreign Secretary under Edward Heath. Appointed Ambassador to France by Harold Wilson, serving from 1968-1972, then becoming Vice-President of the European Commission from 1973-1976.

CHAPTER 4:
Immigration – The End of Empire

1 Brian Cubbon - Permanent Under Secretary of State of the Northern Ireland Office from 1976-1979 and Permanent Under-Secretary of State at the Home Office from 1979-1988. Cubbon was injured in an IRA bomb explosion in which the British Ambassador to Ireland, Christopher Ewart-Biggs, was killed in 1976. Cubbon's Private Secretary, Judith Cooke, was also killed, and his driver, Brian O'Driscoll, injured. He suffered from pain throughout his life. He was a Press Complaints Commission Commissioner from 1995 to 2002. We met regularly in his retirement.

2 Mark Bonham Carter - Grandson of Prime Minister H.H. Asquith, he combined his work as a publisher, at Collins, with his liberal politics. He unexpectedly won the 1958 Torrington by-election, overturning a 9,000 Conservative majority and giving the Liberal Party their first by-election gain since 1929. He became the first chairman of the Race Relations Board, from 1966–1971, and its successor, the Community Relations Commission 1971–1977. He was Vice-chairman of the BBC 1975-80. A wonderful step-

father-in-law, he was a man of decidedly clear views.

3 Peter Hennessy – Formerly a journalist and then a contemporary historian specialising in the history of government. He worked at *The Times, Financial Times* and *The Economist* before founding the Institute of Contemporary British History in 1986 and moving into academia.

4 David Waddington – During his parliamentary career, he worked in government under Margaret Thatcher as Chief Whip, then as Home Secretary and finally as Leader of the House of Lords under John Major. He then served as the Governor of Bermuda between 1992 and 1997. He was surprised by his own success and said to me when I was working with him that he did not expect to be promoted further. How wrong he was.

5 Robert Wade-Gery - Distinguished diplomat, culminating his career as High Commissioner to India. My wife and I stayed with him on various occasions on our visits there.

6 Mark Tully - Bureau Chief of BBC, New Delhi, for 20 years from 1965. He worked with the BBC until 1994, and thereafter as a freelance journalist and broadcaster based in New Delhi. His current and delicious piece of listening is *Something Understood*, broadcast early on a Sunday morning on Radio 4.

7 Percy Cradock – A highly intelligent sinologist, he served as British Ambassador to the People's Republic of China from 1978-1983, playing a significant role in the negotiations which led up to the signing of the Sino-British Joint Declaration in 1984.

8 Peter Carrington - Defence Secretary from 1970-1974, Foreign Secretary from 1979-1982 and Secretary General of NATO from 1984 to 1988. In Margaret Thatcher's first government, he played a major role in negotiating the Lancaster House Agreement that ended the racial conflict in Rhodesia and enabled the creation of Zimbabwe. One of the last British politicians to resign on a point of principle, he was a delightful and amusing man.

9 Tasker Watkins - Lord Justice of Appeal and deputy Lord Chief Justice. He was President of the Welsh Rugby Union from 1993 to 2004, overseeing the switch from amateur to professional, having played himself at outside half for Cardiff and Glamorgan. During the Second World War, he served in the British Army and was awarded the Victoria Cross. A war hero who was prominent in the law and in Rugby Union, he was described as 'The Greatest Living Welshman'.

10 Richard Wilson - Cabinet Secretary from 1998-2002. A contemporary of mine at Cambridge and a lifelong friend, he was immensely supportive and understanding when I had to have a series of major eye operations whilst Permanent Secretary at the Lord Chancellor's Dept.

CHAPTER 5:
Finishing School – The Cabinet Office and Treasury

1 Tessa Blackstone - Master of Birkbeck College, University of London, from 1987-1997, until her appointment to the new Labour government in 1997. She also held research fellowships at the Centre for Studies in Public Policy and the Policy Studies Institute. In 2004, she became Vice-Chancellor of the University of Greenwich.

2 Ballet Russes - An itinerant ballet company begun in Paris and originally conceived by impresario Sergei Diaghilev. From 1909-1929 the company performed throughout Europe and on tours to North and South America. The company never performed in Russia.

3 Frederick Ashton - A ballet dancer and then choreographer with Rambert, Ashton was director of the Royal Ballet from 1963 until 1970. He was widely credited with the creation of a specifically English genre of ballet.

4 Robin Butler - Principal Private Secretary and then Cabinet Secretary under Margaret Thatcher and then Tony Blair. As Cabinet Secretary he organised the most wonderful Permanent Secretary away days, with a heavy emphasis on competitive sport, at Harrow School, where he had been both Head Boy and Chairman of the Governors. He forbade my partnering Dame Barbara Mills as we had won the tennis tournament two years running.

5 Peter Middleton - Permanent Secretary at the Treasury 1983-1991. He joined Barclays in 1991 as Group Deputy Chairman, becoming Group Chairman in 1999.

6 John Moore - He enjoyed a meteoric rise through the ranks of government, which culminated in his serving as a Secretary of State in the Cabinet from 1987 to 1989. He was noted for his film-star good looks, and having spent much time in the US, brought aspects of American corporate culture to Thatcher's government.

7 Ken Clarke - A key figure in all Conservative governments from Thatcher to Cameron, he is well known aficionado of both jazz and suede shoes. I was good on the latter, but not the former. He was one of the most enjoyable ministers I ever worked with.

8 Brian Griffiths - An economist and professor of finance, he resigned as Dean of Cass Business School, to become the Director of the Number 10 Policy Unit from 1985-1990.

9 Rachel Lomax – Following a distinguished Civil Service career – she was Permanent Secretary of the Welsh Office then of Social Security, she became Deputy Governor of the Bank of England from 2003-2008, serving on the Monetary Policy Committee.

10 Thyssen Collection - Acquired by the Spanish state in 1993, the privately assembled Thyssen-Bornemisza Collection provides an overview of Western painting and spans

most European and American styles from the fourteenth to the twentieth century.

11 Neil MacGregor - Director of the National Gallery (1987-2002) and of the British Museum (2002-2015). A wise and perceptive man he became an eloquent broadcaster.

12 Radnor Collection at Longford Castle - A collection of portraits and Old Master paintings built up at Longford Castle, near Salisbury, over the course of the 18th century.

13 Norman Lamont - Chancellor of the Exchequer from 1990-1993 under John Major, and before that a member of cabinet across numerous departments under Margaret Thatcher.

14 Accounting Officer - When parliament calls a public sector organisation to account, it is its Accounting Officer who gives evidence. The Accounting Officer of a public sector organisation is usually its Permanent Secretary or CEO. The post carries personal responsibilities to manage the organisation efficiently and effectively and to report to parliament accurately, meaningfully and without misleading.

15 Michael Howard - Home Secretary (1993-1997) under John Major, then Conservative Leader from 2003-2005.

CHAPTER 6:
A Ministry of Culture

1 David Mellor – Chief Secretary to the Treasury (1990-1992) under John Major, then the first Secretary of State at the Department for National Heritage. He also served as Chairman of the Blair government's 'Football Task Force'. On retiring from frontline politics he pursued a successful career in journalism, both as a newspaper columnist and radio presenter.

2 Heather Wilkinson (now Hancock) - Private Secretary to three Home Secretaries: David Waddington, Kenneth Baker, and Kenneth Clarke, before becoming my Private Secretary at the newly-formed Department for National Heritage. At the Millennium Commission from 1994, and served as its Acting Chief Executive and Deputy Chief Executive. After a successful career in both the public and private sectors she is now the Master of St John's College, Cambridge.

3 Tim Bell - Advertising and public relations guru, best known for his advisory role in Margaret Thatcher's three successful general election campaigns and his co-founding and 30 years of heading Bell Pottinger.

4 Linford Christie - The only male British athlete to have won gold medals in the 100 metres at all four major competitions open to British athletes: the Olympic Games, the

World Championships, the European Championships and the Commonwealth Games. He was the first European athlete to break the 10-second barrier in the 100m and still holds the British record in the event.

5 Sally Gunnell - The only female British athlete to have won all four 'majors'; Olympic, World, European and Commonwealth titles, and was the first female 400 metres hurdler in history to win both the Olympic and World titles. She remains the British record-holder for the women's' 400m hurdles.

6 David Calcutt - An eminent barrister and public servant who reported on the Press Complaints Commission in 1990 and subsequently. He was the Master of Magdalene College Cambridge from 1985 to 1994.

7 Jocelyn Stevens - A magazine publisher and newspaper executive, in 1957 he bought and revamped the British high society publication *The Queen*, renaming it *Queen*. He was then manging director of the *Evening Standard* and *Daily Express* in the 1960s and 1970s, then Rector of the Royal College of Art from 1984–1992 and Chairman of English Heritage from 1992–2000. He was a cheerful, combative colleague and companion.

8 Frank Duffy - A British architect, he founded DEGW, the international architectural and design practice best known for office design and workplace strategy and, for advanced thinking on the programming of educational and arts facilities.

9 John Thaw - An actor best known as the title character in the long-running television series *Inspector Morse*. Thaw married fellow actor Sheila Hancock in 1973.

10 Arnold Goodman – A British lawyer who was Senior Partner in the law firm Goodman, Derrick & Co (now Goodman Derrick LLP). He was solicitor and advisor to politicians such as Harold Wilson. Lord Goodman, as he became in 1965, was chairman of the Arts Council from 1965-1972. He was my wife's stepmother's solicitor.

11 Willard White – Jamaican-born British operatic bass baritone. White sang the role of Porgy in the first stereo recording of *Porgy and Bess*, which received a Grammy Award. He received the Gold Musgrave Medal of the Institute of Jamaica, a CBE in 1995, and was made a Knight Bachelor in the 2004 Birthday Honours.

12 National Heritage Memorial Fund – The NHMF was set up in 1980 to save the most outstanding parts of the British national heritage, in memory of those who have given their lives for the UK. It replaced the National Land Fund which had fulfilled the same function since 1946. The NHMF is funded by grant-in-aid through the Department for Digital, Culture, Media and Sport. In 1993 NHMF was given the responsibility for distributing the share of heritage funding from the National Lottery for the heritage good causes through the National Lottery Heritage Fund.

13 Jacob Rothschild - Investment banker, he was Chairman of RIT Capital Partners plc. From 2003-2008 he was Deputy Chairman of *BSkyB Television* and a Member of the council for the Duchy of Cornwall for the Prince of Wales. He is also Honorary President of the Institute for Jewish Policy Research. A major figure in the cultural world he has overseen the flowering of the collection at Waddesdon.

14 Martin Charteris – After a military career he became Assistant Private Secretary (1954-1972) and then Private Secretary (1972-1977) to Queen Elizabeth II.

15 Young Winston - Winston Churchill's grandson, he was a Conservative MP from 1970-1997, first for Stretford and then for Davyhulme. Before becoming a Member of Parliament, he was a journalist, notably in the Middle East during the Six-Day War, about which he later published a book.

16 Nick Serota - English art historian and curator who served as the Director of the Tate from 1988-2017. He was the creator of Tate Modern. He is currently Chair of Arts Council England, a role which he has held since 2017.

17 Oliver Popplewell - A former judge, he chaired the inquiry into the Bradford City stadium fire and presided over the libel case brought by Jonathan Aitken MP against *The Guardian* which eventually led to Aitken's imprisonment for perjury. He was appointed as Recorder of the Crown Court in 1971 and was a High Court judge from 1983-2003. He played first-class cricket for Cambridge University and was president of the Marylebone Cricket Club from 1994–1996.

18 Richard Rogers - British architect best known for his work on the Pompidou Centre in Paris, the Lloyd's building and Millennium Dome in London, the Senedd building in Cardiff, and the European Court of Human Rights building in Strasbourg. He was awarded the RIBA Gold Medal, the Thomas Jefferson Medal, the RIBA Stirling Prize, the Minerva Medal, and the Pritzker Prize.

19 Jennie Page - Chief Executive of English Heritage from 1989 to 1995, before becoming headhunted to lead the Millennium Dome project. In 2006 she was appointed Vice-chairman of the Cathedrals Fabric Commission for England.

20 Stephen Dorrell - Secretary of State for National Heritage (1994-1995) and then Health (1995-1997) under John Major. He served as Chairman of the House of Commons Health Select Committee from 2010 to 2014. He defected from the Conservatives to join Change UK in 2019, and then the Liberal Democrats

21 John Sainsbury – Chairman & CEO of Sainsbury's from 1969-1992. He led the company on to the London Stock Exchange on 12 July 1973, which was at the time the largest flotation ever. On retirement he remained Life President. A great and wise cultural philanthropist, he and his wife Anya became firm friends.

22 Jack Cunningham - He joined the Shadow Cabinet in 1983 and ran the Labour Party's general election campaign in 1992. After the Labour landslide victory in 1997 he first became Minister of Agriculture, Fisheries and Food and then Minister for the Cabinet Office and Chancellor of the Duchy of Lancaster.

23 Peter Mandelson – Served as the Labour Party's Director of Communications from 1985-1990. MP for Hartlepool from 1992-2004. He served in the Blair cabinet from 1997-2001, then as the European Commissioner for Trade between 2004 and 2008, then in the Brown cabinet from 2008-2010. Much liked by his civil servants, he is a Wiltshire neighbour and friend.

24 The Corrs - An Irish family pop band from County Louth that combined pop rock with traditional Irish music.

25 Georgina Nayler - Joining the National Heritage Memorial Fund as a secretary in her late twenties she rose in just seven years to become it's Director. On leaving in 1996 she became Director of The Pilgrim Trust, a post she held in 2020.

26 Canova's *Three Graces* - Regarded internationally as a masterpiece of neoclassical European sculpture, the Three Graces was carved in Rome by Antonio Canova between 1814 and 1817 for an English collector. This group of three mythological sisters was in fact a second version of an original one commissioned by Joséphine de Beauharnais, first wife of Napoleon Bonaparte.

27 Editors' Code – The Editors' Code of Practice sets out the rules that newspapers and magazines regulated by IPSO have agreed to follow. The Code is written and administered by the Editors' Code Committee, formed in 1990 to draft Britain's first universally-accepted Code of Practice for the Press, to coincide with the birth of the Press Complaints Commission, which administered the new system of self-regulation prior to the launch of IPSO after the Leveson Report.

28 Simon Jenkins – Author, newspaper columnist and editor. He was editor of the *Evening Standard* from 1976-1978 and *The Times* from 1990-1992, and currently writes columns for The Guardian. He chaired the National Trust from 2008-2014.

29 Princess Diana compost – the Royal Parks did the same with the floral tributes to The Queen after her death in 2022.

30 David Puttnam – Film producer best known for *Chariots of Fire*, which won the Academy Award for Best Picture, *The Killing Fields*, *Midnight Express* and *Memphis Belle*. In 2006 he was awarded the BAFTA Fellowship for lifetime achievement, and in the same year became deputy Chairman of Channel 4 Television.

31 Chris Smith - Labour MP for Islington South and Finsbury (1983-2005) and Secretary of State for Culture, Media and Sport (1997-2001). He was Chairman of the

Environment Agency then of the Advertising Standards Authority and since 2015 has been Master of Pembroke College, Cambridge.

32 Virginia Bottomley – Conservative MP for South West Surrey (1984-2005). Secretary of State for Health (1992-1995) and Secretary of State for National Heritage (1995-1997). In 2006, she was elected and installed as Chancellor of the University of Hull.

33 Dickie Attenborough – Actor and filmmaker, he was the president of the Royal Academy of Dramatic Art (RADA) and the British Academy of Film and Television Arts (BAFTA), as well as the life president of Chelsea FC. For his directorial debut, 1969's *Oh! What a Lovely War*, he was nominated for the BAFTA for Best Direction, and he was nominated for his films *Young Winston*, *A Bridge Too Far*, and *Cry Freedom*. He won two Academy Awards for *Gandhi* in 1983: *Best Picture and Best Director.*

34 Andrew Turnbull – Principal Private Secretary to both Margaret Thatcher and John Major, he became Permanent Secretary to the Treasury from 1998-2002 and then Cabinet Secretary from 2002-2005.

35 Michael Bichard - Permanent Secretary at the Department for Education and Employment (DfEE) from 1995 until 2001. He later became Rector of The University of the Arts and director of the Institute for Government.

36 Jack Straw – Home Secretary (1997-2001) and then Foreign Secretary (2001-2006). Through my daughter Flo and her husband we have become friends with Jack's son Will and his wife Claire.

37 Derry Irvine – He became a QC in 1978 and head of chambers in 1981, founding 11 King's Bench Walk Chambers. Among his pupil barristers were Tony Blair and Cherie Booth; at their wedding he dubbed himself "Cupid QC". In the 1980s he became a Recorder and then a Deputy High Court Judge, as well as a legal advisor to the Labour Party. Shadow Lord Chancellor (1992-1997) and Lord Chancellor (1997-2003).

CHAPTER 7:
The Majesty of the Law

1 Michael Beloff QC - A barrister and arbitrator, he is a member of Blackstone Chambers, practising in human rights, administrative law and sports law. He sits on the Court of Arbitration for Sport (CAS), which deals with disputes including doping offences on behalf of the International Olympic Committee. He served as President of Trinity College, Oxford, from 1996 to 2006.

2 Lord Woolf – Master of the Rolls (1996-2000) and Lord Chief Justice of England and Wales (2000-2005).

3 Elizabeth Butler-Sloss – She was the first female Lord Justice of Appeal and was the highest-ranking female judge in the United Kingdom until 2004. President of the Family Division of the High Court of Justice (1999-2005). A cross-bench Peer.

4 Clerk to the Crown in Chancery – A senior House of Lords official who is the head of The Crown Office (see also below).

5 The Crown Office – A section of the Ministry of Justice (formerly the Lord Chancellor's Department) that has custody of the Great Seal of the Realm, and certain administrative functions in connection with the courts and the judicial process, as well as functions relating to the electoral process, the keeping of the Roll of the Peerage, and the preparation of royal documents such as warrants required to pass under the royal sign-manual, fiats, letters patent, etc.

6 Clerk of the Parliaments – The chief clerk of the House of Lords. The position has existed since at least 1315, and duties include preparing the minutes of Lords proceedings, advising on proper parliamentary procedure and pronouncing the Royal Assent.

7 Ian Magee – Second Permanent Secretary at the Department for Constitutional Affairs and Head of Profession for Operational Delivery for the whole Civil Service. He was also a member of the Capability Review team for the Cabinet Office. A close friend - he and I own bits of racehorses together; sometimes successfully.

8 Tom Bingham – Successively Master of the Rolls (1992-1996), Lord Chief Justice (1996-2000) and Senior Law Lord (2000-2008). Played a pioneering role in the formation of the UK Supreme Court. A man of penetrating intellect.

9 Charlie Falconer – After various Ministerial posts he became Lord Chancellor (2003-2007).

10 David Blunkett – Education and Employment Secretary (1997-2001), Home Secretary (2001-2004) and Work and Pensions Secretary (2005).

11 Alastair Darling – Chief Secretary to the Treasury (1997-1998), Secretary of State for Work and Pensions (1998-2002) and Secretary of State for Transport (2003-2006). Chancellor of the Exchequer (2007-2010) to Gordon Brown, including through the financial crisis of 2008.

12 Peter Hain – Born in Kenya Colony to South African parents, Hain came to the United Kingdom from South Africa as a teenager and was a noted anti-fascist and anti-apartheid campaigner in the 1970s. Secretary of State for Northern Ireland (2005-2007), Secretary of State for Work and Pensions (2007-2008) and Secretary of State for Wales (2002-2008 and 2009-2010).

13 Paul Jenkins – A barrister, he was the Treasury Solicitor, the UK Government's principal legal official, in which role he served as the Attorney General's Permanent Secre-

tary and Chief Executive of the Treasury Solicitor's Department (TSol). He was also Her Majesty's Procurator General and, as Head of the Government Legal Service, head of profession for the 2,000 lawyers advising government. He was appointed Queen's Counsel (honoris causa) on 30 March 2009. He was my legal adviser for 10 years. He died too young.

14 Stephen Breyer - US Supreme Court Justice, nominated by Bill Clinton in 1994. Born in San Francisco, Breyer attended Stanford University, the University of Oxford as a Marshall Scholar, and graduated from Harvard Law School in 1964. A long standing Liberal judge.

15 Tom Chandos – Tom sits on the Labour bench in the House of Lords, having been created a life peer as Baron Lyttelton of Aldershot in 2000. Tom was Chairman of the Social Market Foundation from 1989-1991, Chairman of the Esmee Fairbairn Foundation from 2007-2013. He was a Director of English National Opera and President of the National Kidney Research Fund.

16 Bob Moy – Purse Bearer to the Lord Chancellor for over 20 years. The use of a special purse or burse to hold the Great Seal of the Realm, the Lord Chancellor's symbol of Office, can be traced as far back as the end of the 13th Century. The purse is carried before the Lord Chancellor in procession on State occasions. Bob taught me how to get dressed and how best to process.

17 Norah Dobinson – Train Bearer to the Lord Chancellor. As with her colleague Bob Moy, Norah held her position in the House of Lords for over two decades.

18 Lord Hutton – Lord of Appeal (1997-2004) and Lord Chief Justice of Northern Ireland (1989-1997). Lord Hutton represented the Ministry of Defence at the inquest into the killing of civil rights marchers on "Bloody Sunday" and also adjudicated over the 1999 extradition of former Chilean dictator Gen. Augusto Pinochet.

19 Mark Ormerod – Chief Executive of the Supreme Court of the United Kingdom and the Judicial Committee of the Privy Council (2015-2020) He was previously the Chief Executive of the Law Commission and also held posts as Chief Executive of the Probation Associations and was Director of Access to Justice Policy at the Ministry of Justice.

CHAPTER 8:
The Theatre, the City and the Prince

1 Christopher Hogg – Chief Executive of Courtaulds from 1979-1991 and a member of JP Morgan's International Advisory Council from 1988 to 2003. He served as a

Non-Executive Director of the Bank of England from 1992-1996 and a Trustee of the Ford Foundation from 1987-1999.

2 Joan Bakewell – Journalist, television presenter and peer, She first became known as one of the presenters of the BBC2 programme *Late Night Line-Up* 1965–72, then worked across programming at both Granada and the BBC. She presented the ethics documentary series *Heart of the Matter* for 12 years.

3 Nick Hytner – Associate Director of the National Theatre from 1990-2003, then becoming Artistic Director until 2015. Hytner has also worked extensively in opera, with many of his productions achieving critical acclaim and commercial success. He now runs The Bridge Theatre with long-time collaborator Nick Starr. "The Two Nicks" were a joy to work with.

4 Nick Starr – Executive Director of the National Theatre 2002-2014. He has chaired the boards of Battersea Arts Centre (2002-2007) and the Bush Theatre (2009-2014) and has served as a non-executive director of the Society of London Theatre and Nesta.

5 Peter Hall – In 1960, aged 29, Hall founded the Royal Shakespeare Company. He was later director of the National Theatre (1973–88) and artistic director of Glyndebourne Festival Opera (1984–1990). He formed the Peter Hall Company (1998–2011) and became founding director of the Rose Theatre Kingston in 2003.

6 Lloyd Dorfman – Founder of the foreign exchange retailer Travelex in 1976. He is chairman of The Prince's Trust, and Prince's Trust International, chairman of the Royal Opera House, and a trustee of the Royal Academy Trust and of JW3.

7 Vivien Duffield – Chairman of the Clore Foundations in the UK and in Israel since 1976. She founded the Jewish community centre JW3 in London in 2013. She is currently Chairman of the Royal Opera House Endowment Fund, Director of the Southbank Centre board and a Governor of the Royal Ballet. We worked closely together through some difficult times for the ROH.

8 Lord Cottesloe – Chairman of the Arts Council from 1960-65 and Southbank Theatre Board from 1962-1977. He was a Deputy Lieutenant of London from 1951-1976.

9 Simon Russell Beale – He has spent much of his theatre career at the Royal Shakespeare Company and National Theatre. He has received ten Laurence Olivier Award nominations, winning three awards for his performances in *Volpone* (1996), *Candide* (2000), and *Uncle Vanya* (2003). In 2022 he won the Tony Award for Best Actor for his role in *The Lehman Trilogy*. Great fun to be with as well as a brilliant actor.

10 Frances de la Tour – Originally known for her role as Miss Ruth Jones in the television sitcom *Rising Damp* from 1974-1978. She is a Tony Award winner and three-time Olivier Award winner. Upon reprising her *Rising Damp* role in the 1980 film version,

she won Best Actress at the *Evening Standard* British Film Awards.

11 Richard Griffiths – Actor known best for his portrayals of Uncle Monty in *Withnail and I* (1987), Henry Crabbe in *Pie in the Sky* (1994-1997) and the teacher 'Hector' in *The History Boys* (2004-2006)). For his performance in the latter he won a Tony Award, a Laurence Olivier Award, the Drama Desk Award and the Outer Critics Circle Award.

12 James Hanson – Along with business partner Gordon White he started the Hanson Trust (later renamed simply Hanson) in 1960, which specialised in the acquisition of other companies. Hanson's acquisitions included the 1986 purchase of Imperial Group, the British tobacco conglomerate.

13 Bill Staple – Chief Executive of Hanson Westhouse. Formerly an investment banker at N M Rothschild & Sons Ltd and Director-General of the Takeover Panel, which regulates takeover bids in the UK.

14 Dominic Shorthouse – Founder of private equity firm Englefield Capital LLP and a former partner at Warburg Pincus. He launched Channel 5 in 1997 and Cognita, a UK-based private schools operator, in 2004.

CHAPTER 9:
Party Funding – A Farewell to Westminster

1 Andrew McDonald – Also a writer and campaigner, he spent most of his career working in the National Archives and, subsequently, in the Cabinet Office and Ministry of Justice. His last executive role was as CEO of *IPSA*, the regulator established to tackle MPs' expenses crisis. He became a close friend and I paid tribute to him at his Memorial Service in Westminster Cathedral.

2 Ian Gambles – Formerly Director of National Infrastructure at the Planning Inspectorate and Chief Executive Officer of the Forestry Commission (2019-2021). He worked across both public and private sectors, including HM Treasury and as a management consultant. Currently Chair of the James Hutton Institute and a Fellow of the Chartered Institute of Management Accountants.

3 Nick Clegg – Leader of the Liberal Democrats (2007-2015) and Deputy Prime Minister (2010-2015), in coalition with David Cameron's Conservative Party. Currently President of Global Affairs at Facebook.

4 Matthew Parris – Political writer and broadcaster, formerly Conservative MP for West Derbyshire. He joined the Conservative Research Department and moved on to become Correspondence Secretary to Margaret Thatcher. He is now a columnist for *The Times*.

5 Peter Riddell – A journalist and author, he worked for the *Financial Times* from 1970-1991. From 2016-2021 he served as the Commissioner for Public Appointments, and is the former Director of the Institute for Government.

6 Francis Maude – Paymaster General (2010-2015) under David Cameron, then Minister of State for Trade and Investment (2015-2016). Conservative MP for North Warwickshire (1983-1992) and then Horsham (1997-2015). Since leaving government and parliament in 2016 he has run his own consultancy business specialising in government efficiency.

CHAPTER 10:

A Professional After-Life – Advertising, Art and the Movies

1 John Caines – Permanent Secretary of the Overseas Development Administration at the Foreign and Commonwealth Office (1987-1989), the Department of Education and Science (1989-1992) and its successor, the Department for Education (1992-1993).

2 Winston Fletcher – Chairman of the Advertising Association and President of the Institute of Practitioners in Advertising. He was founder Chairman of the World Advertising Research Center, a Vice President of the History of Advertising Trust and Visiting Professor of Marketing at the University of Westminster.

3 Alan Moses – A former Lord Justice of Appeal and Court of Appeal Judge, he was appointed as the first Chairman of IPSO (Independent Press Standards Organisation) from 2014-2018. He is joint Chair of the Spoliation Advisory Panel.

4 Edward Faulks QC – A barrister and unaffiliated peer who is the current Chairman of the Independent Press Standards Organisation (IPSO). Formerly a Conservative peer, he was Minister of State for Justice between from 2013-2016.

5 David Stancliffe – A now-retired Church of England bishop, he was Provost of Portsmouth Cathedral from 1982-1993 and the Bishop of Salisbury from 1993-2010. A close friend he was also ex-officio President of Marlborough College. He is an accomplished musician.

6 Peter Inge – Field Marshal. He was the Chief of the General Staff, the professional head of the British Army, from 1992-1994, and then served as Chief of the Defence Staff before retiring in 1997. Early in his military career he saw action during the Malayan Emergency and Operation Banner in Northern Ireland, and later in his career he provided advice to the British Government during the Bosnian War.

7 Alan Turing – Mathematician and computer scientist who is widely considered to be the father of theoretical computer science and artificial intelligence. He first proposed

the principle of the modern computer with the Turing machine, in his seminal 1936 paper *On Computable Numbers*. He tragically committed suicide in 1954, in the aftermath of his prosecution as a homosexual by the British government.

8 Waverley criteria – The criteria, established in 1952, that enable the Reviewing Committee on the Export of Works of Art to assess whether an object may be allowed to leave the UK. If an object meets one or more of the criteria, it is deemed a "national treasure" and an export bar on the object is established.

9 Cary Fukunaga – An American filmmaker who first gained recognition for writing and directing the 2009 film *Sin Nombre*. In 2014 he won the Primetime Emmy Award for Outstanding Directing for a Drama Series for the HBO series *True Detective*. His films have included *Jane Eyre* (2011), *Beasts of No Nation* (2015) and the 25th James Bond film, *No Time to Die* (2021).

CHAPTER 11:
Government Service in Retrospect

1 1944 Education Act – Also known as the "Butler Act", after the then President of the Board of Education, RA Butler, it made major changes in the provision and governance of secondary schools in England and Wales, ending the fees the general public had to pay for secondary education.

2 TA Critchley – He was Principal Private Secretary to Rab Butler as Home Secretary. In 1963 he was appointed as Secretary to Lord Denning's enquiry into the Profumo Affair. He spent a significant amount of his career in the Police Department of the Home Office where he was credited with modernising the Police Force.

CHAPTER 12:
A Sense of Place

1 Barbara Brooke – She entered politics as a member of Hampstead Council (1948-1965) and was a Joint Vice-chairman of the Conservative Party from 1954-1964. She was also active in a number of health organisations, including the North West Metropolitan Regional Hospital Board (1954-1966), The Queen's Institute of District Nursing (1961-1971) and the North London Hospital Management Committee (1963-1966). More importantly she was a wonderful friend and neighbour.

2 Henry Brooke – Conservative MP for Hampstead (1950-1966). Chief Secretary to the Treasury and Paymaster-General from 1961-1962, then Home Secretary from 1962-

1964 under Harold Macmillan.

3 Homington – A small village on the River Ebble in the Chalke Valley, just off the A354 that runs from Salisbury to Blandford Forum.

4 Earl Radnor - Jacob Pleydell-Bouverie, 8th Earl of Radnor. From 1971 to 2008 he served as Governor of the French Hospital in Rochester, Kent. He was a knowledgeable custodian of an exceptional collection of Old Master paintings at Longford Castle near Salisbury.

5 Joe Fison – An Anglican Bishop who held residentiary canonries at Rochester Cathedral (1945–1952) and Truro Cathedral (1952–1959) before moving to Cambridge to be Vicar of the Great St Mary's (1959-1963) and finally becoming Bishop of Salisbury (1963-1972).

6 Brian Clarke – Painter, architectural artist and printmaker, known for his large-scale stained glass and mosaic projects, symbolist paintings, set designs, and collaborations with major figures in modern and contemporary architecture.

7 Ptolemy Dean – Architect, television presenter and the 19th Surveyor of the Fabric of Westminster Abbey. He specialises in historic preservation, as well as designing new buildings that are in keeping with their historic or natural settings. He is best known for his appearances on two BBC television series, *Restoration and The Perfect Village.*

8 June Osborne – As the Dean of Salisbury from 2004-2017 she was the first woman to head one of England's medieval cathedrals. In 2014, after the vote to allow for the consecration of women as bishops, there was speculation that she could become the first female bishop in the Church of England. She has served as the Bishop of Llandaff since 2017.

9 Nick Papadopoulos – After studying law at City University he worked as a barrister practising criminal law for seven years before studying for ordination at Ripon College. He was the vicar of St Peter's Church, Eaton Square (2007-2013), then Canon Treasurer of Canterbury Cathedral (2013-2018). He has been Dean of Salisbury since 2018.

10 Nicholas Holtam – From 1995-2011 he was the vicar of St Martin-in-the-Fields, where he initiated and led a £36 million buildings renewal. He served as Bishop of Salisbury from 2011-2021.

11 Ledger Stone – An inscribed stone slab usually laid into the floor of a church to commemorate or mark the place of the burial of an important deceased person.

12 Frank Field – Labour MP for Birkenhead for 40 years, from 1979 to 2019. He served as Minister of Welfare Reform (1997-1998) in Tony Blair's government and was Chair of the Work and Pensions Select Committee from 2015-2019.

13 William Pye – British sculptor known particularly for his water sculptures. He has had

major commissions at The Southbank Centre, Gatwick Airport and the All-England Club, Wimbledon. He was elected Honorary Fellow of the Royal Institute of British Architects in 1993.

14 Order of the Bath – A British order of chivalry founded by George I on 18 May 1725. The name derives from the elaborate medieval ceremony for appointing a knight, which involved bathing (as a symbol of purification) as one of its elements. The knights so created were known as "Knights of the Bath". Members belong to either the Civil or the Military Division.

15 Mike Jackson – Commander of NATO's Allied Rapid Reaction Corps (1997-2000) in the Balkans. On his return he became Commander-in-Chief, Land Command (2000-2003) and Chief of the General Staff (2003-2006).

16 Jeremy Davies – Canon Precentor of Salisbury Cathedral for 26 years from 1985-2011. He was brought up in Cardiff, as a Welsh-speaking Baptist until the age of seven, when he was baptised into the Anglican church. He was a chorister at Llandaff cathedral. He read English literature as a choral scholar at Corpus Christi College, Cambridge.

17 Desmond Tutu – Archbishop of Cape Town from 1986-1996, the first black African to hold the position. He played a critical role in the overthrow of apartheid in South Africa and was a world-leading human rights activist.

18 David Willcocks – British choral conductor, organist, composer and music administrator. He was particularly well known for his association with the Choir of King's College, Cambridge, which he directed from 1957 to 1974, making frequent broadcasts and recordings.

19 River Ebble – The smallest of the five chalk streams running into the Avon at Salisbury. Rising at Alvediston to the west of the city, it joins the River Avon at Bodenham, near Nunton, to the south east.

CHAPTER 13:
Boy on a Bicycle – A Cambridge Childhood

1 Roger Norrington – English conductor known for historically informed performances of Baroque, Classical and Romantic music. He was music director of the Kent Opera (1969-1984), the London Classical Players (1978-1997), and the Orchestra of St. Luke's in New York (1990-1994), as well as principal conductor of the Bournemouth Sinfonietta (1985-1989). In Europe, he was principal conductor of the Camerata Salzburg (1997-2006), and the Stuttgart Radio Symphony Orchestra (1998-2011).

2 Richard Norman – British academic, philosopher and humanist. He is currently

Emeritus Professor of Moral Philosophy at the University of Kent, and Vice-President of Humanists UK.

3 Tony Lock - English cricketer who played primarily as a left-arm spinner. He played in 49 Tests for England taking 174 wickets. He played his county cricket firstly for Surrey (1946-1963) and then for Leicestershire (1965-1967).

4 Jim Laker – English right-arm off break bowler who played in 46 Tests for England. Laker is generally regarded as one of the greatest spin bowlers in cricket history. In 1956, he achieved a still-unequalled world record when he took nineteen (of a maximum twenty) wickets in a Test match at Old Trafford.

5 Ray Lindwall – Australian cricketer who played in 61 Tests from 1946 to 1960. He is widely regarded as one of the greatest fast bowlers of all time. A right-arm fast bowler of express pace, he modelled his action on the great England fast bowler Harold Larwood.

6 Roger Waters – English musician, singer-songwriter and composer. In 1965 he co-founded the progressive rock band Pink Floyd. He initially served as the bassist, but following the departure of singer-songwriter Syd Barrett in 1968 he also became their lyricist, co-lead vocalist and conceptual leader until his departure in 1983.

CHAPTER 14:
University Life – Cambridge and Yale

1 Alastair Goodlad – British politician who served as Chief Whip of the House of Commons (1995-1997) and British High Commissioner to Australia (2000-2005). He was Conservative MP for Eddisbury (formerly Northwich) from 1974-1999.

2 Geoffrey Elton - A German-born, British political and constitutional historian, specialising in the Tudor period. He taught at Clare College, Cambridge, and was the Regius Professor of Modern History from 1983-1988.

3 Duncan Robinson – art historian and academic, he was the Director of the Fitzwilliam Museum from 1995-2007 and the Master of Magdalene College, Cambridge, from 2002-2012. He moved to the USA when he retired and, sadly, died on 2 December 2022.

4 Haight Ashbury – A district of San Francisco, named for the intersection of Haight and Ashbury streets. The neighbourhood is known as one of the main centres of the counterculture of the 1960s, particularly over the 1967 'Summer of Love', when as many as 100,000 young people from converged on the neighbourhood from across America.

INDEX

Page numbers followed by *n* refer to footnotes

Academy Awards 199*n*, 200*n*
Addington Palace, Surrey, Royal School
    of Church Music 179–80
Adelaide, Australia 36
advertising, self-regulation 94–5, 142–3
Advertising Association 205*n*
Advertising Standards Authority (ASA)
    140–2, 200*n*
Advertising Standards Board of Finance
    (ASBOF) 140
Africa 167
Agra, Taj Mahal 50
Air Tanzania, aircraft hijacking 38–9
Airlie, David Ogilvy, Earl of 84
Aitken, Jonathan 198*n*
Albert, Prince Consort 147
Alderney 117
Allen of Abbeydale, Philip Allen, Baron
    14
Alvediston, Wiltshire 209*n*
Anglesey 15
Anglo-American Legal Exchange 116
apartheid 201*n*, 208*n*
Aqaba, Jordan 147
The Archers 180
Arizona 187
Armstrong, Sir Robert (later Baron
    Armstrong of Ilminster) 18, 31,
    67, 167
Arts Council 86, 145, 196*n*, 203*n*
    Export Licensing Unit 145
Arts Council England 198*n*
Arundells, Salisbury, Wiltshire 167
Ashby, Sir Eric (later Baron Ashby) 186
Ashton, Sir Frederick 67
Asquith, H H (Herbert Henry Asquith,
    1st Earl of Oxford and Asquith)
    193*n*

Attenborough, Richard Attenborough,
    Baron 98–9
Attlee, Clement Attlee, 1st Earl 191*n*
Australia 36–7, 181, 209*n*
Avon, River 165, 174
Aylsham, Norfolk 185

BAFTA (British Academy of Film and
    Television Arts) 199*n*
Baker of Dorking, Kenneth Baker, Baron
    196*n*
Bakewell, Joan (later Baroness Bakewell)
    126
Ball, Simon 106
Ballets Russes 67
Baltic states 115
Banana, Canaan 44
Bangladesh 51–3
Bank of England 195*n*, 203*n*
Barbury Castle, Wiltshire 88
Barcelona, Olympic Games 81
Barclays Bank 195*n*
Barrett, Syd 209*n*
Bath,
    Holburne Museum 144, 145
    Theatre Royal 145
Bath, Order of the 168
Bauwens, Mona 81
BBC 97, 98, 121–2, 153, 194*n*
    New Delhi 194*n*
    World Service 51
BBC2 203*n*
Beasts of No Nation (film) 206*n*
Beijing 113
    Peking University 114
Belfast 135
Bell Pottinger 196*n*
Bell, Timothy (Tim)

(later Baron Bell) 80
Bellotto, Bernardo, *The Fortress of König-stein from the North* 147
Beloff, Michael 103–4
Bemerton, Wiltshire 169
Bennett, RF 185
Benson, Lady 37
Benson, William 164
Berlin, Checkpoint Charlie 13
Bermuda 194*n*
Bernier, François 66
Bessborough, Madeleine, Countess 171
Bhutan, Supreme Court 114
Bichard, Michael (later Baron Bichard) 100
'Big Bang' 192*n*
Biggles books (W E Johns) 180
Biggs, Kate (grandmother) 176
Bin Laden, Osama 37
Bingham of Cornhill, Tom Bingham, Baron 11, 109
Birkenhead 207*n*
Birmingham 40, 55
    IRA bombing 11
    Stechford constituency 11
Blackstone, Tessa Blackstone, Baroness 64
Blair, Cherie (née Booth) 200*n*
Blair, Tony (later Sir Tony) 120
    and author 135
    and Derry Irvine 110, 117-18, 124
    and "Football Task Force" 196*n*
    Frank Field and 207*n*
    and liberal reform 14, 155
    and Lord Chancellor's Department 111–12
    and Millennium Dome 1, 92
    and party funding 134–5, 138
    Peter Mandelson and 199*n*
    and post of Cabinet Secretary 100, 195*n*, 200*n*
    and review of Honours System 123
    succeeded by Gordon Brown 137
Blake, Robert Blake, Baron 64–5
Bletchley Park, Buckinghamshire 156
"Bloody Sunday" 202*n*

Blunkett, David (later Baron Blunkett) 111
Board for Social Responsibility 54
Bodenham, Wiltshire 208*n*
Bonham Carter, Mark (later Baron Bonham-Carter) 47
Bonham-Carter, Lady (earlier Leslie Nast) 32, 51, 111
Bonn 13
Bosnian War 205*n*
Bottomley, Virginia (later Baroness Bottomley of Nettlestone) 97–8, 99, 158
Bournemouth Sinfonietta 208*n*
BP 67
Bradford 49, 55, 198*n*
Brexit referendum 10, 146
Breyer, Stephen 116
A Bridge Too Far 200*n*
Bristol University 147
Britain in Europe group 13
British Airways 12
British National (Overseas) Passport 53
Brittan, Leon (later Baron Brittan of Spennithorne) 58–9, 158
broadcasting 33, 79, 82, 100
Broccoli, Barbara 153
Brooke, Peter (later Baron Brooke of Sutton Mandeville) 84–5, 86–7, 88, 95, 97, 158
Brooke of Cumnor, Henry Brooke, Baron 162
Brooke of Ystradfellte, Barbara Brooke, Baroness 162–3
Brown, George (Baron George-Brown) 79
Brown, Gordon 137, 199*n*, 201*n*
The Browning Version (Terence Rattigan) 182
Brussels 15, 20, 31, 138, 160, 192*n*
    Berlaymont building 23, 25
    see also European Commission
BSkyB Television 198*n*
Budapest 115
Budd, Zola 58

Bunker, A R 4, 9
Burger, Lisa 127
Burger, Warren 32
Burton, Richard 129, 169
Butler, R A "Rab" (later Baron Butler of
    Saffron Walden) 155, 206*n*
Butler, Robin (later Baron Butler of
    Brockwell) 68, 78–9, 90, 95, 100,
    101
Butler-Sloss, Elisabeth 104
Byron, George Gordon, Lord 135

Cabinet system (France) 19–20, 29, 138
Caines, Sir John 140
Cairo 28
Calcutt, Sir David 81, 94
Calcutta 52
Caldecott, Andrew 163
Callaghan, James (later Baron Callaghan
    of Cardiff) 7, 16, 17
Calne, Sir Roy 69
Cam, River 168, 186
Cambridge 154, 177–83
    Addenbrooke's Hospital 69, 179
    Cambridgeshire High School for
        Boys 180–3
        Cadet Force 183
        corporal punishment at 181
    Cherry Hinton Road 177
    Engineering Labs 184
    Fitzwilliam Museum 186, 209*n*
    Great St Mary's, University
        Church of 55, 165, 186,
        207*n*
    Lichfield Road 178
    Mill Road hospital 177
    railway station 181
    Rock Road Public Library 180
    Romsey County Junior School
        179–80
    Sedley Taylor Primary School 179
Cambridge, University of 9, 65, 144, 194*n*
    Clare College 168, 179–80, 184–6,
        188
        Choristers Fund 185

        Memorial Court 185
    Corpus Christi College 208*n*
    cricket at 198*n*
    Cricket Club ground (Fenner's)
        180
    hockey and rowing at 186
    Jesus College 182
    King's College Chapel Choir 179,
        208*n*
    Latin Reading Prize 182
    Library 185
    Magdalene College 185, 196*n*,
        209*n*
    Pembroke College 141, 200*n*
    St John's College 196*n*
Camelot Group 87
Camerata Salzburg 208–9*n*
Cameron, David 30, 134, 137, 204*n*, 205*n*
Campbell of Pittenweem, Walter Men-
    zies "Ming" Campbell, Baron
    134
Canaletto (Giovanni Antonio Canal) 95
Candide (Leonard Bernstein) 203*n*
Canova, Antonio,
    Napoleon 149–50
    The Three Graces 94
Canterbury, Cathedral 207*n*
Cape Town 170, 208*n*
Card, Brian 106
Cardiff 27, 135, 194*n*, 208*n*
    Millennium Stadium 91
    Senedd building 198*n*
Carey, George, Archbishop of Can-
    terbury (later Baron Carey of
    Clifton) 93, 101, 105
Carrington, Peter Carington, Baron
    53–4, 159, 170
Carter, Jimmy 27, 37
Cass Business School, London 195*n*
Cathedrals Fabric Commission for En-
    gland 166, 167, 198*n*
Central Television 86
Centre for Management and Policy
    Studies 68
Centre for Studies in Public Policy 195*n*

Chalke Valley, Wiltshire 207*n*
     History Festival 171
Chance, Michael 171
Chandos, Tom (Baron Lyttelton of
     Aldershot) 120
Change UK 198*n*
Channel 4 Television 199*n*
Channel 5 Television 204*n*
Channel Islands 112, 116–17
Chariots of Fire (film) 199*n*
Charles I, King 80
Charles, Prince of Wales (later King
     Charles III) 73, 85, 125, 132–3,
     167, 198*n*
Chartered Institute of Management
     Accountants 204*n*
Charteris, Sir Martin (Baron Charteris of
     Amisfield) 88
Chatsworth House, Derbyshire 100
Chelsea Football Club 200*n*
Cherrapunji 53
Chicago 32
The Children's Newspaper 180
China 26–7, 53, 113–14, 157, 194*n*
     Cultural Revolution 47
     Taiping Rebellion 192*n*
Christie, Linford 81
Church of England 104, 205*n*, 207*n*
     General Synod 54
Church Times 174
Churchill, Sir Winston, papers 90
Churchill, Winston (grandson of Sir
     Winston, "Young Winston") 90
Chuter-Ede of Epsom, James Chuter
     Ede, Baron 10
Cinch cars 142
Civil Aviation Authority 35
Civil List 71, 74
Civil Service 4–5, 62, 66, 76, 121, 158
     day-to-day life in 140
     exams 156
     Margaret Thatcher and 155
     pensions 75
     reform 138, 155
     rise in applications to join 161

Civil Service College 8, 68
Clarke, Brian 166–7
Clarke, Kenneth (later Baron Clarke of
     Nottingham) 12, 69, 74, 196*n*
Clegg, Nicholas "Nick" (later Sir Nich-
     olas) 137
Clinton, Bill 202*n*
Clive, Robert Clive, Baron (Clive of
     India) 61, 79
Clore Foundations 203*n*
Clore-Duffield Foundation 129
Cockerell, Michael 55
Cognita 204*n*
Collins (publishers) 193*n*
Columbia University, New York 33
Committee on Standards of Conduct in
     Public Life 137
Common Agricultural Congress 111
Commonwealth Games 196*n*
Community Relations Commission 194*n*
Condé Nast Publications 192*n*
Conservative Party (UK) 134, 135, 136–8,
     193*n*, 196*n*, 198*n*, 204*n*, 206*n*
     Conferences 47
     general election victory (1992) 78
Conservative Research Association 205*n*
Constable, John 111, 174
constitutional reform 121
Cook, Captain James 148
Cooke, Judith 193*n*
Cornwall, Camilla, Duchess of (later
     Queen Consort) 133, 167
Cornwall, Duchy of, Council 198*n*
The Corrs 93
Cottesloe, John Fremantle, 4th Baron
     128–9
Cottesloe, John Fremantle, 5th Baron
     128–9
Court of Arbitration for Sport (CA)
     200*n*
Courtaulds 203*n*
Courtman, Pat 163–4
Covid-19 pandemic 70, 153, 172
Cracow, City Hall 115
Cradock, Sir Percy 53

Craig, Daniel 153
Cranborne, Robert Gascoyne-Cecil,
	Viscount (later 7th Marquess of
	Salisbury) 106
Cranborne Manor, Dorset 106
Critchley, T A 158
Cromwell, Thomas 185
Cry Freedom (film) 200*n*
Cubbon, Sir Brian 43, 45, 46, 47, 60
Cunningham, Jack (later Baron Cun-
	ningham of Felling) 92
Cup Final 80, 177
Currie, Edwina 51

D-Day landings 170
Daily Express 196*n*
Daily Mail 58, 131
Daily Telegraph 120
Dalí, Salvador, *Lips Sofa* 147
Dancing Diggers 115
Darling, Alastair (later Baron Darling of
	Roulanish) 112
Darling, Nurse 178
Davies, Jeremy 168–9, 169
Davignon, comte Étienne, and comtesse
	22
Davis, David 94
Davyhulme 198*n*
de la Tour, Frances 130
de Sancha, Antonia 80
Dean, Ptolemy 166
Decker, Mary 58
DEGW (architectural practice) 196*n*
Delhi 50, 51
Dellow, John 34, 36
Dench, Dame Judi 151
Denning, Tom Denning, Baron 206*n*
Derby 152
Devonshire, Andrew Cavendish, 11th
	Duke of 99–100
Devonshire, Deborah Cavendish, Duch-
	ess of 99–100
Dhaka 52
Diaghilev, Sergei 195*n*
Diana, Princess of Wales 94, 96–7

Dickson, Will 171
Ditchley Park, Oxfordshire 23–4
Dobinson, Norah 121
Dorfman, Lloyd (later Sir Lloyd) 128
Dorrell, Stephen 91–2, 97
Dorset 165, 172
Dover 190*n*
Drama Desk Awards 204*n*
Dublin 27
Duffield, Dame Vivien 128–9
Duffy, Frank 85
Durham Prison 10

Eagle (comic) 180
East Hendred, Oxfordshire 24–5, 65
East India Company, Civil Service 66
Ebble, River 174, 207*n*
The Economist 194*n*
Eddisbury (constituency) 209*n*
Eden Project, Cornwall 91
Edinburgh 27, 135
Editors' Code Committee 199*n*
Editors' Code of Practice 95
Education Act (1944) 155
Edwards, Andrew 71
Egypt 27–8
Elizabeth II, Queen 32, 43, 85, 105, 108,
	198*n*, 199*n*
Elton, Geoffrey (later Sir Geoffrey),
	*Tudor Revolution in Govern-
	ment* 185
Elvetham Hall, Hampshire 64, 65
Ely, Cambridgeshire 186
	Cathedral 178
Emerson, Professor Michael 25
Empress Elizabeth of Austria Hunter
	Chase 99
England cricket team 209*n*
Englefield Capital 132
English Heritage 91, 149, 196*n*, 198*n*
English National Opera 202*n*
English Schools Lacrosse Final 144
Ennals, David (later Baron Ennals) 7
Environment Agency 200*n*
Equity (trade union) 150

Esmee Fairbairn Foundation 202*n*
Establishment Officers Meeting 75
Estonia 115
Euro 25
European Championships 196*n*
European Commission 17, 20–30, 44,
    115, 157, 192*n*, 193*n*
    Information Directorate 25, 27
    Interpretation Service 27
    Legal Services Directorate 25
    Personnel Appointments Commit-
        tee 26
    Porte Parole 25
European Court of Human Rights 48
European Court of Justice 25, 27
European Monetary System 191*n*
European Monetary Union 25
European Parliament 27
European Union (earlier Common Mar-
    ket; European Economic Com-
    munity; European Community)
    115, 117, 156, 157
    Referendum (1975) 13–14, 24, 57,
        156
    Referendum (2016) 14, 156–7
Evening Standard 43, 100, 196*n*
    British Film Awards 204*n*
Ewart-Biggs, Christopher 193*n*
Eyre, Sir Richard 99
Eyres, Mark 174

Facebook 204*n*
Fagan, Michael 32, 43
Falconer of Thoroton, Charlie Falconer,
    Baron 111, 119–21, 122, 158
Farley, Wiltshire 129
    All Saints church 129, 169
Faro 12
Fassbender, Michael 151
Fatehpur Sikri 50
Faulks, Edward Faulks, Baron 143
Field, Frank (later Baron Field of Birken-
    head) 167
Financial Management Initiative (FMI)
    59

The Financial Times 142, 194*n*, 205*n*
Finney, Tom 177
Fison, Joseph, Bishop of Salisbury 165,
    186
Fletcher, Winston 140
Fletcher, Yvonne 53
Florence 25
Foley, Sir John 117
Foot, Michael 16
foot and mouth disease 172
'Football Task Force' 196*n*
Forbes, Duncan 185
Ford Foundation 203*n*
Forestry Commission 204*n*
Foster, Volnay 32
Fox, Stephen 129
France 24
        Post Office *Tabac* monopoly 26
France, SS 187
Freetown, Gold Coast (now Sierra
        Leone) 176
Fukunaga, Cary 150, 152
Fulton, John, Baron Fulton 190*n*
Fulton Report (1967) 8, 68

G7 meetings 24
Gainsborough, Thomas, *The Byam
        Family* 144
Gambles, Ian 135
Gambon, Michael 130
Gandhi (film) 200*n*
'Gang of Four' 191*n*
Garrick, David 145
Gatwick Airport, West Sussex 208*n*
General Elections,
    (1987) 67
    (1992) 78
    (1997) 97
    (2001) 111, 172
George I, King 208*n*
George III, King 148, 163
George VI, King 188
Germany 13, 24
Gibraltar 176
Gilligan, Andrew 121

Gilmour, Ian (later Baron Gilmour of
    Craigmillar) 15
Gimson, Andrew, "Charming wit or oily
    Welshman?" 130–1
Giscard d'Estaing, Valéry 17
Glamorgan 194*n*
Glamour 193*n*
Glyndebourne Festival Opera 203*n*
Goodlad, Alastair (later Baron Goodlad)
    184
Goodman, Arnold Goodman, Baron 86
Goodman, Derrick & Co. 196*n*
Gordon, Charles George 28
government departments,
    Agriculture, Fisheries and Food
        199*n*
    Cabinet Office 60, 79, 112, 118–19,
        122, 133, 138, 199*n*, 200*n*,
        204*n*
        Briefing Room (COBR,
            COBRA) 34, 38, 50
        Capability Review 201*n*
        Civil Service College 61, 65
        Next Steps reform pro-
            gramme 68, 71, 75–6
        room in Treasury building
            61, 79
        Summer Node 62, 67–8
        Top Management Pro-
            gramme 60–8, 130
        Training Division 61
    Constitutional Affairs 201*n*
    Defence 121, 193*n*, 202*n*
    Economic Affairs 79
    Education 71, 79, 86, 192*n*, 200*n*,
        205*n*
    Environment 79, 100
    Foreign and Commonwealth
        Office, Overseas Develop-
        ment Administration 205*n*
    Foreign Office 13, 14, 17, 19, 20, 21,
        50, 53, 98, 192*n*
    Health and Social Security 71, 198*n*
    Home Office,
        Administrative Class 5, 8

and animal welfare 191*n*
and author's visit to US 32
author's application for lead-
    ership of 100–1, 148
Brian Cubbon at 43, 45,
    46-7
and broadcasting 33, 79, 82
and Channel Islands 116–17
David Blunkett at 111
David Mellor at 94
Executive Class 5
expenditure 71
Jack Straw and 108
leadership of 100–1, 158
Lord Hailsham and 42
Mrs Thatcher's visit to 33
Police Department 8, 31–45,
    206*n*
Princess Diana and 97
Prison Service 77
and public expenditure 73
Roy Jenkins at 9–29, 110
see also Phillips, Sir Hayden,
    at Home Office
Immigration and Nationality De-
    partment (IND) 46–60,
    157, 162–3
and Judicial Review 58
Justice 113, 202*n*, 204*n*
    Crown Office 105
Legal Department, *The Judge over
    Your Shoulder* 59
Lord Chancellor's Department
    (LCD; later Department
    for Constitutional Affairs;
    Ministry of Justice) 58, 71,
    101, 103–24, 130, 185*n*
"Concordat" 121, 122–3
proposed abolition of office
    of Lord Chancellor
    119, 122
renamed 112, 120, 122
Metropolitan Police, Programme
    Budgeting System 8
National Heritage (later Digital,

Culture, Media and Sport, DCMS) 78–101, 130, 149, 196*n*
   renamed 94, 96
   search for headquarters 82–3
Northern Ireland 71, 193*n*, 201*n*
Office of Arts and Libraries 71, 79
Power 5
Private Office 7–8, 18–20, 29, 80, 138
Public Administration Committee 123
Scotland Office 71, 112, 135
Social Security 195*n*
Trade and Industry 60, 79
Transport 201*n*
Treasury 82–3, 98, 200*n*, 201*n*, 202*n*, 204*n*
   author at 5, 8, 68–77, 88, 130, 138
   author speaks at 59–60
   building 61
   and Financial Management Initiative 59
   and Lottery funds 149
   permanent secretaries 2
   and Roy Jenkins 16
   Solicitor's Department 202*n*
Wales Office 71, 112, 195*n*, 201*n*
Work and Pensions 201*n*
   Select Committee 208*n*
Government Legal Service 202*n*
Grammy awards 196*n*
Granada Television 203*n*
Grange Festival Opera 171
Granta, River 186
Grantchester, Cambridgeshire 178, 186
Great Exhibition (1851) 91
Great Seal of the Realm 201*n*, 202*n*
Great Storm (1987) 65
Greece 157
Greenwich, University of 195*n*
Griffiths, Brian (later Baron Griffiths of Fforestfach) 69
Griffiths, Richard 130

The Guardian 142, 198*n*
Guernsey 117
Guilin, China 113
Gunnell, Sally 81

Haddon Hall, Derbyshire 150, 151
Haferkamp, Wilhelm 26–7
Hailsham of St Marylebone, Quintin Hogg, Baron 42
Hain, Peter (later Baron Hain) 112
Halifax 191*n*
Hall, Sir Peter 127
Hamburg 13
Hancock, Dame Sheila 196*n*
Hanson, James Hanson, Baron 63, 125, 130–2
Hanson, Robert 132
Hanson Transport 132
Hanson Trust 204*n*
Hanson Westhouse (later Westhouse) 132
Hare, Sir David 127
Harrow School, London 195*n*
Hart, Garry (later Baron Hart of Chilton) 110–11
Hartlepool 199*n*
Harvard University, Massachusetts 21, 188
   Law School 202*n*
Hay-on-Wye 16
HBO 206*n*
Healey, Denis (later Baron Healey) 16
health expenditure 74
Heart of the Matter (TV series) 203*n*
Heath, Edward (Ted) (later Sir Edward) 8, 14, 16, 45, 55, 64–5, 164, 167, 192*n*, 193*n*
   stone in Salisbury Cathedral 167
Hegel, Friedrich 185
Henderson, Sir John Nicholas "Nico" 13
   Mandarin 191*n*
   The Private Office 19–20
Henderson, Lady (Mary) 13
Hennessy, Peter (later Baron Hennessy of Nympsfield) 49, 55

Herbert, George 169
Heseltine, Michael (later Baron Heseltine)
    91, 92
Heywood, Jeremy (later Baron Heywood of
    Whitehall) 71
Highways England 142
History of Advertising Trust 205*n*
The History Boys (Alan Bennett) 128, 129,
    204*n*
Hogg, Sir Christopher 126
Holtam, Nicholas, Bishop of Salisbury
    166–7, 174
Homington, Wiltshire,
    Homington Farm 106, 110–11, 164–5,
    171–4
    St Mary's church 169
Hong Kong 53
Hong Kong Act (1985) 53
Honours System 121, 123
horseracing 98–100
Horsham 205*n*
House & Garden 193*n*
House of Lords Act (1999) 106
Household Cavalry 43
Howard, Michael (later Baron Howard of
    Lympne) 77
Hudson, River 187
Hull 40
    University of 200*n*
Humanists UK 209*n*
Hungary 115
Hurd of Westwell, Douglas Hurd, Baron 12
Hutton, Brian Hutton, Baron, Hutton
    Report 121–2
Hytner, Nicholas (later Sir Nicholas) 127,
    128, 129–30, 171–2

Iceland 150
immigration 54–7, 73, 157
    and arranged marriages 47–9
Immigration Appeal Tribunals 59
Imperial Group 204*n*
The Independent 142
Independent Press Standards Organisation
    (IPSO) 82, 142–3, 199*n*

Appointments Panel 95
Complaints Committee 143
Foundation Group 142
India 114–15, 194*n*
    Civil Service 66
    Holi festival 72
    Supreme Court 114
Indian subcontinent 47, 49–53
Inge, Peter Inge, Baron 144
Innes, Bill 10
Inspector Morse (TV series) 86
Institute of Contemporary British History
    194*n*
Institute for Government 75, 200*n*, 205*n*
Institute of Jamaica 196*n*
Institute for Jewish Policy Research 198*n*
Institute of Practitioners in Advertising
    205*n*
International Olympic Committee 200*n*
Iowa 32
IRA (Irish Republican Army) 9, 10, 43,
    193*n*
Irvine, Lady 111
Irvine of Lairg, Derry Irvine, Baron 101–2,
    103–5, 113–15, 157–8
    author's friendship with 124, 158
    removal as Lord Chancellor 109,
        118–19
Islam, Sunni and Shia
denominations 35
Islamabad 50
Isle of Man 112, 116–17
Italy 25, 157

Jackson, Sir Mike 168, 169
James Hutton Institute 204*n*
James, P D (Phyllis White) 7
Jane Eyre (film) 150–2
Japan 37
Jellicoe, George Jellicoe, 2nd Earl 45
Jenkins, Dame Jennifer (later Baroness
    Jenkins) 12, 95, 105, 111
Jenkins, Paul (later Sir Paul) 113
Jenkins, Roy (later Baron Jenkins of Hill-
    head),

appoints author as his PPS 10, 17,
    138
author's friendship with 111, 158
and author's oath of allegiance to
    Queen 105
and author's visit to US 32
and Birmingham bombings 40
at Bletchley Park 156
Cabinet 19–21, 29, 192*n*
as Chancellor of the Exchequer 29,
    157–8, 158
as Chancellor of Oxford University
    64–5
and Christopher Soames 44
gives dinner for Tony Blair 100
as Home Secretary 9–29, 110
as President of European Commis-
    sion 17, 20–9
Private Office 7–8, 18–20, 29, 138
and SDP 191*n*
on Syd Norris 190*n*
European Diary 29
Jenkins, Simon (later Sir Simon) 95
Jersey 117
John, St, Gospel of 165
Johnson, Boris 10
Johnson, Samuel 124
Jones, Sir William 66
Joséphine de Beauharnais, Empress of
    France 199*n*
Joyner, Alfred (grandfather) 176
Judicial Appointments Advisory Com-
    mission 109, 118–19
JW3 (Jewish Community Centre Lon-
    don) 203*n*

Kalinka (Russian folk song) 188
Kelly, David 121–2
    family 121–2
Kemp, Peter 68, 74, 76
Kennedy, Edward 32
Kennet, River 163
Kent, University of 180, 209*n*
Kent Opera 208*n*
Kentucky Fried Chicken 142

Kenya colony 201*n*
Khartoum, International Trade Fair 28
The Killing Fields 199*n*
King, Sir John (later Lord King of
    Wartnaby) 12
Kinnock, Neil (later Baron Kinnock)
    69–70
Kobbé's Complete Opera Book 173
Königswinter Conference (Bonn, 1975)
    13
Kottawallah, Mr 51
Koussa, Moussa 54

Labour Party (UK) 14, 16, 17, 28, 92,
    96, 135, 136–7, 191*n*, 199*n*, 200*n*,
    202*n*
    as New Labour 111
Lahore 50
Lake Forest, Illinois 32
Laker, Jim 181
Lamb, Lady Caroline 135
Lamont, Norman (later Baron Lamont
    of Lerwick) 74
Lancaster House Agreement 194*n*
Larwood, Harold 209*n*
Last Night of the Proms 115
Late Night Line-Up (TV series) 203*n*
Latvia 115
Laurence Olivier Awards 203*n*, 204*n*
Law Commission 202*n*
Lawrence, D H, *Lady Chatterley's Lover*
    147
Lawrence, T E 147
Lawson, Nigel (later Baron Lawson of
    Blaby) 17, 68–9, 70, 71–2, 76
Leagrave, Bedfordshire 176
Leeds 40, 55
Legal Year, Service to open 104
Legg, Sir Thomas 59, 119
The Lehman Trilogy (Massini) 203*n*
Leicester, Edward Coke, 7th Earl of 149
Leicester City Police 190*n*
Leicestershire County Cricket Club
    209*n*
Lester, Anthony (later Baron Lester of

Herne Hill) 9, 110
Letts, Quentin 131–2
Leveson Report 82, 95, 142, 199*n*
Liberal Democrats (UK) 134, 135, 136, 191*n*, 198*n*, 204*n*
Liberal Party (UK) 191*n*, 193*n*
Libya, Intelligence Services 54
Light, Marcus 172
Lincoln Cathedral 166
Lincolnshire 191*n*
Lindwall, Ray 181
Lithuania 115
Littlecote, Buckinghamshire, fishing syndicate 163
Llandaff 207*n*
Cathedral 208*n*
local government finance 71
Lock, Tony 181
Lofthouse, Nat 177
Lomax, Rachel 72
London,
All-England Club, Wimbledon 80, 208*n*
Apsley House 82–3
Wellington Collection 149–50
Balcombe Street siege 34
Bankside Power Station 90
Banqueting House, Whitehall 80
Battersea 145
Battersea Arts Centre 203*n*
Battersea Park 144
Blackstone Chambers 200*n*
Brent 55
Bridge Theatre 203*n*
British Library 91, 166
British Museum 98, 196*n*
Brixton prison 10
Brixton riots 39–40, 41
Brooks's (gentlemen's club) 10, 11–12, 177
Buckingham Palace 43, 85, 86, 96
Bush Theatre 203*n*
Canary Wharf 95
Central Hall, Westminster 44

City, University of London 207*n*
Clarence House 132, 140
Claridge's 36
Cockspur Street 83
Covent Garden 86
Croydon 46–7
Lunar House 47, 48, 56, 61
Dover House 135
Elizabeth House 83
Garrick Club 140
and Great Storm (1987) 65
Greater London Council 191*n*
Hamleys toy shop 11
Hampstead 208*n*
Council 206*n*
Heathrow airport 35, 55
High Court of Justice 201*n*
Horse Guards Parade 94, 95, 95–6
House of Commons 10, 16, 41, 119, 135, 191*n*, 209*n*
Public Administration Committee 123
Select Committee 198*n*
House of Lords 14, 41–2, 92, 105–6, 158, 166, 191*n*, 194*n*, 202*n*
Law Lords 116, 118
Woolsack 105, 120
Houses of Parliament, State Opening 104–5, 148
Hyde Park 35, 43, 97
Inner Temple 104
IRA bombings 43
Iranian embassy terrorist siege 34–6, 37
Islington South and Finsbury (constituency) 200*n*
Kensington Palace 96–7
King's Bench Walk Chambers 200*n*
King's Road 46, 102, 152
Lambeth Palace 158
Lanesborough Hotel 82
Libyan People's Bureau 53–4
Lloyd's building 198*n*

Lord Mayor 104
Lord's Cricket Ground 5
The Mall 86, 95, 96
Marylebone Cricket Club 198*n*
Metropolitan Police 39, 44, 45,
        190*n*
        Catering Department 38
Middlesex Guildhall 116
Millennium Dome 91–3, 95, 198*n*
Montessori primary school 34
Mosimann's Club 132
National Army Museum 147
National Gallery 73, 83, 95, 98,
        146, 147, 196*n*
National Theatre 72, 89, 124, 138,
        140, 144–5, 150, 203*n*
        Board 126–8, 145
        Cottesloe Room 128–9
        Cottesloe Theatre (later
                Dorfman Theatre)
                128–9
        Finance Committee 127
        Lyttelton Theatre 138
        "NT Live" 128
        Olivier Theatre 138
No 1 Knightsbridge 82
Northumberland Avenue 99
parking law enforcement 8
Parliament Square 116
RAF Club 190*n*
Regent's Park 43
Regent's Park Mosque 35
Rose Theatre Kingston 203*n*
Royal Albert Hall 153
Royal Ballet 203*n*
Royal Collection 149
Royal College of Art 196*n*
Royal Courts of Justice 104, 124
        Great Hall 124
Royal Festival Hall 86
Royal Opera House 94, 98, 203*n*
Royal Parks 95, 96–7, 199*n*
Royal School of Needlework 34
Royal Shakespeare Company 203*n*
St James's Palace 96, 132, 133

St James's Park 61, 79, 86, 95
St James's Street 177
St John's, Smith Square 116, 182
St Martin-in-the-Fields 207*n*
St Paul's Cathedral 90
        Millennium Service 105
Savile Row 156
Seaman's Church, Battersea 30
Southbank Centre 203*n*, 208*n*
Spaghetti House siege 34
Stock Exchange 198*n*
Tate Modern 90, 198*n*
10 Downing Street 96, 97
Tower of London, White Tower 11
Trafalgar Square 83, 96
Twickenham Studios 99
University of Westminster 205*n*
US embassy 37
Victoria & Albert Museum 89, 145,
        147, 181
Victoria Gardens 158
Victoria Memorial 86
visits by European Commission
        officials 27
wartime bombing 150
Waterloo station 93
Wembley Stadium 14
Westminster Abbey 96, 97, 207*n*
        Henry VII Chapel 168
Westminster Cathedral 204*n*
White's (gentlemen's club) 177
London Assurance (Dion Boucicault)
        129
London Classical Players 208*n*
London, University of, Birkbeck College
        64, 195*n*
Longford Castle, Wiltshire 73, 111, 164,
        165
Louth, Co. 199*n*
Luton, Bedfordshire 167, 178
Luton Town Football Club 176–7
Lutyens, Sir Edwin 51, 114
Luxembourg 27
Luxor 28

Macaulay Report (1854) 66
McDonald, Andrew 135
MacGregor, Neil 73, 95, 99, 145
Machinery of Government changes 118
Macmillan, Harold (1st Earl of Stockton)
    208n
Macmillan Cancer 120
McNee, Sir David (Commissioner of
    Metropolitan Police) 39
Madrid, Carmen Thyssen-Bornemisza
    Collection 73
Magee, Ian 108
Magistrates' Courts 112
Magna Carta 166
Magnus, Sir Laurie 149
Major, John (later Sir John),
        cabinet members 194n, 196n,
        198n, 200n
        as Chancellor of the Exchequer
        75
        and David Mellor 80
        and Department of National
        Heritage 78
        friendship with author 158
        and National Lottery 89
        and Peter Brooke 84
        and post of Cabinet Secretary 100
        and press regulation 95
        and public expenditure 72-3
        and Treasury 83
        and Windsor Castle restoration
        85
Malayan Emergency and Operation
    Banner 205n
Manchester 55
    Moss Side riots 40, 41, 159
Mandela, Nelson 109
Mandelson, Peter (later Baron Mandel-
    son) 92, 100, 158
Mao Zedong 47
Margaret and Lionel (South African
    guests) 109
Mark, Sir Robert 8
Marks & Spencer 63
Marlborough College, Malaysia 143

Marlborough College, Wiltshire 143-4,
    180, 205n
Marlborough, Wiltshire, Ducks Toy Shop
    163
Martinware pottery 147
Matthews, Stanley 177
Maude, Francis (later Baron Maude of
    Horsham) 138
Maugham, W. Somerset 145
Maureen (friend) 170
Mayhew, Patrick (later Baron Mayhew of
    Twysden) 42
MCC (Marylebone Cricket Club) 90
Megalayah 50, 53
Melbourne, William Lamb, Viscount 135
Mellon, Paul 187
Mellor, David 79, 80-3, 94, 97
Melody Radio 130
Memphis Belle 199n
Messums Wiltshire 171
Mexico 192n
Middleton, Sir Peter 68, 71, 74-5, 77
Midnight Express 199n
Mildenhall, Wiltshire,
        Glebe House 162-4
        Roman's Halt 163
        St John the Baptist 163-4, 174
Mill, John Stuart 66
Millennium celebrations 87, 88, 91, 105,
    111
Millennium Commission 91, 196n
Mills, Dame Barbara 195n
Milton, John 182
Minerva Medal 198n
Monetary Policy Committee 195n
Monnet, Jean 25
Montefiore, Hugh, Bishop 54, 55, 186
Moore, John (later Baron Moore of
    Lower Marsh) 69, 72
Morgan, J P, International Advisory
    Council 203n
Mortenson, Stan 177
Moses, Sir Alan 143
Moses (play) 182
Moule, C M W 185

Mowl, Mrs 177
Moy, Bob 121
Mueller, Anne (later Dame Anne) 67,
    74–5
Mugabe, Robert 44
Mugg, Isle of 19
Munich 27
Murray-Threipland, Tertius and Clare
    164
Muslims, Uighur 113

Napoleon I, Emperor 149–50, 199*n*
Nast, Condé 32–3
National Archives 204*n*
National Audit Office (NAO) 89
National Health Service (NHS) 68–70,
    76, 89, 176, 185
National Heritage Memorial Fund
    (NHMF) 88, 199*n*
National Kidney Research Fund 202*n*
National Land Fund 196*n*
National Lottery 79, 87–90, 149, 198*n*
National Lottery Charities Commission
    89
National Lottery Heritage Fund 90, 93,
    198*n*
Native Americans 187, 188
NATO 194*n*
    Allied Rapid Reaction Corps 208*n*
Navajo people 187
Naylor, Georgina 93
Nesta (charity) 203*n*
New Delhi 194*n*
    Government Offices 114
    Presidential Palace 114–15
    Rashtrapati Bhavan 114
New Haven Army Depot 189
New Mexico 32
New York City 32, 33, 186–7
    Orchestra of St. Luke's 208*n*
    September 11 attacks 113
    Statue of Liberty 187
New York Times 171
New Yorker 193*n*
Newnham, Cambridgeshire 178

Nile, River 28
Nimeiri, Jaafar 28
No Time to Die (film) 152–3
Noel, Emile 26, 29
Norfolk County Cricket Club 185
Norman, Richard 180
Norrington, Sir Roger 179
Norris, Syd 9, 10
North Korea 157
North London Hospital Management
    Committee 206*n*
North Sea oil rigs 34
North Warwickshire (constituency) 205*n*
North West Metropolitan Regional
    Hospital Board 206*n*
Northcote–Trevelyan Report (1854) 66
Northern Ireland 10, 113, 205*n*
Norwich North 190*n*
NT Live broadcasts 128
Nubian Desert 28
Number 10 Policy Unit 195*n*
Nuneham Courtenay, Oxfordshire 64,
    67
Nunton, Wiltshire, Radnor Arms 164

Oak Furniture Land 141
Obey, André, *Noah* 182
O'Driscoll, Brian 193*n*
Oflot (Office of the National Lottery)
    87
Oh! What a Lovely War (film) 200*n*
Old Trafford Cricket Ground, Greater
    Manchester 209*n*
Olivier, Laurence 127
Olympic Games 196*n*
    (1984) 58
    (1992) 81
Omai (Mai) 148
One Man, Two Guvnors (Richard Bean)
    128
Ootacamund 51
Orme, Robert 66
Ormerod, Mark 123
Osborne, June 166
Outer Critics Circle Award 204*n*

Owen, David Owen, Baron 191*n*
Owen, Syd 177
Oxford, Kenneth (later Sir Kenneth) 40
Oxford, University of 186, 202*n*
    Balliol College 64
    Chancellorship 64–5
    Green College 192*n*
    Magdalen College 99, 116
    St John's College 184
    Trinity College 200*n*

Page, Sir Denys 182
Page, Jennie 91–2
Pakenham, Sir Michael 115
Pakistan 49–50
    Azad Kashmir 49
Palestine Liberation Organization (PLO)
    81
Palitana, Gujarat, Jain temples 50
Palliser, Sir Michael 20
Palmer, Tony 182
Palumbo, Peter Palumbo, Baron 86
Papadopoulos, Nick 166
Paris 27, 191*n*, 195*n*
    Charles de Gaulle airport 12
    Faubourg St Honoré 12
    Musée du Louvre 150
    Pompidou Centre 198*n*
Parris, Matthew 137
party funding 126, 131, 134–8
Pay Review Bodies 75
The People 80
The Perfect Village (TV series) 207*n*
Perth, Australia 36
Peter Hall Company 203*n*
Peterson, Sir Arthur 10, 17
Pevsner, Sir Nikolaus 165–6
Philip, Prince, Duke of Edinburgh 85
Phillips, (?) (grandmother) 175
Phillips, ? (mother) 175–80
Phillips, Alexander (son) 27
Phillips, Cyril (uncle) 177
Phillips, Daisy (née Sutton, paternal
    grandmother) 177
Phillips, Florence (daughter) 32–3, 33,

109, 144, 150, 200*n*
Phillips, Gerald (father) 175–80, 184

Phillips, Sir Hayden,
    birth, childhood and early life
        175–83
    choice of name 175–6
    family's move to Cambridge 177
    love of football 176–7
    as chorister 179–80
    childhood illness 179
    acting at school 182–3
    as head boy at school 183
    teaching post in Norfolk 184–5
    sport at Cambridge 185–6
    awarded Mellon Fellowship 186
    at Yale University 4, 8, 9, 115, 187–9
    and Yale Russian Chorus 187–8
    and American football 188
    Master's degree 189
    return to England 189
    at Cambridge University 165,
        184–6, 194*n*
    at Home Office 1, 4, 5, 7–17, 76,
        112, 132, 158-9
    as PPS to Roy Jenkins 9–17, 138
    Minute on speech-writing 18–19
    at European Commission 20–30
    knowledge of French 20–2, 26
    divorce from first wife 30
    marriage to Laura Grenfell 30
    at Police Department 31–45, 56
    State Department fellowship and
        US trip 32–3
    and anti-terrorism 33–9
    trips to Australia, Japan and USA
        36–7
    as Head of Immigration and
        Nationality Department
        (IND) 46–60, 157, 162–3
    trips to Indian subcontinent 49–53
    illness in Bangladesh 52–3
    as Deputy Secretary of Cabinet
        Office 60
    as Director of Top Management

Programme (TMP) 60–8, 130

at Treasury 70–7, 88, 138

invited to return to Home Office 77

at Department of National Heritage (later Digital, Culture, Media and Sport, DCMS) 78–101, 158

and Windsor Castle fire 84–5

and creation of National Lottery 87–90

unsuccessful application for leadership of Home Office 100–1

at Lord Chancellor's Department 103–24, 130, 132, 195n

as Clerk of the Crown in Chancery 105

as pig farmer 106, 173

eye operations 105

as Permanent Secretary to Scotland and Wales Offices 112–13, 135

visit to China 113–14

visit to India (2003) 113–15

visits to Eastern Europe 115

visits US Supreme Court 116

visits Channel Islands and Isle of Man 116–17

and review of Honours system 123–4

as Permanent Secretary of Department of Constitutional Affairs 120–4

end of Civil Service career 121, 123–4, 155, 158

as Chairman of National Theatre 124, 125–33, 138, 144–5, 150

as consultant to Prince of Wales 125, 132–3

conducts review of party funding 126, 131, 134–8

Times article 136

work with Advertising Standards Authority 140–2

as Chairman of Independent Press Standards Organisation (IPSO) 82, 95, 142–3

as Chairman of Marlborough College 180

as Chairman of Reviewing Committee on the Export of Works of Art and Objects of Cultural Interest 128, 145–9

acting roles in movies 126, 150–3

knighthood 152

purchase of Glebe House 162–4

as Chairman of Salisbury Cathedral Fabric Advisory Committee 166–8, 171

as Lay Canon of Salisbury Cathedral 168–70

performance in *Under Milk Wood* 129, 169–70

as Deputy Lieutenant of Wiltshire 171

and Homington Farm 106, 110–11, 171–4

Phillips, Dorothy Florence, mother known as 'Babs' 175

Phillips, Laura (née Grenfell), in aircraft incident 117

birth of son Tom 67

cast as extra in *Jane Eyre* film 150-3

as chairman of Salisbury International Arts Festival 114, 170

at Ditchley Park 24

family 32–3, 116

at Glebe House 162–3

as High Sheriff of Wiltshire 171

and horse racing 99

and Jennifer Jenkins 12

marriage to author 30

and National Theatre 126

purchase and running of Homington Farm 164, 171–2

as rider 99

travels with author 21, 32–3, 50–1

Phillips, Louisa (daughter) 92, 93, 133, 144
Phillips, Peter (cousin) 177
Phillips, Rachel (daughter) 93
Phillips, Tom (son) 67, 143–4
Phillips of Worth Matravers, Nick Phillips, Baron 142
Picasso, Pablo 29
Pie in the Sky (film) 204*n*
The Pilgrim Trust 199*n*
Pinewood Studios, Buckinghamshire 152
Pink Floyd 181
Pinochet, Augusto 202*n*
Pius II, Pope (Piccolomini) 185
Pleydell-Bouverie, Jane 171
Poland 115, 191*n*
Police Dependents' Trust 7
Policy Studies Institute 195*n*
Poniatowski, Michel 12
Pontormo, Jacopo, *Portrait of a Young Man in a Red Cap* 146
Popplewell, Sir Oliver 90
Porgy and Bess 196*n*
Portsmouth Cathedral 205*n*
Portugal 12, 157
Powell, Jonathan 134
Press Complaints Commission (PCC) 94, 95, 142, 196*n*, 199*n*
press regulation 94–5, 126
Pressbof 95
Preston 40
Prevention of Terrorism (Temporary Provisions) Act (1974) 11, 45
Price, Marian and Dolours 9–10
Primetime Emmy awards 206*n*
The Prince's Trust 203*n*
Prison Service 76–7
Pritzker Prize 198*n*
Probation Association 202*n*
Profumo affair 206*n*
Prorogation 105
PSBR (public sector borrowing requirement) and PDSR (public sector debt repayment) 74
Public Accounts Committee (PAC) 93

public expenditure 15, 68, 70–5, 71–4, 79, 87–9
Puckeridge, HMS 175
Pugin, A. W. N. 42, 106, 158
Puttnam, David Puttnam, Baron 97, 99
Pye, William 167

Qatar 82–3
Queen magazine 196*n*
Queen Elizabeth, RMS 186
Queen's Counsel ceremony 104
The Queen's Institute of District Nursing 206*n*

Race Relations Board 47, 194*n*
RADA (Royal Academy of Dramatic Art) 200*n*
Radley College, Oxfordshire 143
Radnor, Anne, Countess of 165
Radnor, Jacob Pleydell-Bouverie, 8th Earl of 111, 164
Radnor Collection 73
Ragwort Control Act (2003) 105
Rambert (ballet company) 195*n*
Raverat, Gwen, *Period Piece* 154
Rayner, Derek Rayner, Baron 59, 63–4
Restoration (TV series) 207*n*
Reviewing Committee on the Export of Works of Art and Objects of Cultural Interest 128, 145–8
Waverley Criteria 145, 148
Reynolds, Sir Joshua, *Portrait of Omai* 148–9
Rhodesia 194*n*
Riddell, Peter (later Sir Peter) 137–8
Riga 115
Rio Grande 32
Ripon College, North Yorkshire 207*n*
Rising Damp (TV series) 203–4*n*
RIT Capital Partners plc 198*n*
Roberts, Sir Hugh 149
Robinson, Duncan 186–7
Robinson, Lisa 187
Roche Court, Winterslow, Wiltshire 171
Rochester, Kent,

Cathedral 207n
French Hospital 207n
Rodgers, Silvia (later Baroness Rodgers) 13
Rodgers, William (later Baron Rodgers of Quarry Bank) 13
Rogers of Riverside, Richard Rogers, Baron 91
Rolls, Charles 147
Ronald, Susan 193n
Rose, Michael (later Sir Michael) 34, 35–6, 36, 38, 193n
Ross, Sir Malcolm 96
Rothschild, Jacob Rothschild, Baron 88, 90, 93, 132
Rothschild, N M, & Sons Ltd 204n
Rothschild, Serena Rothschild, Baroness 88
Royal Academy Trust 203n
Royal Air Force 38
Royal Assent 201n
Royal Ballet 195n
Royal Institute of British Architects (RIBA) 208n
RIBA Gold Medal 198n
RIBA Stirling Prize 198n
Royal Opera House Endowment Fund 203n
Royal Parks Review Group 95
Royal School of Church Music 179
Royce, Henry 147
Runcie, Robert, Archbishop of Canterbury 54
Russell Beale, Sir Simon 129, 169

Sainsbury of Preston Candover, Anya, Baroness 199n
Sainsbury of Preston Candover, John Sainsbury, Baron 92
Sainsbury's (supermarket chain) 141, 198n
Salisbury, Wiltshire 102, 110, 152
Cathedral 111, 126, 165–9, 168–71, 208n
Council 166
Fabric Advisory Committee

(FAC) 166–8, 171
Major Repair Programme 167
re-founding anniversary 167
South Canonry 165
as vaccination centre 171
District Hospital 174
International Arts Festival 114, 170
Salvation Army band 164
Salmond, Alex 135
Salvation Army 164
Samode, Rajasthan, India 72
San Diego, California 187
San Francisco, California 202n
Haight-Ashbury 188
'Summer of Love' 209n
Sapri, Campania, Italy 153
Sark 117
Scarman, Leslie Scarman, Baron 39–40
Schmidt, Helmut 17
Scotland 113
Scots Guards 54, 156
Second World War 156, 190n, 194n
Serota, Sir Nicholas 90
Seth, Leila 114
Seth, Vikram 114, 169
Shackleton, Sir Ernest 147
Nimrod expedition 147
Shadowlands (film) 99
Shakespeare, William 171–2, 182
Henry IV Part 2 130
Sheppard of Liverpool, David Sheppard, Baron, Bishop 193n
Better Together and *With Hope in our Hearts* (with Derek Worlock) 193n
Sherborne Abbey, Dorset 165
Shillong 50
Shorthouse, Dominic 132
Silberstein, Dr 179
Sino-British Joint Declaration 194n
Six-Day War 198n
Smith, Chris (later Baron Smith of Finsbury) 97–8, 140, 141, 158
Soames, Christopher Soames, Baron 44

Soames, Mary Soames, Baroness 89, 126
Social Democratic Party (SDP) (UK)
191n
Social Market Foundation 202n
Society of Labour Lawyers 109
Society of London Theatre 203n
Somerset 172
Somerset County Cricket Club 106
South Africa 58, 109, 170, 201n
South West Surrey (constituency) 200n
Southbank Theatre Board 203n
Southern Rhodesia, elections 44
Soviet Union 175
Army 13
Spain 157
special advisers, rise of 158–60
The Spectator 130–1
Spencer, Charles Spencer, Earl 9
Spey, River 163
Spoliation Advisory Panel 205n
Sports Council 87
Stalingrad 175
Stancliffe, David, Bishop of Salisbury 111,
144, 168–9
Stancliffe, Sarah 111
Stanford University, California 202n
Stansted airport 38
Staple, Bill 132
Starbucks 142
Starr, Nick 127
Stevens, Jocelyn (later Sir Jocelyn) 85,
91–2
Stockwood, Mervyn, Bishop 186
Stonham, Victor John Collins, Baron 7
Strasbourg 27
European Court of Human Rights
building 198n
Straw, Jack 101, 108, 138
Straw, Will and Claire 200n
Stretford 198n
Stuart, Nick 26
Stuttgart Radio Symphony Orchestra
209n
Sudan 27–8
Suez Crisis 178

Summerskill, Shirley 10
Sunningdale, Berkshire 61–2
Supreme Court (Offices) Bill
(1997) 104
Surrey County Cricket Club 209n
Sutherland, Francis Egerton, Duke of, art
collection 73
Sylhet 52

Takeover Panel 204n
Tallinn 115
Church of St Nicholas 115
Tehran, hostage crisis 37
Tesco (supermarket chain) 141
Texas 32
TGV (rail service) 192n
Thames, River 91, 158
Thatcher, Margaret (later Baroness
Thatcher),
and Air Tanzania hijacking 38–9
cabinet members 54, 191n, 192n,
194n, 195n, 196n, 200n
and Civil Service 155
and Derek Rayner 59
election campaigns 67, 196n
"going on and on" 128
and Lord Hanson 130
Mr Kottawallah and 51
Matthew Parris and 205n
and National Lottery 88
and review of NHS 68–9
and riots of 1981 41
and Thyssen Collection 73
and Top Management Programme
64
and Treasury 75–6
visit to Home Office 33
and William Whitelaw 54
and *Yes Minister* 159
Thaw, John 86
Thick, David 174
Thomas, Dylan, *Under Milk Wood* 129,
169–70
Thomas Jefferson Medal 198n
Thorpe, Jeremy 14

Thyssen, Countess Carmen (née Cervera) 73
Thyssen-Bornemisza Collection 73
Tickell, Crispin (later Sir Crispin) 21, 25, 27
The Times 95, 110, 131, 136, 137, 138, 194*n*, 205*n*
Tisbury, Wiltshire, Tithe Barn 171
Titian, *Danaë* 149
Tokyo 37
Tomkins, Sir Edward 12
Tomkins, Lady (Gillian) 12
Tony Awards 203*n*, 204*n*
Torrington by-election (1958) 193*n*
Towcester Racecourse, Northamptonshire 99
Toxteth, Liverpool, riots 40, 159
Toyota 142
trade union movement 60, 75, 136
Travelex 203*n*
Tripura 50
Trollope, Anthony 111
True Detective (TV series) 206*n*
Truro, Cathedral 207*n*
Tugendhat, Christopher Tugendhat, Baron 21
Tully, Mark (later Sir Mark) 50
    Something Understood (radio series) 194*n*
Turing, Alan 148
    On Comparable Numbers 206*n*
Turnbull, Andrew (later Baron Turnbull) 100, 118, 123
Tutu, Desmond, Archbishop 170

Uncle Vanya (Anton Chekhov) 203*n*
United Kingdom,
    British Army 194*n*, 205*n*
    SAS (Special Air Service) 33–4, 193*n*
    Hereford HQ 34–6, 37–8
    coalition government 137, 138
    Driver and Vehicle Licensing Agency (DVLA) 176
    HM Customs and Excise (later HM Revenue and Customs, HMRC) 76, 176
    Inland Revenue 76, 138
    Privy Council 202*n*
    riots of 1981 40–3, 159
    Royal Air Force 190*n*
    Royal Collection 149
    Supreme Court 118–19, 142, 201*n*, 202*n*
United Nations 192*n*
United States of America 8, 32–3
    Federal government 160
    Freedom of Information Act (1966) 14
    Navy 187
    September 11 attacks 113
    Supreme Court 32, 116, 202*n*
University of the Arts 200*n*
UNPROFOR Bosnia 193*n*
Uplands conference centre, Buckinghamshire 64

Valley of the Kings 28
Value for Money programme 71
Van Hoof, Renée (later Haferkamp) 26–7
Vanity Fair 193*n*
Varanasi 52
Victoria, Queen 135
    Coronet 147
Victoria Cross 194*n*
Vietnam War 188, 189
Villefranche-sur-Mer 21
Vilnius 115
Vogue magazine 32
Volpone (Ben Jonson) 203*n*

Waddesdon Manor, Buckinghamshire 116, 198*n*
Waddington, David (later Baron Waddington) 48, 50, 51–2, 77, 196*n*
Waddington, Gillie 50
Wade-Gery, Sir Robert 50
Wales 113
Walker, Mr (teacher) 182

Walters, Sir Peter 67
War Horse (Michael Morpurgo) 128
Warburg Pincus 204*n*
Warne, Mr (teacher) 182
Washington, D.C. 14, 116, 191*n*
    Supreme Court 32, 116
Wasserman, Gordon (later Baron Wasserman) 8
Waterloo, Battle of 150
Waters, Roger 181
Watkins, Sir Tasker 59
Waugh, Evelyn, *Officers and Gentlemen* 18, 19
Waverley, John Anderson, 1st Viscount 145, 148
Wellesley family 149
Wellington, Arthur Wellesley, 1st Duke of 149–50
Wellington, Charles Wellesley, 9th Duke of 149
Wellington, Dukes of 82–3
Wellington Collection Management Committee 149
Wellington College, Berkshire 143
Wellington Museum Act (1947) 149
Welsh Rugby Union 194*n*
West Derbyshire (constituency) 205*n*
West Germany 191*n*
"Westminster Palace of Varieties" 120
White, Gordon 204*n*
White, Willard (later Sir Willard) 86
Whitehall Dining Club 67
Whitelaw, William (later Viscount Whitelaw) 1, 12, 14, 15, 38, 40–5, 54, 56, 57, 71, 156, 158
    memoirs 47
    on special advisers 159–60
Whitmore, Clive (later Sir Clive) 41, 82
Wilbury Park, Wiltshire 164
Wilkes, John 66
Wilkinson, Heather 79, 83, 84
Willcocks, Sir David 170
Williams, Shirley (later Baroness Williams of Crosby) 14, 16–17, 191*n*
Wilson, Harold (later Baron Wilson of

Rievaulx) 14, 16, 17, 28, 158, 192*n*, 193*n*, 196*n*
Wilson, Richard (later Baron Wilson of Dinton) 59–60, 69, 100, 108, 111, 118, 123
Wiltshire 162, 165, 199*n*
Windsor Castle, Berkshire, fire (1992) 84–5
    Restoration Committee 85
Withnail and I (film) 204*n*
Wolverhampton 40
Woolf, Harry Woolf, Baron 104, 114, 121, 122–3
Workers' Playtime (radio series) 180
Working for Patients (White Paper) 69
World Advertising Research Center 205*n*
World Championships 196*n*
Worlock, Bishop Derek 40, 193*n*
    Better Together and *With Hope in our Hearts* (with David Sheppard) 193*n*
Wren, Sir Christopher 169
Wright, Sir Peter 99

Xian, China 113

Yale University 4, 8, 9, 186–9
    Elizabethan Club 189
    Mellon Fellowship 4, 186, 187, 188
    Russian Chorus 115, 187–8
    St Anthony Hall (Sigma chapter, Delta Psi) 188–9
    Saybrook College 187
Yearley, Alison 79
Yes Minister 120, 159, 182
Yes, Prime Minister 159
Young Winston (film) 200*n*
Yugoslavia, former 193*n*

Zimbabwe 44, 194*n*
Zoffany, Johan 145